.

LIBRARY OF NEW TESTAMENT STUDIES

558

formerly the Journal for the Study of the New Testament Supplement series

Editor
Chris Keith

The Davidic Shepherd King in the Lukan Narrative

Sarah Harris

Bloomsbury T&T Clark
An imprint of Bloomsbury Publishing Plc

B L O O M S B U R Y
LONDON · OXFORD · NEW YORK · NEW DELHI · SYDNEY

Bloomsbury T&T Clark

An imprint of Bloomsbury Publishing Plc

Imprint previously known as T&T Clark

50 Bedford Square	1385 Broadway
London	New York
WC1B 3DP	NY 10018
UK	USA

www.bloomsbury.com

BLOOMSBURY, T&T CLARK and the Diana logo are trademarks of Bloomsbury Publishing Plc

First published 2016

© Sarah Harris, 2016

British Library Cataloguing-in-Publication Data
A catalogue record for this book is available from the British Library.

ISBN:	HB:	978-0-56766-734-2
	ePDF:	978-0-56766-735-9
	ePub:	978-0-56766-868-4

Library of Congress Cataloging-in-Publication Data
A catalog record for this book is available from the Library of Congress.

Series: Library of New Testament Studies, volume 558

Typeset by Fakenham Prepress Solutions, Fakenham, Norfolk NR21 8NN
Printed and bound in Great Britain

For Craig

CONTENTS

ACKNOWLEDGEMENTS

This book represents a revision of my doctoral thesis accepted by the University of Otago, Dunedin, New Zealand in 2012. This research would not have been possible without the support of many people. I wish to thank Dominic Mattos, the Commissioning Editor at T&T Clark, for accepting this book for publication, and Miriam Cantwell, whose efficiency and skill has brought the manuscript smoothly through the publishing process.

I owe sincere thanks to my supervisors, Professor Paul Trebilco from the University of Otago and Dr Mark Keown from Laidlaw College, whose guidance, encouragement and scholarship has enabled me to finish this race. Deepest gratitude is also due to the members of the examination committee, Professor I. Howard Marshall, Professor Craig L. Blomberg, and Dr Kevin Waldie for their advice and encouragement, which has been of invaluable challenge and assistance.

I would especially like to record my deepest thanks to Professor Steve Walton who has guided and supported my journey through the Lukan narrative to the point of hosting me in Cambridge on several occasions. Together with Ali, your friendship and hospitality has been a special delight and gift.

During this research I was fortunate to have support from several fellowships and scholarships which made my journey richer and which helped the development of this project. Firstly, I am deeply grateful to the Rev. John Fairbrother and Vaughan Park for hosting me as their Scholar-in-Residence in 2009. Three months at the beach writing is such a treasure to a mother and I still miss the peace and beauty of the community and the beach. Many thanks are also due to the Rt. Rev. John Patterson and the Janet Hancock Fund for assistance with travel to Cambridge to study at Tyndale House. My heartfelt thanks go to the warden of Tyndale House, Dr Peter Williams, the ever-patient librarian, Dr Elizabeth Magba and fellow colleagues at the library; your warm fellowship and immense kindness and grace have been one of God's greatest gifts to me on this wonderful journey. Especial thanks to Dr Diane Hakala for her wonderful hospitality which enabled me to return to Tyndale House each summer, and fellow students Dr Myrto Theochorus, Dr Nicki Wilkes and Michelle Stinson, whose company and discussion added colour to the evenings after long days in the library. Thanks are due to the Te Kotahitanga scholarship fund for their financial assistance from 2010 until 2012 which assisted with many of the costs of academic study. My thanks also to the Bible College of New Zealand where I first found my love of biblical studies, and Carey Baptist College who have employed me to teach and challenge a new generation of students. Thank you all!

However, my deepest thanks go to my family who have let me be a semi-absent wife and mother while I pursued my dreams. First, to my parents David and

Alwyn Gray Young: you have always believed in me and encouraged me to follow my passions from my childhood to the present, and I thank you. To Dad, who died after a valiant but difficult struggle with Parkinsons as I wrote my final chapter, your love and quiet presence has always been a stable rock in my life and I still miss your wisdom and company. *Ma Ihowa koe e manaaki.*

To my children Samuel, James, Lydia and Jeremy: thanks for believing I would make it to the finish line and for helping Dad and me around the house. And for Craig, my husband: it is hard to express how much your patience, generosity and encouragement has kept me fuelled on this long path. I know how much you have sacrificed so that I could pursue my dreams, and I know this is a debt that will be hard to repay. Like the woman of Luke 7.36-50 who could only pour out her love to Jesus for all that he had done for her, I think I will spend the next several years paying off a very large bill.

ABBREVIATIONS

AB	Anchor Bible
ABD	*Anchor Bible Dictionary.* Freedman, Noel. (ed.) *Anchor Bible Dictionary* (6 vols; New York: Doubleday, Logos Edition, 1992).
ABRL	The Anchor Bible Reference Library
ALGNT	*Analytical Greek New Testament: Greek Text Analysis.* Friberg, Barbara, Timothy Friberg, Kurt Aland, and Institute for New Testament Textual Research (U.S.), *Vol. 1, Analytical Greek New Testament: Greek Text Analysis* (Baker's Greek New Testament Library; Cedar Hill: Silver Mountain Software, 2001).
ANET	*Ancient Near Eastern Texts Relating to the Old Testament.* Pritchard, James B. (ed.), *Ancient Near Eastern Texts Relating to the Old Testament* (Princeton: Princeton University Press, 3rd edn with supplement, 1978).
ANTC	Abingdon New Testament Commentaries
BA	*Biblical Archaeologist*
BBR	*Bulletin for Biblical Research*
BDAG	*A Greek-English Lexicon of the New Testament and Other Early Christian Literature.* Bauer, W., W. Danker, W. F. Arndt and F. W. Gingrich, *A Greek-English Lexicon of the New Testament and other Early Christian Literature* (Chicago: University of Chicago Press, 3rd edn 2000).
BDB	*A Hebrew and English Lexicon of the Old Testament.* Brown, F., S. Driver and C. Briggs. (eds), *A Hebrew and English Lexicon of the Old Testament.* (Oxford: Clarendon Press, 1906).
BETL	Bibliotheca Ephemeridum Theologicarum Lovaniensium
BIB	*Biblica*
BIBINT	*Biblical Interpretation*
BSAC	*Biblioteca Sacra*
BST	The Bible Speaks Today
BTB	*Biblical Theology Bulletin*
CBQ	*Catholic Biblical Quarterly*
CIG	*Corpus Inscriptionum Graecarum*
EDNT	*Exegetical Dictionary of the New Testament.* Horst Robert Balz, and Gerhard Schneider, *Exegetical Dictionary of the New Testament* (3 vols; Grand Rapids: Eerdmans, 1990–3).
EEC	Eerdmans Critical Commentary
ENCJUD	*Encyclopaedia Judaica* (17 vols; Jerusalem: Keter Publishing House, 1972).
EJT	*European Journal of Theology*
ETL	*Ephemerides Theologicae Lovanienses*
EUS	European University Studies
EXPT	*Expository Times*

GELNT	*Greek-English Lexicon of the New Testament: Based on Semantic Domains.* Louw, Johannes P. and Eugene Albert Nida, *Greek-English Lexicon of the New Testament: Based on Semantic Domains* (New York: United Bible Societies, electronic edn of the 2nd edn 1996).
GELS	*Greek-English Lexicon of the Septuagint.* Muraoka, T., *A Greek-English Lexicon of the Septuagint* (Louvain: Peeters, 3rd edn 2009).
HBM	Hebrew Bible Monographs
HCOT	Historical Commentary on the Old Testament
HNT	Handbuch zum Neuen Testament
ICC	International Commentary Series
INT	*Interpretation*
JAAR	*Journal of the American Academy of Religion*
JBL	*Journal of Biblical Literature*
JCTCR	Jewish and Christian Texts in Contexts and Related Studies
JETS	*Journal of the Evangelical Theological Society*
JPTSS	Journal of Pentecostal Theology Supplement Series
JSNT	*Journal for the Study of the New Testament*
JSNTSS	Journal for the Study of the New Testament Supplement Series
JSOT	*Journal for the Study of the Old Testament*
JSOTSS	Journal for the Study of the Old Testament Supplement Series
LCL	Loeb Classical Library
LHBOTS	Library of Hebrew Bible, Old Testament Studies
LNTS	Library of New Testament Studies
LXX	Septuagint
MT	Masoretic Text
NA	*Novum Testamentum Graece.* E. E. Nestle, B. and K. Aland (eds), *Novum Testamentum Graece* (Stuttgart: Deutsche Bibelgesellschaft, 27th edn 2001).
NCBC	The New Century Bible Commentary
NETS	*A New English Translation of the Septuagint; And the Other Greek Translations Traditionally Included under that Title.* Pietersma, Albert and Benjamin G. Wright (eds), *A New English Translation of the Septuagint; And the Other Greek Translations Traditionally Included under that Title* (New York: Oxford University Press, 2007).
NICNT	New International Commentary on the New Testament
NICOT	New International Commentary on the Old Testament
NIGNTC	New International Greek New Testament Commentary
NOVTSUP	Supplements to Novum Testamentum
NT	New Testament
NTS	*New Testament Studies*
OGIS	*Aktualisierende Konkordanzen zu Dittenbergers Orientis Graeci Inscriptiones Selectae (OGIS) und zur dritten Auflage der von ihm begründeten Sylloge Inscriptionum Graecarum (Syll.3).* Wilfried Gawantka (ed.) *Aktualisierende Konkordanzen zu Dittenbergers Orientis Graeci Inscriptiones Selectae (OGIS) und zur dritten Auflage der von ihm begründeten Sylloge Inscriptionum Graecarum (Syll.3)* (Hildersheim: Georg Olams Verlag, 1977).

OT	Old Testament
PBM	Paternoster Biblical Monographs
SBEC	Studies in the Bible and Early Christianity
SBL	Society of Biblical Literature
SBLDS	*Society of Biblical Literature Dissertation Series*
SBLEJL	Society of Biblical Literature Early Judaism and its Literature
SBLSCS	Society of Biblical Literature Septuagint and Cognate Studies
SBLSP	*Society of Biblical Literature Seminar Papers*
SBT	Studies in Biblical Theology
SJSJ	Supplements to the Journal for the Study of Judaism
SNTSMS	Society for New Testament Studies Monograph Series
SP	Sacra Pagina
SSEJC	Studies in Scripture in Early Judaism and Christianity
SVTP	Studia Veteris Testamenti Pseudepigrapha
TDNT	*Theological Dictionary of the New Testament*. Kittel, Gerhard, Geoffrey W. Bromiley and Gerhard Friedrich. (eds) *Theological Dictionary of the New Testament* (10 vols; Grand Rapids: Eerdmans, electronic edn 1964–76).
THEM	*Themelios*
TPINTC	Trinity Press International New Testament Commentaries
TTZ	*Trierer theologische Zeitschrift*
TYNBUL	*Tyndale Bulletin*
UBSGNT[4]	*United Bible Society Greek New Testament,* 4th edn
VT	*Vetus Testamentum*
VTSUP	Supplements to Vetus Testamentum
WBCOM	Westminster Bible Companion
WBC	Word Biblical Commentary
WTJ	*Westminster Theological Journal*
WUNT	Wissenschaftliche Untersuchungen Zum Neuen Testament

1

THE DAVIDIC SHEPHERD KING IN LUKE'S NARRATIVE

While sitting in an undergraduate class and discussing the Lukan birth narrative I became intrigued with why Luke places such a narrative emphasis on the shepherds on the hillside (2.8-20). The birth of Jesus is told simply and with little narrative space, while the shepherds are prominent figures whose experiences and movements fill the text. I began to wonder how Luke viewed the shepherds. At that time I was aware that Lukan theology emphasized the gospel coming to the poor, visible in many texts including the programmatic saying in 4.18-19, and that first-century Palestinian shepherds were examples of just such people. However, the more I heard echoes of Jewish scripture in the narrative, the more I became convinced that the role of the shepherds meant something more for Luke. I further noted that Luke placed considerable emphasis on the Davidic motif in the infancy narrative with many direct statements and echoes. Also, I recalled how David's role as a shepherd was central to his kingship. It made me wonder if Luke was suggesting something about Jesus' kingship and the kingdom he came preaching and proclaiming.

As my study continued I became intrigued with the parable of the lost sheep in Luke 15 and how this parable, which Bovon notes falls at the midpoint of the Gospel,[1] seems to return to the shepherd tones of the infancy narrative. Then when I reached the story of Zacchaeus, the place most scholars define as the final encounter in the travel narrative, and I heard the strong echo of the Davidic shepherd king in 19.10, I decided that it would be valuable to explore Luke's theological interest in the motif of the shepherd in a comprehensive and systematic way.

I. H. Marshall has previously suggested that Luke 19.10, where the reader hears the well-supported Davidic shepherd king echo, 'sums up the central message of the Gospel'.[2] More recently, Yuzuru Miura, in his study on David in Luke-Acts, writes that, 'in Luke 19, Jesus' earthly ministry is summarized with Davidic

---

1. François Bovon, *Das Evangelium nach Lukas 1. Teilband Lk 1,1-9,50* (EKKNT; Zürich: Benziger, 1989), pp. 15–16.

2. I. Howard Marshall, *Luke, Historian and Theologian* (Downers Grove: IVP, 1988), p. 116.

Shepherd imagery,[3] while not explaining how this is true. I agree with these two statements and recognize that these scholars have noted something significant for reading Luke; but no study, including their own, has fully explored the Davidic shepherd king in the Lukan narrative. This study aims to fill that lacuna.

The problem of recognizing the Davidic shepherd king in the narrative comes because there is no direct statement where Jesus is named as a 'shepherd' in the Gospel. In contrast, the Gospel of Matthew has one verse where Jesus is named as shepherd of Israel (Mt. 2.6) and so studies have explored the motif in that Gospel.[4] However, Luke's lack of a direct reference does not necessarily mean that he has not woven this theme into his narrative. As the curtain goes up in the Gospel, the reader steps into the Septuagintal world grounded firmly in the stories of Israel, where one cannot but recall the story of David, God's chosen shepherd king with Luke's sixfold repetition of *David* (1.27, 32, 69; 2.4 [twice], 11).

Bovon's survey of christological titles for Jesus from the last fifty-five years identifies the Lukan Jesus as Prophet, Master, Son of Man, Servant, Son of David, Son of God, Messiah, Lord, Saviour, and even Guide.[5] These categories are further identified in major biblical commentaries. As Tuckett rightly points out, 'Luke does not present a single Christology but rather a whole variety of Christologies'.[6]

This study aims to show that Luke's portrayal of Jesus as David is implicitly coloured by his nature as a shepherd king, which Luke demonstrates in explicit and implicit ways. While Luke 4.18-19 describes Jesus' mission to the poor, Luke 19.10 summarizes how he brings good news. That is, he does so as God's faithful shepherd king who always seeks out and saves the lost sheep. The Lukan Jesus, whom all scholars note is constantly reaching out to the margins of society, does so at least in part because he is God's faithful shepherd. This mission continues into Acts where it begins in Jerusalem, then continues into Judea, Samaria, and to the ends of the earth (Acts 1.8).

---

3. Yuzuru Miura, *David in Luke-Acts: His Portrayal in Light of Early Judaism* (WUNT II/232; Tübingen: Mohr Siebeck, 2007), p. 240.

4. Francis Martin, 'Image of Shepherd in the Gospel of Saint Matthew', *ScEs* 27 (1975), pp. 261–301; John Paul Heil, 'Ezekiel 34 and the Narrative Strategy of the Shepherd and the Sheep Metaphor in Matthew', *CBQ* 55 (1993), pp. 698–708; J. R. C. Cousland, *The Crowds in the Gospel of Matthew* (NovTSup 102; Leiden: Brill, 2002); Young S. Chae, *Jesus as the Eschatological Davidic Shepherd: Studies in the Old Testament, Second Temple Judaism, and in the Gospel of Matthew* (WUNT II/216; Tübingen: Mohr Siebeck, 2006); Joel Willitts, *Matthew's Messianic Shepherd-King: In Search of 'The Lost Sheep of the House of Israel'* (BZNW 147; Berlin: Walter de Gruyter, 2007).

5. François Bovon, *Luke The Theologian: Fifty-Five Years of Research (1950-2005)* (Waco: Baylor, 2006), pp. 199–219.

6. Christopher M. Tuckett, 'The Christology of Luke-Acts', in *The Unity of Luke-Acts* (ed. J. Verheyden; BETL, 142; Leuven: Leuven University Press, 1999), p. 139.

1.1 Methodology

This study will use a narrative critical methodology that relies heavily on exegetical discussions to recover the picture of Jesus as the Davidic shepherd king. In using this methodology I acknowledge that the biblical narrative is not a mere compilation of unconnected stories, but is a carefully crafted narrative. Furthermore, it takes seriously Luke's specific intention given in 1.1 to write a διήγησις (an orderly account), and therefore it aims to follow Luke's lead by drawing attention to his narrative landmarks, structure and detail. Beginnings, middle and endings of narrative units and the greater Gospel narrative must be considered. A balanced exegesis relies on contextual interpretation, and this study assumes that not only the pericopae that immediately surround a text are necessary for interpretation, but also the entire Gospel narrative. That is, Luke's Gospel from 1.1 to 24.53 is a narrative unity, and it is also in unity with the second volume in the Acts of the Apostles.[7]

While narrative concerns have not been entirely absent from Lukan scholarship,[8] in the late 1950s scholars began to consider Luke's theological concerns more systematically and to 'pick up one of the loose threads left by form criticism'.[9] *Redaktionsgeschichte* helped uncover the role of the author/s who created a unified story through editing their sources. This method of study has given special emphasis to the way insertions, modifications, reordering and shaping give theological meaning to a Gospel.

The rise of biblical narrative criticism in the last three decades arose within the greater movement of literary criticism. Scholars such as Martin Buber, Franz Rosenzweig, Erich Auerbach, Robert Alter, Meir Sternberg, Kenneth Gros Louis, Shimon Bar-Efrat and Yairah Amit[10] have spearheaded study in the Hebrew

---

7. I agree with major scholarly thought that Luke and Acts are written by the same author and contain an authorial unity. Green, *Gospel*, pp. 6–10; Fitzmyer, *Luke*, p. 35; John Nolland, *Luke 1–9:20* (WBC, 35A; Dallas: Word, 1989), p. xxxiii; Marshall, *Historian and Theologian*, 13. Generic, narrative and theological unity are however open to question, and this has been opened up by the work of Parsons and Pervo. See Mikeal C. Parsons and Richard I. Pervo, *Rethinking the Unity of Luke and Acts* (Minneapolis: Fortress Press, 1993).

8. For example H. Cadbury and M. Dibelius paid attention to Lukan language and style. Mark Coleridge and Beverly Roberts Gaventa acknowledge Cadbury's foreshadowing of a literary approach and Gaventa and Joseph B. Tyson of Dibelius' similar attention. Mark Coleridge, *The Birth of the Lukan Narrative: Narrative as Christology in Luke 1–2* (JSNTSS, 88; Sheffield: JSOT, 1993), p. 12; Beverley Roberts Gaventa, 'The Peril of Modernizing Henry Joel Cadbury', in *SBLSP 87* (ed. K. H. Richards; Atlanta: Scholars Press, 1987), p. 64; Joseph B. Tyson, *Death of Jesus in Luke-Acts* (Columbia: University of South Carolina, 1986), p. 25.

9. Marshall, *Historian and Theologian*, 14.

10. Martin Buber and Franz Rosenzweig, *Scripture and Translation* (trans. Lawrence Rosenwald with Everett Fox; Bloomington: Indiana University Press, 1994); E. Auerbach,

Bible, while NT scholarship turned with great interest to the narrative in its texts.[11]

Narrative and literary methodologies have become well accepted, and within the field of Lukan studies there have been a plethora of books written using narrative methodologies in full or in part.[12] Therefore, the choice of methodology

Mimesis: The Representation of Reality in Western Literature (trans. W. Trask; New York: Anchor Books, 1957); E. M. Sternberg, *The Poetics of Biblical Narrative: Ideological Literature and the Drama of Reading* (Bloomington: Indiana University Press, 1985); Robert Alter, *The Art of Biblical Narrative* (London: George Allen and Unwin, 1981); K. R. R. Gros Louis, J. S. Ackermann and T. S. Warshaw (eds), *Literary Interpretations of Biblical Narrative Volume I* (Nashville: Abingdon Press, 1974); K. R. R. Gros Louis and J. S. Ackermann (eds), *Literary Interpretations of Biblical Narrative Volume II* (Nashville: Abingdon Press, 1982); S. Bar-Efrat, *Narrative Art in the Bible* (trans. Dorothea Shefer-Vanson; JSOTSS, 70/BLS, 17; Sheffield: Almond Press, 1989); Y. Amit, 'The Multi-Purpose "Leading Word" and the Problems of its Usage', *Prooftexts* 9 (1989): 99–114.

11. Tremper Longman III, *Literary Approaches for Biblical Interpretation* (Grand Rapids: Academie Books, 1987); Scot McKnight, *Interpreting the Synoptic Gospels* (Grand Rapids: Baker Books, 1988); Steven D. Moore, *Literary Criticism and the Gospels: The Theoretical Challenge* (New Haven: Yale University Press, 1989); Norman R. Petersen, *Literary Criticism for New Testament Critic* (Philadelphia: Fortress Press, 1978); Mark Allan Powell, *What is Narrative Criticism?* (Minneapolis: Fortress Press, 1990).

12. Charles H. Talbert, *Literary Patterns, Theological Themes and the Genre of Luke-Acts* (SBLMS, 20; Missoula: Scholars Press, 1974); Robert F. O'Toole, *The Unity of Luke's Theology* (Wilmington: Glazier, 1984); Robert C. Tannehill, *The Narrative Unity of Luke-Acts: A Literary Interpretation* (2 vols; Philadelphia: Fortress Press, 1986, 1990); Roland Meynet, *L'Évangile selon Saint Luc: Analyse Rhétorique Commentaire* (Paris: Cerf, 1988); Susan R. Garrett, *The Demise of the Devil* (Minneapolis: Fortress, 1989); David P. Moessner, *Lord of the Banquet: The Literary and Theological Significance of the Lukan Travel Narrative* (Minneapolis: Fortress Press, 1989); Luke Timothy Johnson, *The Gospel of Luke* (SP3; Collegeville: Liturgical Press, 1991); Mark Coleridge, *The Birth of the Lukan Narrative: Narrative as Christology in Luke 1–2* (JSNTSS, 88; Sheffield: JSOT, 1993); William S. Kurz, *Reading Luke-Acts: Dynamics of Biblical Narrative* (Louisville: Westminster John Knox Press, 1993); William H. Shepherd Jr., *The Narrative Function of the Holy Spirit as a Character in Luke-Acts* (SBLDS, 147; Atlanta: Scholars Press, 1994); David Lertis Matson, *Household Conversion Narratives in Acts: Pattern and Interpretation* (JSNTSS, 123; Sheffield: Sheffield Academic, 1996); Robert C. Tannehill, *Luke* (ANTC; Nashville: Abingdon, 1996); Fernando Méndez-Moratalla, *The Paradigm of Conversion in Luke* (JSNTSS, 252; London: T&T Clark International, 2004); Craig G. Bartholomew, Joel B. Green, and Anthony C. Thiselton (eds), *Reading Luke: Interpretation, Reflection, Formation* (Scripture and Hermeneutics Series 6; Grand Rapids: Zondervan, 2005); Kenneth Duncan Litwak, *Echoes of Scripture in Luke-Acts: Telling the History of God's People Intertextually* (JSNTSS, 282; London: T&T Clark International, 2005); Robert C. Tannehill, *The Shape of Luke's Story: Essays on Luke-Acts* (Eugene: Cascade, 2005); Gary Yamasaki, 'Point of View in a Gospel Story: What Difference Does It Make? Luke 19:1-10 as a Test Case', *JBL* 125

for this study stands in a growing tradition of narrative studies which are adding greatly to Lukan scholarship.

1.2 The contours of narrative methodology used in this study

There are six key narrative features which will be considered in this study; each is a tool an author uses to convey meaning to a reader. They are:

1. The cumulative nature of narrative
2. The cohesive structure of a narrative
3. The order of a narrative
4. Gaps and blanks in the text
5. The role of repetition
6. Echoes within the text

First, narrative methodology takes seriously the cumulative nature of a story which has a beginning, middle and end that are inextricably linked. It recognizes the causal connections between situations and events in Luke's writing. This means one event or situation gives rise to another and the causal chain leads to the 'goal' in the sense of the conclusion of the story line.[13] The significance of each event in the narrative is therefore incomplete if it is viewed apart from the whole.[14]

This approach has merit, because an original audience is likely to have heard a Gospel story in its entirety and not as isolated pericope, thus allowing the cumulative *telos* of the story to emerge.[15] This will be important for this study of the Davidic shepherd king motif, because the motif is not centred in one text. Luke begins the picture in the infancy narrative, but focus and detail are added as the narrative moves toward its goal.

(2006): 89–105; Elizabeth V. Dowling, *Taking Away the Pound: Women, Theology and the Parable of the Pounds in the Gospel of Luke* (LNTS 324; London: T&T Clark, 2007); Gary Yamasaki, *Watching Biblical Narrative: Point of View in Biblical Exegesis* (New York: T&T Clark, 2007); C. Kavin Rowe, *Early Narrative Christology: The Lord in the Gospel of Luke* (Grand Rapids: Baker Academic, 2009); Kazuhiko Yamazaki-Ransom, *The Roman Empire in Luke's Narrative* (LNTS, 404; London: T&T Clark, 2010); Geir Otto Holmås, *Prayer and Vindication in Luke-Acts: The Theme of Prayer within the Context of the Legitimating and Edifying Objective in the Lukan Narrative* (LNTS, 433; London: T&T Clark, 2011).

13. Litwak notes there can be multiple causal chains in a narrative. Litwak, *Echoes*, pp. 41–2.

14. Green, *Gospel*, p. 11.

15. David B. Howell, *Matthew's Inclusive Story: A Study in the Narrative Rhetoric of the First Gospel* (JSNTSS, 42; Sheffield: JSOT, 1990), p. 32; Kathy Reiko Maxwell, *Hearing Between the Lines: The Audience as Fellow-Workers in Luke-Acts and its Literary Milieu* (LNTS, 425; London: T&T Clark, 2010), pp. 128–9.

Secondly, a narrative approach assumes – as this study does – that Luke wrote a cohesive story of Jesus crafted to shape his readers' understanding. We cannot expect that the author ever intended for Luke to be read in one hand, with Mark's Gospel in the other hand for comparison. Therefore, the primary context for interpreting any part of the text is the text itself. Verseput writes of the Synoptic context that 'the exegete who wishes to confront the Evangelist face to face must do so on the grounds of the entire text ... It is the completed text which stands between the author and the reader, and it is that text against which all meaning must ultimately be measured.'[16]

Narrative criticism understands the text as a coherent unity in comparison to a redaction critical approach which tends toward seeing the text's lesions and parts.[17] Critics of this methodology suggest narrative scholars can try to make the text more homogeneous than it really is and can deny the possibility of internal contradictions.[18] To guard against this the narrative critical approach in general, and this study in particular, must allow the proof of unity to come from a cumulative rather than a singular strand of thought in the narrative. This approach also does not preclude analysing a triple tradition or Q passage where there is a shared tradition. Rather, this approach ensures that these are the appetizer and not the main course.

Thirdly, narrative methodology assumes that the order of the narrative is essential for semantic understanding. This is consistent with Luke's prologue where he states he has written καθεξῆς (an orderly account).[19] The use of καθεξῆς conveys the notion of sequential action.[20] This does not necessarily imply a chronologically ordered narrative, neither does it exclude it, but it does point to an account that has been deliberately ordered to convey meaning.[21] Narrative methodology, therefore, is appropriate as it highlights narrative direction and location as possible rhetorical devices. For example, Luke's geographical structure is well known in its movement first from Galilee toward Jerusalem (9.51) and later in Acts, out from Jerusalem to the ends of the earth (Acts 1.8).[22] This is an example of ordering the text where there is a spatial centre in Jerusalem and a progression to and from it that is woven into the text. However, for Luke this structure is less

---

16. Donald Verseput, *The Rejection of the Humble Messianic King: A Study of the Composition of Matthew 11–12* (EUS; Frankfurt am Main: Peter Lang, 1986), pp. 5–8.

17. Coleridge goes so far as to say that redaction criticism shows a 'deeply fissured collection of a diversity of elements'. Coleridge, *Birth*, p. 18.

18. S. D. Moore, 'Are the Gospels Unified Narratives?' in *SBLSP 1987* (ed. K. H. Richards; Atlanta: Scholars Press, 1987), pp. 443–58.

19. Kurz, *Reading Luke-Acts*, pp. 24–6; Tannehill, *Narrative Unity*, pp. 1:1–12; Rowe, *Early Narrative Christology*, pp. 11–15.

20. 'καθεξῆς', *BDAG*, p. 490.

21. Tannehill is in agreement here with Dillon that this does not have to imply a chronological order that is historically accurate. Tannehill, *Narrative Unity*, pp. 1:9–10; Richard J. Dillon, 'Previewing Luke's Project From his Prologue', *CBQ* 43 (1981): 221–2.

22. Johnson, *Gospel*, pp. 14–15.

about geography than the universal scope of the Gospel. Another example of narrative order is the 'royal section' where I argue Luke has ordered and connected stories at the end of the travel narrative to enable the reader to identify Jesus as king, and specifically the Davidic shepherd king. This section begins in 18.35 with the story of the blind man who names Jesus as the Son of David (18.35-43). This is followed by the Zacchaeus pericope where, as I will show, Jesus is the Davidic shepherd king (19.1-10); the parable of the minas, which is full of the language of power and kingdom (19.11-27); climaxing in the triumphal entry into Jerusalem where Jesus is named as ὁ βασιλεύς (19.28-44).

In studying the order of a narrative, attention will also be paid to the special role of the beginning of a narrative. This effect was recognized as early as Plato in the *Republic*,[23] who noted that first impressions are formed at the beginning of a work, and so they are of primary importance. There has been much work undertaken on the effects of narrative beginnings.[24] Perry has shown that information situated at the beginning of a message persuades and change people's attitudes and impressions. More importantly he has demonstrated how beginnings affect one's comprehension, and how people's tendency is to persist in a direction when a trajectory has been set.[25] He says:

> The first terms set up in most subjects a *direction* which exerts a continuous effect on the latter terms. When the subject hears the first term, a broad, uncrystallized but directed impression is born. The next characteristic comes not as a separate item but is related to the established direction ... later characteristics are fitted – if conditions permit – to the given direction.[26]

Sternberg's comments on life and literature are also helpful where he says:

> In literature, as in life, we tend to judge people based on the first impression they make on us; but there is in this respect a basic difference between the two ... The impressions we receive in life come in an essentially unplanned, accidental, and sporadic manner ... In literature, unlike life, it is therefore not only profitable but necessary to pose such questions as: Why has this complex of events been presented first and that delayed? Why has this facet of character been portrayed before that? Why has this piece of (verbal, actional, structural, or even generic)

---

23. Plato, *Republic* II.377b.

24. Menakhem Perry, 'Literary Dynamics: How the Order of a Text Creates its Meanings', *Poetics Today* 1 (1979): 35–64, 311–61; Meir Sternberg, *Expositional Modes and Ordering in Fiction* (Baltimore: Johns Hopkins University Press, 1978), pp. 93–112; Coleridge, *Birth*, pp. 28–9; Litwak, *Echoes*, p. 66; Paul S. Minear, 'Luke's Use of the Birth Stories', in *Studies in Luke-Acts: Essays in Honour of Paul Schubert* (eds L. E. Keck and J. L. Martyn; London: SPCK, 1978), pp. 111–30; Joseph B. Tyson, 'The Birth Narratives and the Beginning of Luke's Gospel', *Semeia* 52 (1990): 103–20.

25. Perry, 'Literary Dynamics', p. 53.

26. Ibid., p. 55.

information been conveyed – or on the contrary, suppressed or ambiguated – at precisely this point?[27]

Sternberg points out that authorial choices require the reader to ask questions of the text's beginning. Maxwell has recently demonstrated that this is an ancient rhetorical tool where the reader is given access to privileged information early in the narrative, and that such omniscient knowledge becomes important as the story progresses.[28]

This study stresses the literary force of the *primacy effect* and the effect it has on reading a narrative whole. As a result, we will pay particular attention to the beginning of David's story from Kingdoms in Chapter 2, and the story of the Lukan Jesus in Chapter 3.

Fourthly, a narrative methodology allows the reader to approach gaps and blanks in the text, not primarily as the writer's inability to handle his sources or write coherent narrative, but as a deliberate decision to place a gap in the narrative that the reader is expected to fill.[29] The laconic nature of the text, therefore, is an opportunity and an invitation for the reader to make links between words and phrases. Maxwell has recently shown that ancient writers used gaps or omissions in a text; Aristotle believed audiences were more persuaded by arguments when they required some effort on behalf of the audience (*Rhet.* 3.10.4).[30] She quotes Theophrastus, the ancient rhetorician on this practice, saying:

> Not all possible points should be punctiliously and tediously elaborated, but some should be left to the comprehension and inference of the hearer, who when he perceives what you have left unsaid becomes not only your hearer but your witness, and a very friendly witness too. For he thinks himself intelligent because you have afforded him the means of showing his intelligence. It seems like a slur on your hearer to tell him everything as though he were a simpleton (*Eloc.* 222).[31]

This has become an accepted strand of literary study in the last twenty or thirty years,[32] with Wolfgang Iser of the Constance School of reception theory becoming

27. Sternberg, *Expositional Modes,* pp. 96–7.

28. Maxwell, *Hearing,* p. 49.

29. This does not entirely rule out the possibility that: (1) textual corruption could occur; or (2) that there is incorrect information. For example, there is the possibility that the census in 2.1 is not correctly recorded.

30. Ibid., pp. 51–8.

31. Ibid., p. 51. The quote can be found in *Demetrius On Style* who records Theophrastus' rhetorical views from a lost work. See W. Hamilton Fyfe and W. Rhys Roberts, *Aristotle the Poetics, Longinus on the Sublime and Demetrius On Style* (LCL; Cambridge, MA: Harvard University Press, 1991), p. 439.

32. Alter, *Art,* p. 179; Wolfgang Iser, *The Acts of Reading: A Theory of Aesthetic Response* (London: Routledge and Keegan Paul, 1978), pp. 180–231; Sternberg, *Poetics,*

well known for this identification.[33] In an elementary form, biblical scholarship has been doing this for years by noticing the change of scenes in the Gospels where Jesus' story has time lapses or scene and location shifts. For example, in the birth narrative we are given limited knowledge or windows with which to view and interpret Jesus' early life, and yet, from the sparse details we can faithfully imagine this time. Iser calls these gaps in the narrative and describes them much like scene shifts between chapters of a novel.[34]

Iser also identifies other types of structured blanks in the narrative. He describes these as unseen joints of a text that are to be connected even though the text does not say so. These require the reader to construct meaning from the narrative's *implicit* connections, to fill in gaps, to draw inferences and test hunches while drawing on their growing body of prior knowledge.[35] This process is dynamic and requires more than a linear reading movement, since in the process of foregrounding and excluding units or items in a text, the reader must be able to allow a retrospective transformation to take place. Yet this creates new possibilities as the reader engages with the task of creating new meaning. This process may not be as radical as it seems. As Iser rightly notes of literature, 'No author worth his salt will ever attempt to set the *whole* picture before his reader's eyes'.[36]

This style of reading allows for considerable freedom to make links in the text, and yet Iser is clear that for those links to be true, there must be internal consistency. Indeed, this whole process is one of establishing norms and reducing the polysemantic potential to one of order and not one of limitless possibilities.[37] He explains that:

> The discontinuities of textual segments trigger synthesizing operations in the reader's mind, because the blanks lead to collisions between the individual ideas formed, thus preventing 'good continuation', which is a prerequisite for

pp. 186–229; Rowe, *Early Narrative Christology*, pp. 37–9; Terry Eagleton, *Literary Theory: An Introduction* (Minneapolis: University of Minnesota Press, 2008), pp. 65–78; Anthony C. Thiselton, *New Horizons in Hermeneutics: The Theory and Practice of Transforming Biblical Reading* (Grand Rapids: Zondervan, 1992); Kurz, *Reading Luke-Acts*, pp. 31–6; Rowe, *Early Narrative Christology*, pp. 37–9.

33. Wolfgang Iser, *How To Do Theory* (Oxford: Blackwell Publishing, 2006); 'The Reading Process: A Phenomenological Approach', in *Modern Criticism and Theory: A Reader* (ed. David Lodge; London: Longman, 1988), pp. 211–28; originally published in *New Literary History* 3 (1972): 279–99.

34. Iser, *Theory*, p. 64.

35. Eagleton, *Literary Theory*, p. 66; Iser, *Act of Reading*, pp. 180–231.

36. Wolfgang Iser, *The Implied Reader: Patterns of Communication in Prose from Bunyan to Beckett* (Baltimore: Johns Hopkins University Press, 1974), p. 282.

37. Sternberg writes similarly of norms and directives that give interpretation plausibility. Meir Sternberg, *Poetics*, p. 188. Coleridge holds a similar position. Coleridge, *Birth*, p. 17.

understanding. These colliding ideas condition each other in the time flow of reading.[38]

This process is open to critique as a reader can claim a God-like gnostic knowledge in the text that is somehow denied to other readers; the possibility that the reader is simply taking her own knowledge or 'concretization' into the text and therefore in measuring the text can ever only deal with one's own concretization.[39] As Eagleton vividly describes, it is the age-old problem of how one can know the light in the refrigerator is off when the door is shut![40]

Eagleton suggests that Iser's view is made viable by the reader who must be 'logically constrained to the text itself', and not wander into total indeterminacy.[41] He notes that there are constraints on readers' interpretations through the academy which legitimate ways of reading works;[42] however, this argument must be tempered by his opening challenge that literature cannot be viewed as an unchanging object.

Fifthly, narrative criticism also notices the role of both direct and implied repetition of words and phrases as a literary semantic tool. Martin Buber's well-known identification of the role of repetition of a leading word (*Leitwort*) both in close proximity and over a large narrative area will be important for this study.[43] He describes a 'lead word' as 'a word or word root that is meaningfully repeated within a text or a sequence of texts or complex of texts; those who attend to these repetitions will find a meaning of the text revealed or clarified, or at any rate made more emphatic'.[44]

The purpose of a *Leitwort*, then, is to direct the reader's attention to the themes of the narrative.[45] This device allows for a writer to establish and shape themes, to give emphasis by indirect means and to let the narrative proceed without disruption or distortion. Buber describes the device as allowing the message to be 'infused by the descending spirit'[46] – a particularly apt description for the Lukan narrative which favours allusions and echoes over direct quotes.[47] For Buber and other scholars, repetition is not incidental to the narrative but is skilfully interwoven and is one of the strongest of all techniques for making meaning.[48] These

38. Iser, *Theory*, p. 66.
39. Eagleton, *Literary Theory*, p. 73.
40. Ibid.
41. Ibid.
42. Ibid., pp. 76–7.
43. Buber, *Scripture*, pp. 114–28.
44. Ibid., p. 114.
45. Ibid., pp. 114–15; Amit, 'Multi-Purpose', p. 109.
46. Buber, *Scripture*, p. 115.
47. The UBSGNT 4th rev. edn. notes that the Lukan Gospel uses 34 direct quotes, while it conservatively suggests there are 267 allusions. See the 'Index of Allusions and Verbal Parallels', pp. 887–901.
48. Alter, *Art*, pp. 92–7, 148; Bar-Efrat, *Narrative Art*, pp. 136, 212; Amit, 'Multi-Purpose',

repeated words can come from a single or root word. Buber even suggests that when there is diversity in the use of a word or 'paronomasia', this strengthens its overall semantic effect.[49] He pays particular attention to the nature of parono-masia at a distance in a text showing how repetition at a distance works to create semantic connection between stories. He cites the example of Egyptian Hagar's flight (Gen. 16.6, 9, 11), where the repetition does not occur until ch. 29. This creates a connection in the story that draws together the history of the patriarchs with the history of the people.[50] We will come to see that Luke establishes the Davidic shepherd motif clearly in the infancy narrative, and though the motif recurs in occasional places, it does so most clearly at the end of the travel narrative when Jesus enters Jerusalem as the Davidic shepherd king. Thus, the vision cast at the beginning of the narrative is reestablished and further shaped in the later narrative so that a semantic connection between the stories reaffirms Luke's theological interest in Jesus as the Davidic king. With a prior understanding of Iser's theory of retrospective transformation, we note how this Davidic shepherd king motif casts a shadow backward into the period of Jesus' ministry and new meaning is both reinforced and created. We will also see that Luke uses paronomasia at a distance with 19.10 recalling 4.18-19. The use of repetition thus supports Iser's insights into gaps and blanks and gives further reasoning for celebrating the cohesive and cumulative nature of the narrative.

As repetition is an inherent part of language, the process of classification of a word as a 'leading word' is problematic when innumerable leading words can hypothetically be found. Restrictions therefore need to be made to enable a balanced analysis.[51] They are:

1. The use of estrangement, where two remote texts are related and their meaning is recalled by the reader. The function of estrangement is to attract the reader to what is unique or exceptional, or what is altered or is being altered, and to allow for significant emerging meaning. However, Buber also allows for two adjoining stories to work in a similar manner,[52] calling them a 'matrix of homonyms' which work to bring phonetic focus. These he also calls a form of estrangement.
2. The identification of 'leading words' must bring coherence to the narrative. That is, you must be able to reach the same semantic reasoning by other means. He labels the leading word as a 'directing tool' which reveals more emphatically a conclusion that is already plausible.

pp. 99-114; Jan Fokkelman, *Reading Biblical Narrative: An Introductory Guide* (trans. Ineke Smit; Louisville: Westminster John Knox Press, 1999); William Freedman, 'The Literary Motif: A Definition and Evaluation', *Novel* 4/2 (1971): 123-31; Rowe, *Early Narrative Christology*, pp. 197-9.

49. Buber, *Scripture*, p. 114.
50. Ibid., pp. 114, 125.
51. Amit discusses Buber's theory and his restrictions in, 'Multi-Purpose', pp. 101-5.
52. Buber, *Scripture*, p. 125.

Buber further acknowledges that not every repetition can be viewed as a leading word, and that some leading words carry more weight. He also acknowledges that not every leading word has equal status.[53]

Robert Alter expanded upon Buber's application of repetition to include the repetition of motifs, themes, sequences of action, and type scenes,[54] as does William Freedman in his work on literary motif.[55] Freedman makes a useful observation, that repetition can be a single unchanging motif or an associated cluster of words.[56] This is helpful because it is not always one unchanging word that an author uses to build an idea or theme, but it can be a collection of related words which act subtly and cumulatively, as we will see in Chapter 3, in which I discuss Luke's motif of David.[57] Freedman rightly says that a motif can be slipped into the author's vocabulary, dialogue and imagery where it becomes part of the total perspective, 'part of the book's atmosphere, and becomes an important thread in the fabric of the work'.[58]

As with Buber's identification of the repetition of leading words, there are the possibilities of multiple motifs that the author may or may not have intended. Freedman therefore suggests three criteria to help determine a motif's efficacy which will help us ascertain Luke's Davidic motif.[59] First, the more frequently the motif is used, the greater the effect. This is a logical first step in assessing its strength; however, Buber's work on estrangement must be held in tension as two carefully connected ideas or phrases can be used powerfully in shaping writing. Frequency is therefore a valuable tool, but low frequency does not have to exclude a word or associated cluster from being identified.

Secondly, he draws attention to the greater efficacy of a motif when it is placed at significant or climactic points in the narrative. This is significant for this study, as we will see how Luke has placed the motif strategically in his narrative, suggesting he views its efficacy highly.

Thirdly, Freedman stresses that a motif carries more weight when it is relevant to the principal purpose of the narrative as a whole. This is consistent with Buber's idea of coherence and Hays' test for satisfaction.[60] As we are working with the

53. Yairah Amit notes that Buber does not create a system to distinguish how a leading word's weight can be evaluated. See Amit, 'Multi-Purpose', p. 102.

54. Alter, *Art*, pp. 88–113; Mara H. Benjamin, 'The Tacit Agenda of a Literary Approach to the Bible', *Prooftexts* 27 (2007): 262–4.

55. Freedman, 'Literary Motif', pp. 123–31. Freedman's methodology is referred to by David Rhoads, 'Narrative Criticism and the Gospel of Mark', *JAAR* 50 (1982), pp. 411–34.

56. Freedman, 'Literary Motif', p. 124.

57. Fokkelman describes 'varied repetition' as having the purpose of expanding the richness of meanings and keeping surprises in store for the reader by avoiding monotony. Fokkelman, *Reading Biblical Narrative*, p. 112.

58. Freedman, 'Literary Motif', p. 125.

59. Ibid., pp. 126–7.

60. Richard Hays, *Echoes of Scripture in the Letters of Paul* (New Haven: Yale University Press, 1989), p. 30.

statement that Luke 19.10 is summative for the Gospel, this study will show that this repeated Davidic shepherd king motif resonates with the Lukan Jesus who has come to bring good news to the poor. These considerations will help assess the likelihood and strength of a motif in the Lukan narrative.

Finally, a narrative focus in the Lukan text helps the reader enter not only into the Lukan narrative but the narrative world of Israel.[61] Luke's extensive use of the

---

61. Many studies have identified Luke's use of OT Scripture. These include Paul Schubert, 'The Structure and Significance of Luke 24', in *Neutestamentliche Studien für Rudolf Bultmann* (ed. W. Eltester; Berlin: Alfred Töpelman, 1954), pp. 165–86; William J. Larkin, 'Luke's Use of the Old Testament in Luke 22–23', (PhD diss., University of Durham, 1974); William J. Larkin, 'Luke's Use of the Old Testament as a Key to his Soteriology', *JETS* 20 (1977), pp. 325–35; Charles H. Talbert, 'Prophecy and Fulfillment in Lukan Theology', in *Luke-Acts: New Perspectives from the Society of Biblical Literature Seminar* (ed. C. H. Talbert; New York: Crossroad, 1984), pp. 91–103; Darrell L. Bock, *Proclamation From Prophecy and Pattern: Lukan Old Testament Christology* (JSNTSS, 12; Sheffield: Sheffield Academic, 1987); B. J. Koet, *Five Studies on Interpretation on Scriptures in Luke-Acts* (Leuven: Leuven University Press, 1989); W. J. C. Weren, 'Psalm 2 in Luke-Acts: An Intertextual Study', in *Intertextuality in Biblical Writings: Essays in Honour of Bas van Iersel* (ed. S. Draisma; Kampen: J. H. Kok, 1989), pp. 189–203; Thomas L. Brodie, 'Luke-Acts as an Imitation and Emulation of the Elijah-Elisha Narrative', in *New Views on Luke and Acts* (ed. Earl Richard; Collegeville: Liturgical Press, 1990), pp. 78–85; F. Bovon, 'The Role of the Scriptures in the Composition of the Gospel Accounts: The Temptations of Jesus (Luke 4:1-13 par.) and the Multiplication of the Loaves (Luke 9:10-17)', in *Luke and Acts* (eds Gerald O'Collins and Gilberto Marconi; New York: Paulist Press, 1991), pp. 26–31; Johnson, *Gospel*, pp. 15–16; Craig A. Evans and James A. Sanders, *Luke and Scripture: The Function of Sacred Tradition in Luke-Acts* (Minneapolis: Fortress Press, 1993); Charles A. Kimball, *Jesus' Exposition of the Old Testament in Luke's Gospel* (JSNTSS, 94; Sheffield: Sheffield Academic, 1994); Robert Brawley, *Text to Text Pours Forth Speech: Voices of Scripture in Luke-Acts* (Bloomington: Indiana University Press, 1995); Rebecca I. Denova, *The Things Accomplished Among Us: Prophetic Tradition in the Structural Pattern of Luke-Acts* (JSNTSS, 141; Sheffield: Sheffield Academic, 1997); Darrell L. Bock, 'Proclamation from Prophecy and Pattern: Luke's Use of the Old Testament for Christology and Mission', in *The Gospels and the Scriptures of Israel* (eds Craig A. Evans and W. Richard Stegner; JSNTSS, 104; Sheffield: Sheffield Academic, 1999), pp. 280–307; Thomas L. Brodie, *The Crucial Bridge: the Elijah-Elisha Narrative as an Interpretive Synthesis of Genesis-Kings and a Literary Model for the Gospels* (Collegeville: Liturgical Press, 2000); Joel B. Green 'The Problem of a Beginning: Israel's Scriptures in Luke 1-2', *BBR* 4 (1994): 61–85; David W. Pao, *Acts and the Isaianic New Exodus* (Tübingen: J. C. B. Mohr, 2000); Charles H. Talbert, *Reading Luke-Acts in the Mediterranean Milieu* (Leiden: Brill, 2003), p. 294; Scott Hahn, 'Kingdom and Church in Luke-Acts', in *Reading Luke: Interpretation, Reflection, Formation* (eds Craig G. Bartholomew, Joel B. Green and Anthony C. Thiselton; Scripture and Hermeneutics Series 6; Grand Rapids: Zondervan, 2005), pp. 294–326; Peter Mallen, *The Reading and Transformation of Isaiah in Luke-Acts* (LNTS, 367; London: T&T Clark, 2008); Frederick S. Tappenden, 'Aural Performance, Conceptual Blending, and Intertextuality : the (non)-use of Scripture in Luke 24:45-48', in

style, vocabulary and stories from the LXX is well known,[62] and therefore, this study will use and explore the LXX text and not the MT as the basis for reading Luke.[63] Furthermore, although this is the appropriate text with which to engage the Lukan narrative, previous studies on the shepherd king motif in Matthew's Gospel have focused on recovering the Davidic shepherd king motif from the MT as Matthew's audience was predominantly Jewish-Christian.[64] We will see that the LXX has an unexplored narrative subtlety.

Luke's use of the LXX stories is so profound that they have been recognized as the hermeneutic by which he weaves and reinterprets the LXX narratives in light of Jesus Christ. Indeed Luke states that he writes περὶ τῶν πεπληροφορημένων ἐν ἡμῖν πραγμάτων (1.1), suggesting to the reader that he sees something of their fulfilment in the story of Jesus. Del Agua identifies this when he says, 'the Old Testament tradition ... is the hermeneutic reference of meaning sought in his narration',[65] and goes on to say that 'the author's profound knowledge of biblical traditions, as well as his expertise in the art *of reapplying and updating them for the Christian community,* constitutes his theological and hermeneutical world'.[66] Similarly, Litwak states, 'the Scriptures of Israel pervade Luke-Acts from its beginning until its end ... and that they play a critical *hermeneutical* role in shaping the entirety of Luke's narrative'.[67]

In appreciating Luke's use of scripture, scholars have noted his profound

---

Biblical Interpretation in Early Christian Gospels: Volume 3, The Gospel of Luke (ed. Thomas R. Hatina; LNTS, 376; London: T&T Clark, 2010), pp. 194–5.

62. Jacques Dupont, *The Salvation of the Gentiles: Studies in the Acts of the Apostles* (trans. John Keating; New York: Paulist Press, 1979), pp. 153–4; Litwak, *Echoes,* p. 7; Mallen, *Reading,* pp. 4–5; Steve Moyise, *The Old Testament in the New: An Introduction* (New York: Continuum, 2001), pp. 45–62; Fitzmyer, *Luke,* pp. 114–16; Vernon K. Robbins, 'The Social Location of the Implied Author of Luke and Acts', in *The Social World of Luke-Acts: Models for Interpretation* (ed. Jerome H. Neyrey; Peabody: Hendrickson, 1991), pp. 323–6; Kurz, *Reading Luke-Acts,* p. 16; Brawley, *Text to Text,* p. ix; Robert F. O'Toole, 'The Parallels Between Jesus and Moses', *BTB* 20 (1990): 22; Bill T. Arnold, 'Luke's Characterizing Use of the Old Testament in the Book of Acts', in *History, Literature and Society in the Book of Acts* (ed. Ben Witherington III; Cambridge: Cambridge University Press, 1996), pp. 300–23.

63. Where there is a Göttingen version of the LXX, I will follow this, and where there is not yet or this is not yet published, I will use Alfred Rahlfs, *Septuaginta: With Morphology* (Stuttgart: Deutsche Bibelgesellschaft, 1996).

64. John Nolland, *The Gospel of Matthew* (NIGTC; Grand Rapids: Eerdmans/Bletchley: Paternoster, 2005), p. 17.

65. Augustín del Agua, 'The Lucan Narrative of the "Evangelisation of the Kingdom of God": A Contribution to the Unity of Acts', in *The Unity of Luke-Acts* (ed. J. Verheyden; BETL, 142; Leuven: Peeters, 1999), pp. 639–62 (643); Hahn, 'Kingdom and Church', p. 294.

66. del Agua, 'Lucan Narrative', p. 641, n. 8. Emphasis added.

67. Litwak, *Echoes,* p. 1. Emphasis original.

mastery of the Jewish scriptures,[68] which suggests not only he, but his named recipient Theophilus (Lk. 1.3; Acts 1.1) had considerable knowledge of the scriptures. This resonates with Kurz when he says, 'Luke generally alludes to Old Testament passages without announcing he is doing so',[69] and that he presupposes readers with a knowledge of the LXX. In acknowledging this, it is necessary to clarify that while Luke makes reference and pays some attention to his temporal world, it is primarily the story of God and God's people within which he seeks to interpret the story of Jesus. Therefore, uncovering these stories, identifying echoes, and then assessing their strength and significance is an important task. The process is not an exact science, however, and requires a framework within which to work. This study will employ Hays' seven tests for hearing echoes which allow us to test an echo's strength.[70] These are tests of: availability, volume, recurrence, thematic coherence, historical plausibility, history of interpretation, and satisfaction. The final test of satisfaction is particularly significant; it asks whether the echo creates a resonant reading with the surrounding narrative context. That is, does the echo create a satisfying end-result for the reader? This test may be regarded as subjective; but informed by the previous six tests, it may become the most important in keeping alive the possibility of new intertextual connections.

Hays' seven tests are concluded with a final note that there are occasions when an intertextual connection has a dynamic power that cannot be contained, and meaning has a way of leaping over a carefully maintained hedge.[71] In many ways, this acknowledges that interpretation is also an art and a matter of intuition. This dynamic is made even more appropriate by Luke's emphasis upon the role of the Spirit for Jesus (1.35; 3.16; 4.1, 14, 18; 10.21) and the disciples (1.15, 41, 80; 2.25, 26; 11.13; 12.12; Acts 1.2, 5, 8; 2.4).[72] This study seeks to open up narrative possibilities and to leave room for life beyond the hedges.

One last thing to be considered is the relationship between narrative methodology and history. A valid critique is levelled that narrative criticism is too distant from an historical anchor and, at its extremes, can be totally removed from history.[73] Here it is helpful to state my assumptions. The Gospel is a product of its culture which is rooted in time and space and therefore understanding the historical matrices remain an essential part in reading an ancient text.[74] It is

---

68. For Strelan this led him to posit that Luke must be a Jewish priest and not a Gentile God-fearer. Rick Strelan, *Luke the Priest: The Authority of the Author of the Third Gospel* (Aldershot: Ashgate, 2008).

69. Kurz, *Reading Luke-Acts*, p. 16.

70. Hays, *Echoes of Scripture*, pp. 29–32.

71. Ibid., pp. 32–3.

72. This is not an exhaustive list of Luke's emphasis on the Holy Spirit in Acts as the emphasis is so extensive. For a review of the importance of the Holy Spirit in Luke-Acts see Max Turner, *Power From On High: The Spirit in Israel's Restoration and Witness in Luke-Acts* (JPTSS, 9; Sheffield: Sheffield Academic, 1996).

73. Osborne, *Hermeneutical Spiral*, pp. 213–14; Hays, *Echoes of Scripture*, pp. 26–7.

74. Green, *Gospel*, p. 11.

between these two worlds of narrative and the ancient soil that I seek to navigate. Luke's Gospel is a text that is firmly linked to historical markers in the Greco-Roman world where Herod is King of Judea (1.5), Augustus is Caesar (2.1) and the Emperor Tiberius reigns (3.1). Luke makes an effort to assure his hearers that he has fully investigated the stories in his narrative (1.3) and his accuracy as an ancient historian is well supported.[75] Therefore, any study of Luke's writing must follow his lead and consider his 'text in the world'.[76] As a result we will pay particular attention to the historical use of the shepherd king motif in Chapter 2 and then consider the historical references in the Gospel, particularly in the infancy narrative, in Chapter 3. As this narrative methodology aims to rely on a solid exegetical base, this methodology will also ensure historical-grammatical considerations are met.

This study assumes Markan priority and that there is a likely common and separate source that both Luke and Matthew knew, known as Q. I do not assume Luke knew Matthew's Gospel and so Matthew will not play a significant role in this study, but may be used as a comparison.

1.3 The outline of this study

In assessing the Lukan use of the Davidic shepherd king motif, this study acknowledges the shepherd motif is repeatedly used in the LXX, God is understood as the shepherd of Israel, and Israel's hope was for a Davidic king as expressed in Ezekiel 34.23-24.[77]

In Chapter 2 we examine the narrative of David in the book of Kingdoms. This will highlight that David's nature as a shepherd is intertwined with his kingship,

---

75. There is much support for Luke as an ancient historian who gave careful attention to the accuracy of his sources. Colin J. Hemer, *The Book of Acts in the Setting of Hellenistic History* (ed. Conrad Gempf; WUNT, 49; Tübingen: J. C. B. Mohr, 1989); Bruce W. Winter and Andrew D. Clarke (eds), *The Book of Acts in its Ancient Literary Setting* (Grand Rapids: Eerdmans, 1993); Green, 'Internal Repetition', pp. 283–99; Marshall, *Historian and Theologian*, pp. 53–76; Bock, *Luke*, pp. 52–64; Ben Witherington III, *The Acts of the Apostles: A Socio-Rhetorical Commentary*, Grand Rapids: Eerdmans, 1998), p. 52; E. Plümacher, 'Luke as Historian', *ABD* 4, p. 398. *Contra*, Fitzmyer, *Luke*, p. 17; Susan Marie Praeder, 'Jesus-Paul, Peter-Paul, and Jesus-Peter Parallelisms in Luke-Acts: A History of Reader Response', in *Society of Biblical Literature Seminar Papers 1984* (ed. Kent H. Richards; Chico: SBL, 1984), pp. 23–39; Richard I. Pervo, *Acts* (Hermeneia; Minneapolis: Fortress Press, 2009), pp. 5–7.

76. Ulrich Luz, *Studies in Matthew* (trans. Rosemary Selle; Grand Rapids: Eerdmans, 2005), p. 3.

77. A full survey of the shepherd motif in the LXX and Second Temple period is found in the doctoral dissertation, 'The Davidic Shepherd King in the Lukan Narrative' (PhD diss., University of Otago, 2011). See also the comprehensive study of Jack Wayland Vancil, 'The Symbolism of the Shepherd in Biblical, Intertestamental and New Testament Material' (unpublished PhD diss., Dropsie University, 1975).

and the LXX translator takes care to make this explicit at the end of David's life as Israel's king.

In Chapter 3 we turn to the opening of Luke's narrative in Luke 1–2 taking our understanding of the Davidic shepherd king, and consider how Luke uses his many echoes and references to David. We will especially evaluate the various ways in which scholars have understood the function of the shepherds in the birth narrative and then consider how the echo of David as a shepherd king helps us read the Lukan narrative with fresh eyes.

In Chapter 4 we will note where the motif continues in Luke-Acts. We will first turn to the household mission in Luke 10 where the disciples are sent out as lambs into the midst of wolves, a text which prefigures the Acts household mission into Gentile territory, and then how Jesus calls his disciples τὸ μικρὸν ποίμνιον when he teaches them about God's provision (12.32). At the mid-point of the Gospel we will explore the parable of the faithful shepherd who goes into the wilderness to find the lost sheep (15.3-7), and see how Jesus enacts this parable in his ministry by being God's faithful shepherd. In Acts we will note the motif recurs in Paul's Miletus speech, suggesting it is not only a useful motif to describe Jesus' ministry years, but it maintains currency in the early stages of the church (Acts 20.28-29). Finally, we will ask why Luke omits Mark 6.34 and 14.27, shepherd texts which were available to him.

In Chapter 5 we examine the story of Zacchaeus, the final event in Jesus' ministry outside Jerusalem, and explore its nature as a salvation story where the Davidic shepherd king has come to seek out and save the lost sheep. We explore how 19.10 sums up the message of the Gospel and how the story finally demonstrates the fullness of the universal salvation offered by the Lukan Jesus. While our study acknowledges that this is only one of the motifs that Luke has given the reader to understand Jesus, we do suggest that Luke's use of shepherd imagery is more cohesive and systematic than has been acknowledged. The motif comes at key places in the narrative and gradually builds a picture whereby the reader can see the Lukan Jesus as God's faithful Davidic shepherd king extending salvation to the lost sheep.

2

DAVID: THE NARRATIVE IN THE LXX

The story of Israel, like that of its ANE neighbours, used elements from daily life to explore their understanding of rulers and deities. As Vancil says, 'Man's religious quest does not start from scratch, but he rather stands in relation to his past and his heritage'.[1] Civilization grew up around rivers which supplied fresh water for daily life, and so one of the lenses was that of farmers or shepherds who cared for flocks and crops. The motif is used sparsely in the early OT narrative,[2] and yet many of the earliest characters in the scriptures are shepherds. Abel is a shepherd (Gen. 4.2), so too are Abram (13.7), Lot (13.7), Laban (29.1-10), and Jacob and his sons (46.32, 34; 47.3). Even Jethro, who was a priest and Moses' father-in-law, kept a flock (Exod. 3.1). Many Israelites in Egypt were shepherds and so when the Israelites were released from slavery, they left with their flocks (12.32, 38).

The shepherd motif is firmly established in the use of ῥάβδος in the exodus narrative. This is a simple shepherding tool, but the text uses it to embody symbols of authority and power which is consistent with Egyptian and Mesopotamian cultures. Moses was known as God's shepherd in the wilderness (Num. 27.14-17), the Psalms especially theologize God as shepherd (22; *Targum Psalms* 23.1; 27.9; 47.15; 67.8; 76.21; 73.1; 77.52-54, 70-72; 79.2; 94.7; 99.3; 120.4), and David's story focuses on his shepherd identity; to this we now turn. Brueggemann writes that 'the entire narrative of David's rise is staged from shepherd boy (1 Kgdms 16:11) to shepherd king'.[3] He is correct; to talk of David *is* to talk of his story as the faithful shepherd king of Israel. Yet, this study suggests it is not only in the story of David's rise that the motif is significant, but the ongoing story of David which maintains the narrative shepherd thread until David says to the Lord, ἐγώ εἰμι ὁ ποιμήν (2 Kgdms 24.17). From David's earliest introduction to the final curtain call, he is a shepherd.

---

1. Vancil, 'The Symbolism of the Shepherd', p. 2.

2. Timothy S. Laniak, *Shepherds After My Own Heart: Pastoral Traditions and Leadership in the Bible* (NSBT, 20; Nottingham: Apollos/Downers Grove: IVP, 2006), p. 77.

3. Walter Brueggemann, *First and Second Samuel* (Interpretation; Louisville: John Knox Press, 1990), pp. 237–8.

2.1 Literary features in 'The History of David's Rise'

We first meet David as a young faithful shepherd to his father's sheep in 1 Kingdoms 16, the first story in the HDR. The unit 1 Kingdoms 16–2 Kingdoms 5 is marked by a recurring and cumulative interest in David as a shepherd,[4] with both the beginning and the end highlighting David's identity as shepherd. This creates a literary *inclusio* where the first identity the reader is presented with is David as a shepherd, and then this same motif is reiterated at the conclusion of the narrative, providing an intentional return of the motif.[5] Bar-Efrat is correct when he says, 'contrary to real life no accidental and irrelevant facts are included and the incidents are connected with each other both temporally and causally'.[6] This interest in David as a shepherd in the HDR has been clearly structured.

David is repeatedly introduced in the first three stories which could suggest a multiplicity of sources,[7] yet as we consider the narrative's final form, it is most likely that the author uses the reintroduction of David as a repetitive device whereby the reader engages with varying aspects of David's life.[8] This leads us to the conclusion that the writer has carefully crafted the reader's first impressions of David, and the initial setting and characterization is the hermeneutical filter the author provides for the reader to understand the wider narrative.[9]

2.2 David the shepherd in the HDR (1 Kgdms 16.1-2 Kgdms 5)

2.2.1 David as shepherd of his father's flock (1 Kgdms 16.1-13)

The setting for David's introduction has been prepared by the story of Samuel's miraculous birth and his career as prophet whereby he is the one who anoints the first king of Israel Saul, and most especially, his successor and God's elect king David. We meet David after Saul is rejected as king (1 Kgdms 15) when the Lord sends Samuel to anoint a new king from the house of Jesse the Bethlehemite

---

4. Tony W. Cartledge, *1 & 2 Samuel* (Smyth and Helwys Bible Commentary; Macon: Smyth and Helwys, 2001), p. 199; Brueggemann, *First and Second Samuel*, p. 120.

5. Willitts has explored this motif where the early narrative shows David's youth and inexperience as a shepherd and in 2 Sam. 5.2 where he is a military and political shepherd ruler. His emphasis is on the political ramifications of the shepherd king motif and ultimately shows this in the context of Matthew's Gospel. See Willitts, *Messianic Shepherd-King*, pp. 4, 54–8.

6. Shimon Bar-Efrat, 'Some Observations on the Analysis of Structure in Biblical Literature', *VT* 30 (1980), p. 163.

7. McCarter, *I Samuel*, pp. 282–3, 295–8; Tsumura, *Samuel*, pp. 434–6.

8. Brueggemann, *First and Second Samuel*, p. 120; Keith Bodner, *1 Samuel: A Narrative Commentary* (HBM, 19; Sheffield: Sheffield Phoenix Press, 2008), p. 176.

9. Sternberg, *Expositional Modes*, pp. 8, 56–128; Lyle Eslinger, *Kingship of God in Crisis: A Close Reading of 1 Samuel 1–12* (Sheffield: Almond Press, 1985), p. 50.

(16.1). This is the highlight of Samuel's career, and his final and most significant prophetic task.[10] In many respects this may also be seen as a long prelude before David is anointed king. The narrative is structured to parallel and contrast the story of Saul and David's anointing, with the latter as superior.[11]

Both men are anointed privately (9–10; 16.3) while the Lord sends Saul to Samuel in ch. 9, but Samuel to David in ch. 16. The men are both anointed with oil although the containers vary; the oil for Saul is from a cooking container (φακὸν τοῦ ἐλαίου; 10.1) while a horn of oil (κέρας τοῦ ἐλαίου; 16.13) is used to anoint David. It is possible these two containers point to David's anointing as more important.[12] Κέρας signifies considerable strength[13] while φακός means either lentils or a container that is in the shape of lentils,[14] a household object of no particular interest. Κέρας is used repeatedly in the biblical narrative with respect to sacrificial offerings or the tabernacle (Gen. 22.13; Exod. 27.2; 29.12; 30.2, 3, 10; Lev. 4.7, 18, 25, 34; 8.15). Conversely, φακός occurs only ten times in the LXX and, in all but Jehu's anointing in 4 Kingdoms 9.1 and 3, relates to objects from everday life (Gen. 25.34; 1 Kgdms 26.11, 12, 16; 2 Kgdms 17.28; 23.11; Ezek. 4.9). While it is used of Jehu's anointing as king, Jehu is yet another example of a king who fails in his role and whose kingship is marred (4 Kgdms 9.11-31). It is therefore possible that the object of anointing does symbolize the nature of the king's reign. Like Saul, Jehu too will fail in his role as king, while David is positioned as a superior king who the Lord continues to bless.

The details of Saul and David's physical appearance continue the narrative contrast. In 16.7 the reader hears the divine voice say that God does not look upon the human attributes of appearance and size as criteria in the election of a king. This directly corresponds with the information given about Saul's appearance at his anointing when he is described as handsome and tall (9.2; 10.23). When Eliab is rejected by God due to his external appearance (16.6), this resonates with the story of Saul who has been rejected as king. The narrative also uses ἐξουδενόω to describe both Saul and Eliab's rejection as king (15.23, 26; 16.1, 7) which is contrasted by the use of ἐκλέγω[15] to describe David. Saul was chosen by human criteria in the same way Samuel was quick to choose Eliab due to his appearance. However, David is chosen by God who views the heart.

This internal contrast is further accentuated in the repetitive use of ὁράω, where the reader is encouraged to *see* David's election through God's eyes. The first two pericopae of the HDR both use the verb ὁράω in the context of election (16.1, 6, 7, 17 [twice], 18), and the idea of sight becomes a guiding feature of the

10. Bodner, *1 Samuel,* p. 166.

11. Moshe Garsiel, *The First Book of Samuel: A Literary Study of Comparative Structures, Analogies and Parallels* (Jerusalem: Rubin Mass, 1990), pp. 107–37.

12. Bodner, *1 Samuel,* p. 167.

13. *GELS,* p. 395.

14. *GELS,* p. 710.

15. ἐξουδενόω means to consider to be of no account. *GELS,* p. 254; ἐκλέγω means to pick, select or to confer a unique status. *GELS,* pp. 210–11.

text where God is the one who truly *sees* a person.[16] 1 Kgdms 16.1 opens with God sending Samuel to Jesse for God has already *seen* the one who will become king, and this is based on an internal understanding (seeing) of the heart (16.7). The word also occurs in David's selection as a musician for Saul's court with the servant responding Ἰδοὺ ἑόρακα υἱὸν τῷ Ιεσσαι Βηθλεεμίτην (16.17). The linguistic use of ὁράω thus links the two texts and shows God's point of view in David's election as king and his suitability to come into Saul's court.

The final contrast between Saul and David relates to the use of the word ποίμνιον. The reason the Lord replaces Saul as king is because he has kept some of the Amalekites' ποίμνια when the Lord asked him to kill all living things (15.9, 14, 15, 21); the narrative repeats ποίμνια four times, showing a linguistic emphasis. Even though Saul's intention for these sheep was to give them as a sacrifice to the Lord, this act seals his downfall and contrasts David, who is Jesse's faithful shepherd. It may also be of note that the verb ποιμαίνω is used to describe David but it is never used of Saul (16.11; 2 Kgdms 5.2; 7.7; 1 Chron. 11.2). Thus 1 Kingdoms 15 is the defining event in Saul's demise as king, and the entry point whereby the narrative introduces the new king, the faithful shepherd David.

These parallels and contrasts are built up over a long narrative period, and ultimately point to God's choice of David as Israel's king. In 16.1-13 the reader hears that he is Jesse's youngest son, a ποιμήν (16.11), ruddy with beautiful eyes and of good appearance to the Lord (16.12). The narrative describes the youth's appearance, and yet in 16.7 the Lord explicitly stated that it was not the outward appearance that mattered to God. This could suggest that God is fickle and has changed his mind, or that the author admired David so much that he included details of his good looks anyway.[17] With the close narrative proximity of such contradictory statements however, I suggest that there may be another explanation. It may be possible that it is the other attributes of David listed in 16.11 that indicate why he is chosen as Israel's new king, and these attributes outplay the details of his appearance. Appearance, as 16.7 says, is no indicator of the state of the heart. So what are these other attributes?

First, David is the youngest of Jesse's sons, and second, he is ποιμήν. The textual focus on David's shepherd background will continue to be important, and so may be significant here.[18] As Firth notes, the knowledge that David was with the

16. David G. Firth, *1 and 2 Samuel* (AOTC, 8; Nottingham: Apollos/Downers Grove: IVP, 2009), p. 181; Garsiel, *Samuel*, pp. 111–15; Ralph W. Klein, *1 Samuel* (WBC, 10; Waco: Word, 1983), p. 160; Robert Polzin, *Samuel and the Deuteronomist: A Literary Study of the Deuteronomic History.* Part Two: 1 Samuel (Indiana Studies in Biblical Literature; Bloomington: Indiana University Press, 1989), pp. 153–4; Tsumura, *Samuel*, pp. 424–43.

17. Scholars quickly note the irony here, but generally suggest that the author's admiration for David is such that the information was included anyway. Brueggemann, *First and Second Samuel*, p. 122; Cartledge, *1 and 2 Samuel*, p. 202; Firth, *1 and 2 Samuel*, p. 184; Klein, *1 Samuel*, p. 161.

18. Firth, *1 and 2 Samuel*, p. 184; Klein, *1 Samuel*, p. 161. *Contra*, Tsumura, *Samuel*,

sheep may have created a sense of hope as ANE kings routinely styled themselves as shepherds,[19] and, Alter writes, 'the tending of flocks will have symbolic implication for the future leader of Israel.[20] As we will come to see, when David is anointed king he will be named as *shepherd* king (2 Kgdms 5.2) and therefore, it may be possible that it is this knowledge that is more significant than the reference to David's physical appearance.

Furthermore, being young was not a barrier to serving God. The exodus narrative leads us to understand that Moses was protected by God as a young baby so that he would later be able to rescue the Israelite people from slavery in Egypt (Exod. 1–3). Similarly, Joshua was Moses' young assistant when he was chosen to lead the Israelites across the Jordan and into Canaan (Exod. 33.11). David's youth has kept him hidden in the narrative thus far,[21] but now his youth is removed as a barrier to his kingship.

In 1 Kgdms 16.13 Samuel anoints David in the midst of his brothers, while his destiny as king is known only to Samuel. The reason the Lord gives for the anointing is simply that David is ἀγαθός. The Spirit springs upon him at this point as with Saul (10.6, 9), but remains with him unlike Saul, from whom the Spirit departed (16.14). It is only after the anointing that David is named in the account. Until then he was known only as Jesse's youngest son and the ποιμήν of his flock.

2.2.2 From the shepherd fields to Saul's court (1 Kgdms 16.14-23)

The story of David's anointing (16.1-13) and David at Saul's court (16.14-23) are closely related narratively and thematically,[22] with the story immediately shifting from David who has the Spirit on him, to Saul, from whom the Spirit has departed and who is plagued by an evil spirit. The interplay of good and bad spirits forms a pivot between the texts and brings the stories of the two men together. The court attendants set about solving the problem of the evil spirit on Saul and one attendant proposes finding a skilful musician whose music can alleviate the king's distress. The son of Jesse is suggested and after his resume is given, David is summoned. David is so successful in Saul's court that Saul asks Jesse if he might remain with him. David then becomes Saul's trusted armour-bearer and musician.

p. 422. Tsumura believes the roles of shepherd and king are contrasted in 2 Sam. 7.8 and so it is unlikely here that there is any sense of David's future role being alluded to. However, this position seems unlikely as shepherd and king are linked in 2 Kgdms 5.1-3.

19. Firth, *1 and 2 Samuel*, p. 184.

20. Robert Alter, *The David Story: A Translation and Commentary of 1 and 2 Samuel* (New York: Norton, 1999), p. 97.

21. Firth, *1 and 2 Samuel*, pp. 184–5.

22. Klein, *1 Samuel*, p. 164; Peter D. Miscall, *1 Samuel: A Literary Reading* (Bloomington: Indiana University Press, 1986), p. 115; Garsiel, *The First Book of Samuel: A Literary Study of Comparative Structures, Analogies and Parallels* (Jerusalem: Rubin Mass, 1990), p. 111; Tsumura, *Samuel*, p. 425.

Questions have been raised regarding how a servant of Saul knew so much about a youth from an insignificant Judean village such as Bethlehem.[23] While no definitive answer can be given, this information does paint David as having the necessary attributes for a future king.

This pericope both introduces new information about David and repeats details we have already heard (16.18). The servant describes David as συνετός conveying the sense of sage-like wisdom or being able to understand with discernment,[24] as πολεμιστής, information that will be important in the following chapter, and as σοφὸς λόγῳ.

The narrative repeats that he is a shepherd (16.11, 19), that the Lord is with him (16.13, 18) and he is good in appearance (16.12, 18). The knowledge that ὁ κύριος μετ᾽ αὐτοῦ (16.18) will have further importance in the narrative (16.18; 17.37; 18.14, 18; 2 Kgdms 5.10),[25] and is an attribute that marks David out as a divinely endowed leader.[26] David is presented as 'good': ἀγαθὸς ὁράσει κυρίῳ (16.12), and ἀνὴρ ἀγαθὸς τῷ εἴδει (16.18); the use of ἀγαθός contrasts Saul who is tormented by πνεῦμα πονηρός (16.14).

David is affirmed as a shepherd with the king himself saying, Ἀπόστειλον πρός με τὸν υἱόν σου Δαυιδ τὸν ἐν τῷ ποιμνίῳ σου (16.9). Although this information is not listed in the resume, the pleonastic recollection functions as a *Leitwort*, keeping the reader's attention on David's shepherd identity.[27] As Bar-Efrat points out, repetition serves to emphasize an important aspect in the story and hints at implied meanings.[28] Garsiel notes that 'biblical narrators are very sparing of physical descriptions unless they are relevant to events',[29] and Freedman's tests for a significant motif note that the frequency and the placement of the motif at key points in a narrative strengthen its efficacy. Here both criteria are satisfied.

2.2.3 David fights Goliath (1 Kgdms 17)

This pericope is especially important in the HDR as it is the turning point in David's rise as king when he enters the public stage, and popular support is given to David over Saul. There is a sharp theological focus with David's victory in battle attributed to the Lord's power rather than his own strength. From this point David's destiny as a leader for Israel is sealed and it is only a matter of time before Saul is brought down and David is anointed king.

23. Bodner, *1 Samuel*, p. 173; Brueggemann, *First and Second Samuel*, p. 125.

24. 'συνετός,' BDAG, p. 970.

25. 1 Kgdms 17.37 is verbally similar but not an exact repetition.

26. Firth, *1 and 2 Samuel*, p. 189; McCarter, *1 Samuel*, p. 281; Tsumura, *Samuel*, p. 430.

27. Alter, *Art*, pp. 92–7, 148; Buber, *Scripture*, pp. 114–28; Bar-Efrat, *Narrative Art*, pp. 136, 212; Amit, 'Leading Word', pp. 99–114; Freedman, 'Literary Motif', pp. 123–31; Rowe, *Early Narrative Christology*, pp. 197–9.

28. Bar-Efrat, *Narrative Art*, pp. 116–17.

29. Garsiel, *First Book of Samuel*, p. 115.

The story continues the focus on David as a shepherd and explains to the reader how this background makes him suitable to become God's chosen shepherd for all Israel. We see this first, in the repetition of direct shepherding language.[30] David is ποιμαίνων ἦν ὁ δοῦλός σου and ἐν τῷ ποιμνίῳ (17.34), and he puts his stones ἐν τῷ καδίῳ τῷ ποιμενικῷ (17.40). These ποιμήν cognates, together with the substantial narrative space given to describe the outdoor setting for the battle (17.1-3), paint a vivid pastoral scene.

Sizeable narrative space is given to a detailed description of Goliath and his armoury (17.4-7), which is contrasted with David's laconic shepherd identity. This builds suspense and creates the idea that Goliath is well-prepared and is likely to be successful in battle.[31] Goliath wears a helmet, and he has a coat of chain mail of bronze and iron weighing five thousand shekels (57 kg).[32] He has moulded bronze greaves to protect his legs, a bronze shield protecting his shoulders, an immense spear of iron weighing approximately 6.8 kilos, and he even has a man who went before him to carry his armour.[33] With the biblical text rarely giving such detailed descriptions, the differences between the two characters are accentuated; Goliath is heavily armed and a physically imposing warrior, and David is the young shepherd armed only with the natural objects from the fields. McCarter concludes it 'emphasises further the inequality of the coming contest … (and) divulge(s) to the alert reader the one vulnerable spot on the giant's body, viz. his forehead'.[34] It is this undefended spot David exploits with the simple weapons of a shepherd. He takes his shepherd staff, a sling and five smooth stones, which are likely the size of tennis balls, from the wadi (17.40).[35] While a sling was a homemade weapon most youths in the fields would have carried, it was also a military weapon common in the ANE, able to kill or maim. Egyptian evidence from the second millennium BCE records the sling as a military weapon,[36] and Judges 20.16 records seven hundred ambidextrous slingers who could all throw a stone at a hair and not miss. David clearly had confidence in his tools of shepherding, while the text notes his confidence was in the Lord's ability to bring victory in battle (17.37). The description of the skilled mighty warrior with all the up-to-date technology poses a suggestive comparison to the faith-filled shepherd armed only with a shepherd's pouch.[37] As David is the clear hero of the story, Goliath's long description ultimately functions to accentuate David's success in battle.

---

30. Klein, *1 Samuel*, p. 179; Willitts, *Messianic Shepherd-King*, p. 55.

31. Firth, *1 and 2 Samuel*, p. 196; Tsumura, *Samuel*, p. 442; Bar-Efrat, *Narrative Art*, p. 121.

32. Tsumura, *Samuel*, p. 442.

33. Ibid., pp. 442–4.

34. McCarter, *I Samuel*, p. 292.

35. Firth, *1 and 2 Samuel*, p. 199.

36. Tsumura, *Samuel*, p. 460.

37. Shimon Bar-Efrat, 'First Samuel', in *The Jewish Study Bible* (eds Adele Berlin and Marc Zvi Brettler; Oxford: Oxford University Press, 2004), p. 595.

Secondly, the plot of the story gives details of David's earlier years as a shepherd. David claims that his ability to fight Goliath is due to his success in fighting bears and lions during his shepherding years (17.34-37). 'David's boast' is divided into two sections. In the first part, David describes the dangerous aspects of a shepherd's life (17.34-35), and in the second part, David appeals to the evidence of this shepherd experience as suitable preparation for fighting Goliath (17.36-37).[38] This repeated information is in dialogue form which slows the narrative down, and is the first time we hear David speak – both important features of a text.[39] David claims that his years as his father's shepherd have prepared him as an expert warrior. This information is given three times (17.34, 36, 37), making David's first speech lengthy and conveying some measure of narrative weight.

Finally, David explains that his success as a shepherd warrior came from the Lord's protection, and so he shows confidence that God will protect him against Goliath (17.37); he perceives that his spirituality and his shepherding are connected. The narrative describes David's clothing and armour as that of a shepherd, and this suggests that in fighting Goliath, his years as a shepherd have also spiritually prepared him for battle. David says to Goliath: 'The Lord does not save by spear and sword; for the battle is the Lord's and he will ultimately give you into our hand' (17.47). The section ends with David reaching into his shepherd's pouch and taking the stone that kills Goliath. This links the power of the name of the Lord with David's identity as shepherd and recalls David's earlier ability to fight off Saul's evil spirits (16.14-23). Both textual units maintain the connection between David as a shepherd and his faithfulness to the Lord.

After this pericope Saul quickly starts to lose power (18.7), displays ungodly attributes (18.8; 20.30), is ravaged by evil spirits and tries to kill David (18.11; 19.10), and consults a medium (28). He eventually commits suicide (31.4). David, in contrast, finds success with Michal and Jonathan (18.28; 20.42; 23.17-18), in battle (18.7, 13-16; 23.1-15; 2 Kgdms 3.1), over evil (16.23; 17.47) and finally over Saul.

2.2.4 David's public rise and Saul's public decline (1 Kgdms 18.6-16)

This new section is really a coda to the epic fight from ch. 17. In this passage David's victory over Goliath is met with rejoicing from the women who were dancing and singing, Ἐπάταξεν Σαουλ ἐν χιλιάσιν αὐτοῦ καὶ Δαυιδ ἐν μυριάσιν αὐτοῦ (18.7). This refrain continues the contrast between Saul and David from the previous two pericopae, but whereas the contrast was private, now it is public. Alter comments:

> It is a fixed rule of biblical poetry that when a number occurs in the first verset, it must be increased in the parallel verset, often, as here, by one decimal place.

38. Anthony R. Ceresko, 'A Rhetorical Analysis of David's "Boast" (1 Samuel 17:34-37): Some Reflections on Method', *CBQ* 47 (1985), pp. 59-74.
39. Polzin, *Samuel and the Deuteronomist*, p. 169.

Saul shows himself a good reader of biblical poetry: he understands perfectly well that the convention is a vehicle of meaning, and that the intensification or magnification characteristic of the second verset is used to set David's triumphs above his own. Saul, who earlier had made the mistake of listening to the voice of the people, now is enraged by the people's words.[40]

The contrast is further evident in the fear Saul exhibits of David (18.12), as opposed to David who shows no fear as he went out and in before the people (18.13, 16). It is ironic that because of his fear, Saul sends David out to be an officer of a thousand, the number the narrative has linked to Saul's poetic battle tally in 18.7, yet the result of this is that David gains even greater popular support. From this point in the narrative Saul's public decline begins and inversely, David's rise begins.

The use of ἐξεπορεύετο καὶ εἰσεπορεύετο ἔμπροσθεν τοῦ λαοῦ forms an intertextual link to Numbers 27.15-17[41] where Moses asks God to appoint his successor for the congregation who will, 'go out (ἐξελεύσεται) before them and come in (εἰσελεύσεται) before them ... so that the congregation of the Lord shall not be like sheep without a shepherd'. There is good evidence for an intertextual link here.

First, the same pattern of going out and coming in is used in Numbers 17.15, while Numbers uses the verbs ἐξέρχομαι and εἰσέρχομαι and Kingdoms uses ἐκπορεύω and εἰσπορεύω. The notion of 'going out and coming in' within a battle context will be used again by the writer of Kingdoms (8.20; 29.6; 2 Kgdms 3.25; 5.2, 24).[42] This may have been prefigured in Exodus 3.8 when Moses brings them out (ἐξάγω) and in (εἰσάγω), as this expression of going out and coming in 'is often used to describe military movements led by the shepherd'[43] (cf. Exod. 3.10, 11, 17; 6.6, 13, 26; 7.5; 12.42; 17.3; 23.23; Num. 20.5; Deut. 4.38; 20.1; 21.10; 28.25; Judg. 4.14; 2 Kgdms 5.2, 24; 4 Kgdms 19.9). Chae therefore describes this as 'technical language for a shepherd's role that echoes YHWH's own redemptive leadership'.[44]

Secondly, ἐξεπορεύετο καὶ εἰσεπορεύετο ἔμπροσθεν τοῦ λαοῦ is used twice in the Kingdoms narrative (1 Kgdms 18.13, 16). This double usage strengthens the phrase's efficacy and also encourages the reader to: (1) take careful note of what it encases; and (2) ask why it is important enough to be used twice. The material encased between the repeated phrase is another comparison between the two warriors with David as the hero; David acts prudently and the Lord was

---

40. Alter, *David*, p. 113. *Contra*, McCarter who suggests the couplet shows equality rather than priority as in Ps. 90.7, while he agrees that for David to be considered Saul's equal was enough of a threat to create suspicion and jealousy. McCarter, *1 Samuel*, pp. 311–12; Cartledge, *1 and 2 Samuel*, p. 230.

41. McCarter, *1 Samuel*, p. 313; Tsumura, *Samuel*, p. 480; Willitts, *Messianic Shepherd-King*, pp. 56–7; Chae, *Davidic Shepherd*, p. 27.

42. Tsumura, *Samuel*, p. 480.

43. Chae, *Eschatological Davidic Shepherd*, p. 27.

44. Ibid., p. 28.

with him (18.14) and Saul acknowledges David's prudence while he himself, was afraid (18.15).

Thirdly, the rhetorical stress the writer places on the phrase by sandwiching it around the refrain κύριος μετ αὐτοῦ should not be underestimated. David's story begins with the spirit rushing on him and staying with him (16.13) and the refrain κύριος μετ αὐτοῦ is used to describe him in 1 Kingdoms 16.18 and 2 Kingdoms 5.10. It is knowledge that the Lord was with David which confirmed to the Israelites that David was the chosen king for Israel (2 Kgdms 5.2). Furthermore, there are similarities between the textual units of Numbers 27.15-23 and 1 Kingdoms 16–18, as Joshua is filled with the Spirit and commissioned by the priest Eleazar to lead the Israelite people (Num. 27.18-23), and the Spirit is on David and he is anointed by the priest Samuel to lead the Israelite people (1 Kgdms 16.13). Joshua is an important figure in Israel's history as he leads the Israelites into the promised land, and this parallel suggests David is being presented as another significant figure who is leading the Israelite people by the power of the God's Spirit.

Fourthly, as a considerable part of 1 Kingdoms describes David's rise as shepherd king of Israel, then it is quite conceivable that the writer might appeal to the story of Moses' request for a shepherd leader for Israel in Numbers 27.17 when defending the rise of David the shepherd. Hollander notes that the 'revisionary power of allusive echo generates new figuration'.[45] Moses is the defining figure in the exodus, and his story held great significance for the nation of Israel. This intertextual link strengthens the defence of David's legitimate rise to power.

Finally, there is awareness among scholars who also make this intertextual link.[46] Chae notes the same intertextual link in 2 Kingdoms 5.2 and that 'the OT usage of shepherd imagery for human leaders finds its ideal type in the son of Jesse (2 Kgdms 5.2; 7.5-7, 12-16)'.[47] Firth does not make this connection while he does suggest that the women dancing and singing are reminiscent of Miriam (Exod. 15.20-21) and that this shows the victory is from the Lord.[48] This early exodus story may in fact strengthen the likelihood of the echo of Numbers 27.17, as both are stories of Moses and the exodus.

This makes the link viable through Hays' test for echoes providing good evidence that the shepherd motif continues into ch. 18. This forms the final narrative where David is foregrounded as shepherd in the beginning of the HDR. The narrative now moves to show David's military rise and succession as king, from which he has been prepared in Jesse's field.

---

45. John Hollander, *The Figure of Echo: A Mode of Allusion in Milton and After* (Berkeley: University of California Press, 1981), p. ix.

46. Klein, *1 Samuel*, p. 188; McCarter, *I Samuel*, p. 313; Willitts, *Messianic Shepherd-King*, pp. 56-7.

47. Chae, *Eschatological Davidic Shepherd*, p. 28.

48. Firth, *1 and 2 Samuel*, p. 197.

2.2.5 David anointed as shepherd king (2 Kgdms 5.1-10)

2 Kingdoms 5.1-10 is the climax to the HDR and David is anointed as Israel's shepherd ruler.[49] He was first anointed king over Judah at Hebron (2.4) but now the northern elders recognize that all the tribes of Israel have a flesh and blood relationship and formalize this unity with David. They acknowledge that even when Saul was king, it was David who had led them 'out and in' (cf. 1 Kgdms 8.20; Num. 27.17), and therefore was already functioning as a leader in their midst. This recollection of David's earlier acts and the link with the story of Moses shows the elders have discerned another important leader.[50] Chae writes: 'once again we discover the language of "leading out" and "leading in" clearly associated with the shepherd image.'[51]

At the anointing the Lord says: 'It is you who shall '*shepherd* my people Israel, and it is you who shall become a ruler over Israel' (5.2). By placing the words into the divine mouth, the phrase is given both theological and narrative freight; furthermore, it creates a narrative *inclusio* recalling David's initial anointing by Samuel (1 Kgdms 16).[52]

This central statement in 2 Kingdoms 5.2 is surrounded by a repetition of information. In 5.1 all the tribes of Israel came to David and then in 5.3 all the elders of Israel came to him. Some scholars have questioned if there were two source traditions used by the MT at this point and suggest that 5.1-2 are an independent tradition which was added later to 5.3.[53] However, a narrative reading shows that this repetition is more likely to be a rhetorical device which functions to draw attention to the central saying in 5.2 where David is named as the Lord's shepherd king.[54] Alter labels this device as resumptive repetition and further notes:

> the move to confirm David as king of Israel, with which the episode began, after the insertion of the tribes' dialogue (vv.1, 2) is carried forward. It is the role of the tribal rank and file to proclaim fealty, but of the elders to sign a pact and anoint David, and so 'elders' is now substituted for 'tribes' of the first verse.[55]

49. Brueggemann, *First and Second Samuel*, p. 236; Cartledge, *1 and 2 Samuel*, p. 409; Firth, *1 and 2 Samuel*, p. 363; Willitts, *Messianic Shepherd-King*, p. 54

50. Brueggemann, *First and Second Samuel*, p. 2.

51. Chae, *Eschatological Davidic Shepherd*, p. 28.

52. Cartledge, *1 and 2 Samuel*, 410.

53. Hans William Hertzberg, *I and II Samuel: A Commentary* (trans. J. S. Bowden; Philadelphia: Westminster Press, 1964), pp. 266–7; Gnana Robinson, *Let Us Be Like the Nations: A Commentary on the Books of 1 and 2 Samuel* (International Theological Commentary; Edinburgh: Eerdmans/Grand Rapids: Handsel, 1993), pp. 170–1.

54. Alter, *David*, p. 220; David M. Gunn, *The Story of King David: Genre and Interpretation* (JSOTSS, 6; Sheffield: JSOT, 1978), p. 71.

55. Alter, *David*, pp. 220–1.

David is the one the Lord has chosen for Israel and, as Firth astutely notes, this repetition foregrounds David's status as shepherd ruler of Israel.[56]

The language for ruler in 5.2 is ἡγούμενον (to lead, rule) while 5.3 uses βασιλεύς. Cartledge suggests the possibility that when the tribes came to David at Hebron, they may have been 'dancing around the use of the word king' with the intention to limit David's power, then in an older tradition, represented by 5.3, there are no qualms using the word.[57] Firth comments that David served a preparatory status as 'leader' but in 5.3, is now named as king.[58] However, ἡγούμενον will be used of David again in 2 Kingdoms 6.21 so Firth's reasoning is not likely, and it appears the two terms are used interchangeably.

Therefore, in understanding the nature of David who will be known as Israel's greatest king, we must do this within the understanding of him as the Lord's shepherd king. 2 Kingdoms 5.2 makes this explicit, while the narrative framework of the HDR uses an *inclusio* whereby David is anointed king while he is a shepherd of Jesse's flock at the beginning of the unit, and he is named as *shepherd king* when the elders anoint him shepherd king at the end of the unit. Freedman's criterion for a *Leitwort* is one whereby its placement at significant points adds to the efficacy of the motif, as does the volume of repetition of this shepherd identity. This is highly suggestive that God's choice of king implies care, provision and protection. These combined literary features suggest Brueggemann is correct in saying that 'the entire narrative of David's rise is staged from shepherd boy to shepherd king,'[59] and furthermore, that the HDR sets the standard for David's ongoing kingship.

2.3 The Davidic covenant and beyond

There are three further passages where the shepherd motif is visible and all are significant to the wider story of David. The first is the Davidic covenant (2 Kgdms 7.1-17; cf. 1 Chron. 17.4-14), the second is in a parable when David's first sin as king is recorded (2 Kgdms 12), and the third is David's sin over the census (24.15-17). Each is significant and points to the ongoing nature of David's reign as Israel's shepherd.

2.3.1 The Davidic covenant (2 Kgdms 7.1-17)

In the 'covenant' the eternal nature of the Davidic kingdom is described with reference to David's shepherd roots (7.8) in the longest divine speech since God spoke to Moses. The use of direct speech creates a sense of immediacy and

56. Firth, *1 and 2 Samuel*, p. 363.
57. Cartledge, *1 and 2 Samuel*, p. 411.
58. Firth, *1 and 2 Samuel*, p. 363.
59. Brueggemann, *First and Second Samuel*, p. 237.

priority,[60] and the recollection of factors from the HDR highlights the significance of what is being said.[61]

The word διαθήκη is not used in 2 Kingdoms 7, but the language contained within it suggests this was understood as a formal covenant. The use of τῷ δούλῳ μου (7.5, 8) is language common to suzerain-vassal treaties and has a perlocutionary effect whereby Nathan goes to speak to David. Firth notes this in the treaty between Mursilis and Duppi-Teshub in the second millennium BCE where Mursilis requires that on his death Duppi-Teshub become vassal (or servant) to his son.[62] Gerbrandt shows that it is a phrase used repeatedly of David and demonstrates his close relationship with YHWH, but also that Moses is the other figure to be described as τῷ δούλῳ μου frequently in the Deuteronomistic History and places the two figures on an equal footing.[63] That is, Gerbrandt describes Moses as the founder of Israel's faith, although this may be underplaying Abraham, and David as the founder of a new era in the history of Israel. Certainly they are two primary figures in Israel's history and this connection is helpful. The repeated use of τῷ δούλῳ μου in 7.8 when there is a new stage in the discourse only confirms the importance of the servant relationship.[64]

David hears that the Lord has been with him throughout his battles with his enemies, another feature in suzerain-vassal treaties where the suzerain shows the benefits to his vassals. As Firth says, this demonstrates that the Lord has been David's suzerain through a long period of time.[65] The expression κύριος παντοκράτωρ (7.8), a title which is used repeatedly when the Lord's power and authority is described, points to the solemnity of the word to David and the authority with which it is given.[66]

There are also many connections between the promise to Abraham and 2 Kingdoms 7 which suggest a formal covenant is being initiated here by the Lord. The promise to David in 7.9-10b move from personal promises to those for the nation as a whole. This may allude back to Abraham's promise (Gen. 15.1-15) which begins with his own progeny and then refers to the promise of land and peace for the nation. We also read of both individuals being μέγας (Gen. 12.2; 2 Kgdms 7.9). One of the strongest parallels to the Abrahamic covenant is when

60. Robert D. Bergen, *1, 2 Samuel*, (NAC; Nashville: Broadman and Holman, 1996), p. 336; Firth, *1 and 2 Samuel*, p. 384.

61. David G. Firth, 'Speech Acts and Covenant in 2 Samuel 7:1-17', in *The God of Covenant: Biblical, Theological and Contemporary Perspectives* (ed. Jamie A. Grant and Alistair I. Wilson (Leicester: Apollos, 2005), p. 86.

62. Ibid., p. 87.

63. Gerald Eddie Gerbrandt, *Kingship According to the Deuteronomistic History* (SBLDS, 87; Atlanta: Scholars Press, 1986), p. 170.

64. Firth, 'Speech Acts', p. 88.

65. Ibid., p. 89.

66. The title is used in 2 Kingdoms 5.10 after David's anointing as king of Israel, and later in David's prayer (2 Kgdms 7.25, 27). It is a prominent title in the writings of the prophets, with Zechariah using it forty times.

David wants to build the Lord an οἶκος, and in reply the Lord says he will do so from his σπέρμα (Gen. 15.3, 5, 13, 18; 2 Kgdms 7.12). This is also a feature of a Hittite treaty,[67] though its intertextual echo to Abraham's story is most likely stronger here alongside other echoes of the promise to Abraham. The eternal nature of the Abrahamic and Davidic covenants is also paralleled (Gen. 17.13; 2 Kgdms 7.13, 16, 25, 29), as is the close relationship to the Lord (Gen. 17.8b; 2 Kgdms 7.14). Finally, as we have already noted, David appears to understand the exchange as διαθήκη when in his last words he refers to the everlasting covenant (διαθήκην γὰρ αἰώνιον ἔθετό μοι; 2 Kgdms 23.1-7).

The covenant is also recalled using διαθήκη in many other passages in the scriptures (2 Kgdms 23.1-7; 3 Kgdms 2.4; 8.22-26; 9.4-5), Psalms (2; 71, at the end of Book II; 77.70-72; 88, at the end of Book III; 131.1-18), and in the Prophets (Isa. 8.23–9.6; 11.1-9; Amos 9.11; Mic. 5.2-5; Jer. 17.24-27; 23.5-6; 30.8-9; 33.14-26; Ezek. 37.24-28), and frequently with reference to David's shepherd role.

The covenant names several promises from the Lord to David; the Lord says he will make David's name renowned (2 Kgdms 7.9), will appoint a place for his people (7.10), give rest from his enemies (7.11), an everlasting house and kingdom (7.12, 16) and a father–son relationship (7.14). In the covenant there is deliberate play on the idea of 'house' with the parallel ideas of a physical place of a temple and David's dynastic line.[68]

This promise of an eternal throne for David's house, as Chae rightly notes, coincides with YHWH entrusting David as the shepherd of Israel.[69] The recollection of David's call from the sheepfolds acts as a filter through which the narrative of covenant can be viewed. The Lord makes this covenant with David because leaders are called to function as faithful shepherds of the Lord's flock. Ultimately, as the narrative will reveal, David very quickly demonstrates his weakness in carrying out this shepherd duty when he sins with Bathsheba and this escalates into murder of her husband, Uriah (2 Kgdms 11). It is therefore appropriate that Nathan's response will cause him to recall his anointing to be a faithful shepherd.

2.3.2 Nathan's parable and David's first sin (2 Kgdms 12.1-15)

David's sin of adultery with Bathsheba and this cycle of sin which leads to Uriah's murder results in quick judgement from the Lord via the prophet Nathan. In 2 Kingdoms 12 Nathan speaks to David, beginning with a parable of the rich man and the poor man. The rich man has ποίμνια καὶ βουκόλια πολλὰ σφόδρα (12.2) while the poor man ἀμνὰς μία μικρά ἦν ἐκτήσατο (12.3). There are many points of contrast which point to a favourable view of the poor man. He owns

---

67. Firth, 'Speech Acts', p. 92.

68. Alter, *David*, p. 233; Firth, *1 and 2 Samuel*, p. 382; P. Kyle McCarter Jr. *II Samuel: A New Translation with Introduction, Notes and Commentary* (AB, 9; Garden City: Doubleday, 1984), p. 205; Robinson, *Let Us Be Like*, p. 190.

69. Chae, *Eschatological Davidic Shepherd*, p. 28.

only one female lamb as opposed to the rich man's flocks and herds, and this he has acquired for himself indicating personal effort. Furthermore, the poor man is pictured as a faithful shepherd who takes care of the lamb by preserving it (περιποιέω), rearing it (ἐκτρέφω), and treating it as one of his family. The parable says, 'it used to eat from his bread and drink from his cup and sleep in his bosom, and it was like a daughter to him'. This language personifies the lamb and is highly evocative, and emotive leading the reader to be sympathetic to the poor man.

In contrast, the text tells the reader nothing of how the rich man acquired his flocks nor how he cared for them. This is a clear narrative indicator of how David and the reader are to respond to each character.[70] Nathan takes until the end of 12.3 to set the scene for the narrative turn when the traveller enters into the story.

The traveller comes only to the rich man who, in response, does not use one of his ποίμνιον or βουκολία to prepare a meal, but instead takes the only lamb from the poor man (12.4). A faithful Israelite was expected to provide for the poor, or alien travellers (Lev. 19.10, 33, 34), because God had provided for the Israelites when they were aliens in the land (Gen. 26.3; Exod. 22.21; 23.9). Hospitality is an attribute of God and should be also of his people and yet it is entirely missing in the rich man's response when he steals a lamb to provide for the traveller. This will become an important theme in Luke, which we will see in Chapters 4 and 5.

David responds with harsh words saying this rich man is υἰὸς θανάτου and demands that he restore the poor man sevenfold for his misdeeds (12.6). The term υἰὸς θανάτου implies the man deserves death as in 1 Kingdoms 26.16, and the call for a sevenfold restitution is equally extreme. Tradition says that if a sheep is stolen, a fourfold restitution must be made (Exod. 22.1) or an added fifth (Lev. 6.5), making the reader aware that David views this sin as very great when he demands a sevenfold restitution. There is no excuse for the rich man's actions; he has many resources of his own, and yet he exploits the poor man and hoards his flocks for himself. Other OT texts also have a great deal to say about God's concern for the poor and conversely his judgement on those who oppress the poor or the alien (Exod. 22.21; 23.9; Isa. 14.30; Pss. 24; 35.10; 131.15; Amos 4.1; 5.12; 8.4),[71] and so the parable is even more shocking.

Nathan then reveals that David is the rich man in the parable because he has taken Uriah's wife when he has many wives of his own (2 Kgdms 12.7). Nathan uses a strong introductory formula: τάδε λέγει κύριος ὁ θεὸς Ισραηλ, and reminds David of the grace that has been afforded him. First, Nathan talks of his anointing as king over Israel implying not only God's blessing to him in his election, but his responsibility for the Israelite people (12.7). Secondly, he reminds David that it was God who rescued him from Saul (12.7), which the narrative of 1 Kingdoms 18–31 has already mentioned. Finally, David is reminded that he already has the gift of wives and the house of Israel and Judah (12.8), implying he has no right or need to take anything from anyone else. There is a repetition of the word μικροί which had described the poor man's lamb (12.3) but is now used to question

---

70. Firth, *1 and 2 Samuel*, p. 427.
71. J. David Pleins, 'Poor', *ABD* 5, p. 402.

whether David views the Lord's blessings to him as too μικροί (12.8). After the list of God's blessings to David, this twofold use of μικροί is highly charged. David is also described as βασιλεύς (12.7), and as king his first responsibility is to protect his subjects, and to act justly to all, especially the poor.[72] Clearly David had failed to do this. The ANE understood kings as shepherds, and this has been conveyed repeatedly (2 Kgdms 5.2; 7.8); David has failed as a *shepherd* king because of his injustice toward the poor man.

This parable and proclamation from Nathan leads to David's repentance for Uriah's death and so to God's forgiveness (12.13). The narrative goes on to describe the consequences for David's household when his son dies (12.14-23).

Nathan's shepherd setting for his parable should be considered deliberate.[73] The parable is classified as a *juridical parable* which is designed to target the hearer so that they will pass judgement on themselves.[74] There are three other juridical parables which act in a similar manner (2 Kgdms 14.1-20; 3 Kgdms 20.39-40; Isa. 5.1-7); each is effective because the audience identifies themselves in the parable and so personally hears the voice of judgement. As the reader comes to the text with the view of the narrator, the reader also hears the gavel fall for David.

In Nathan's parable the writer appeals to David's sense not only as Israel's king, as Roth and McCarter suggest, but specifically as their *shepherd* king who should exhibit faithfulness and justice to the flock.[75] As a king he is wealthy and powerful, but neither wealth nor power allow for an abuse of that position. The parable reveals that it is the poor man and not David who is a faithful shepherd. While the shepherd setting of the parable should not be overplayed, it should be considered. Nathan chose a setting that exposed David's role as shepherd king, for with self-understanding comes sound judgement.

2.3.3 David's sin at the census (2 Kgdms 24)

2 Kingdoms 24 is the final pericope we will consider; it records David's sin in counting the people.[76] It comes after the hymns of 1 Kingdoms 22 and 23 which

---

72. Alter, *David*, p. 257.

73. Cartledge, *1 and 2 Samuel*, pp. 410–11. McCarter stresses it is a juridical parable which plays upon David as 'king' rather than 'shepherd'. Mc Carter, *II Samuel*, p. 305.

74. Cartledge, *1 and 2 Samuel*, p. 514; McCarter, *II Samuel*, p. 305. See also Wolfgang Roth, 'You Are the Man! Structural Interaction in 2 Samuel 10-12', *Semeia* 8 (1977), pp. 1–13. Roth notes that the tradition of David as Israel's military leader, though he does not specify shepherd leader, presents David as the hero of 2 Samuel 10–12, and therefore his sin with Bathsheba and Uriah is the reversal of expectation for the reader. It is this expectation which the parable subverts. Roth, 'You are the Man!', pp. 10–11.

75. Roth, 'You are the Man!', pp. 10–11; Mc Carter, *II Samuel*, p. 305.

76. This can be considered the end of David's life even though his finals days and death come in 3 Kgdms 1, as the last words of David are recorded in 2 Kgdms 23.1-7. The census is the final event in his time as king.

signify the end of David's story and balance with Hannah's song in 1 Kingdoms 1, and so this final event in David's life stands alone as a distinct coda to David's life. This passage makes the clearest narrative statement from David, who says of himself, ἐγώ εἰμι ὁ ποιμήν.

It is not entirely clear why counting the people is considered a sin as elsewhere we do not see a negative reaction to a census.[77] In 2 Kingdoms 24.1 the Lord incited David to do this when he was angry with Israel, yet David's actions in counting the people are presented as acting directly against the Lord's wishes. Firth suggests it may be that Israel was not at war and David initiated an action that was not necessary, while McCarter, Alter and Brueggemann acknowledge that we simply are not given the reason for such wrath.[78]

As a result of his actions, David is called to choose a consequence for his sin from a limited range of options, and he chooses that death will come to the land for three days. However, the result is so devastating when seventy thousand people die that David calls out to the Lord to stop, saying: Ἰδοὺ ἐγώ εἰμι ἠδίκησα καὶ ἐγώ εἰμι ὁ ποιμὴν ἐκακοποίησα, καὶ οὗτοι τὰ πρόβατα τί ἐποίησαν᾽ ('Behold, I am – I did wrong, and I am the shepherd – I did evil, and these are the sheep; what did they do?') (2 Kgdms 24.17).

This LXX text uses an addition to the MT with the clarifying words ἐγώ εἰμι ὁ ποιμήν. In a narrative which has traced David's rise from shepherd boy to shepherd king and made great use of the language of shepherding, this narrative statement of David should not be underestimated. The LXX translators have recorded David's own voice declaring before God that he is the Lord's ποιμήν, and the Israelites are the Lord's sheep. He knows that seventy thousand Israelites have died because of his sin and that he has failed as their shepherd, therefore, he appeals to God to punish him rather than the people; it is he as God's *shepherd* who has failed; it is the leader who is accountable for the sheep and not the sheep for the shepherd.

The phrase ἐγώ εἰμι ὁ ποιμήν is supported by 4QSam[a] which says: 'It is I, the shepherd, who did evil.'[79] The LXX reading is from LXX[L] but is taken up by NETS in their recent translation. It is also supported by OL and Josephus, *Ant.* 7.328.[80] The LXX translators clearly understood David as the shepherd king, as evidenced by this explicit statement at the end of David's life. Further, as this is the final event in David's life, from a narrative perspective, this forms an echo and perhaps a final *inclusio* with David's early years as Jesse's shepherd.

---

77. In Exod. 30.11-16 there is a census for taxation purposes and Num. 1 and 26 record a census taken regarding numbers for military service.

78. Firth, *1 and 2 Samuel*, p. 541; McCarter, *II Samuel*, p. 509; Alter, *David*, p. 353; Brueggemann, *First and Second Samuel*, p. 351.

79. Alter, *David*, p. 357; McCarter, *II Samuel*, p. 507.

80. Josephus, *Ant.* 7.328 says: 'the king said to God, that it was he, the shepherd (ὁ ποιμήν) who was rightly to be punished, but the flock, which had committed no sin, should be saved and he entreated him to cause his anger to fall upon him and all his line, but to spare the people.'

This pericope finishes with David making a costly offering to the Lord of an altar from the threshing floor of Araunah, the Jebusite (2 Kgdms 24.18-25). Here David worships the Lord and prays for his mercy, and the Lord answers by averting the plague. The narrative leaves the reader acknowledging that it is the Lord who ultimately protects the Israelites, and saves the flock; it is God who is ultimately the faithful shepherd who saves the flock.

2.4 Summary

While the story of David could be summarized with several different ideas,[81] the narrative consistently highlights his identity as shepherd. This identity functions as a *Leitwort*, which is used repeatedly at key places in the narrative, and draws the reader into its significance for David's role as king of Israel. We must agree with Buber that repetition is not accidental and is one of the strongest techniques for making meaning.[82] The author has deliberately used the beginning of the narrative to set the trajectory and to provide a key to understand how to interpret the events in the narrative. It bears out the Aristotelian notion of connectedness in narrative which has a beginning, a middle, and an end. This ending is intricately connected to its beginning in the sheepfolds of Jesse's household. It also bears witness to the *primacy effect* where key ideas are established at the beginning of a narrative and these affect the reader's perception of a character. David is the shepherd king of the Israelite people, who is called to be a faithful shepherd and put the needs of the flock ahead of his own needs. It is this very realization that David makes at the end of his life when he is punished after he sins at the census. This is also the thrust of Nathan's juridical parable after his first recorded sin. David had put his needs ahead of other people and therefore was not faithful to his high calling as God's shepherd.

David was known as Israel's greatest king,[83] and yet his reign was not perfect. He failed God's flock, but still the Davidic kingdom is said to last forever. As we now turn to the Third Gospel, we find that Luke presents Jesus on the everlasting throne of David (Lk. 1.32-33), and it is Jesus who is the faithful Davidic shepherd king who will succeed where David failed.

---

81. David can be seen as the ideal king, a warrior king, a pious king, a righteous king and a chosen king. Miura, *David*, pp. 118–21.

82. Buber, *Scripture*, p. 115.

83. David M. Howard Jr., 'David', *ABD* 2, p. 41.

3

THE BIRTH OF THE DAVIDIC SHEPHERD KING

As we have seen in the previous chapter, to talk of David must include an understanding of him as shepherd king of Israel. While Luke's richly allusive writing bears echoes of the whole of Israel's story, he emphasizes the story of David which brings with it a shepherd kingdom setting that Lukan scholarship has largely overlooked.

In this chapter we first consider how scholars have understood the Davidic theme in Luke-Acts. This review will show that there has been no study undertaken which has explored the nature of David as a shepherd king. We will then examine Luke's infancy narrative for evidence of David's story and argue that Luke 1–2 introduces Jesus as the Davidic Messiah, the Saviour and Lord, which should be read against the backdrop of David as shepherd king.

We will establish the crucial role David plays in the Lukan infancy narrative by exploring the direct and indirect references to David in the text. The story has six direct references to David (1.27, 32, 69; 2.4 [twice], 11) and many implicit references making this *Leitwort* prominent. These Davidic references, coupled with the implicit language from the David story (Mary's song, Bethlehem, shepherd, Davidic covenant language especially of sonship), form a strong causal chain which functions as a transumed echo of the Davidic shepherd king of the LXX. Luke establishes at the beginning of his narrative that Jesus is the Davidic Messiah, forming a thematic trajectory, ensuring that in his ministry years one way Jesus is to be viewed is as the shepherd king who seeks out and saves the lost sheep.

3.1 Recent study of David in Luke-Acts

In recent years there has been considerable interest in the figure of David in Luke's writing. The monograph of Strauss, *The Davidic Messiah in Luke-Acts*,[1] has become an important work establishing Jesus as the Davidic Messiah, while also a prophet like Moses and the suffering servant. His work on the Davidic Messiah focuses on references to David in the infancy narrative, the main body

---

1. Mark Strauss, *The Davidic Messiah in Luke-Acts* (JSNTSS, 110; Sheffield: Sheffield Academic, 1995).

of the Gospel and the speeches in Acts, making it the most comprehensive study of its type and the first study to demonstrate how the Davidic theme is extended into the main body of the Gospel.[2] He primarily establishes Luke's genealogical interest in David, and demonstrates how central echoes of David are crucial in understanding the infancy narrative. He also notes the importance of the birth narrative in the structure and theology of Luke-Acts, and how key christological passages are Davidic in character. Strauss goes on to say, however, that how Jesus will fulfil the Davidic promise is 'barely suggested' in the infancy narrative, and that the reader must wait for Acts to see Jesus enthroned in heaven at the right hand of God.[3] This study aims to show that, while agreeing broadly with Strauss' argument, this statement is not correct, for the reader is given indications of how Jesus will fulfil this promise in the infancy narrative; he comes as the messianic shepherd.

Bock's *Proclamation From Prophecy and Pattern*[4] explores Luke's use of the OT in presenting a christological view of Jesus. He establishes Luke's initial christological position where Jesus is the promised Davidic Messiah in Luke 1–2 (1.32-53, 68-71, 79; 2.4, 11), which he says is modified by the motif of Jesus as the victorious Servant (2.29-32, 34-35).[5] He notes that Luke paints this picture through images, ideas and allusions, and not citations.[6] Bock argues, however, that ultimately these titles give way to Luke's primary christological characterization, ὁ κύριος, which is confirmed in Acts (2.21, 34-36; 10.36), while having its roots in 2.11.[7] As Rowe points out, his thesis is flawed when he fails to recognize the hermeneutical importance of κύριος in the infancy narrative.[8] I would add that the thrust of Bock's thesis is a justification for viewing Jesus as Lord, and therefore his lens for understanding the Davidic heritage of Jesus is diminished when he fails to explain satisfactorily the father–son relationship Luke presents (2.41-52; 10.21-22). His reasoning takes insufficient account of 2.50 where Luke says Jesus grew in wisdom and in years, and as a result Bock explains away a close relationship between a father and a son.[9] Bock states that 'we distinguish between Luke's presentation of Jesus' self-understanding at an early age and Luke's portrayal of the revelation of Jesus' person in his ministry.'[10] He explains that 'Jesus' deep self-understanding ultimately becomes comprehensible to men through his teaching about himself, as

2. Ibid., pp. 199–336.

3. Ibid., p. 124.

4. Darrell L. Bock, *Proclamation From Prophecy and Pattern: Lucan Old Testament Christology* (JSNTSS, 12; Sheffield: JSOT Press, 1987).

5. Ibid., p. 88.

6. Ibid., p. 55.

7. Ibid., pp. 262–70. Bock notes especially that 'the turning point in the book [of Acts] is reached with the confession that Jesus is Lord of all, the climax of a carefully crafted OT christology'. Ibid., p. 240.

8. Rowe, *Early Narrative Christology*, p. 8.

9. Bock, *Proclamation*, p. 267.

10. Ibid.

that teaching is reflected in what Jesus is doing and in what the Scriptures show'.[11] This interpretative lens undervalues the role of the infancy narratives as a part of Luke's theological schema and the elevation of Jesus' teaching as the preeminent way Luke reveals truths about Jesus seems rather overplayed. This father–son relationship which is established in the infancy narrative is an essential part of the Lukan Jesus.

N. T. Wright draws a clear typological relationship between Luke's narrative of Jesus and the narrative of David's story in 1 Samuel in a brief analysis.[12] While he acknowledges the book of 1 Samuel is not Luke's only parallel,[13] he demonstrates that Luke uses this account to explain how Jesus is the climax of the Jewish story and how Jesus is the 'true David'.[14]

Wright notes that the story of Elizabeth and Zechariah (1.5-25, 39-45, 57-80) parallels that of Hannah and Elkanah (1 Kgdms 1.1–2.11) and that Hannah and Mary's songs function as triumphant conclusions of both stories (1.46-55; 1 Kgdms 2.1-10). He finds ongoing parallels between Samuel's and John the Baptist's judgements (3.7-9; 1 Kgdms 3.1-18), and David's and Jesus' message of judgement to the people in temporal power. He comments that both stories look toward messages of salvation, Jesus' baptism parallels David's anointing (1 Kgdms 16.13; Lk. 3.21-22) and Jesus' battle with Satan is similar to David's battle with Goliath (1 Kgdms 17.1-52; Lk. 4.1-13). He aligns the beginning of Jesus' Galilaean ministry where there is acceptance and then rejection with David's return from the battle with Goliath (1 Kgdms 18.6-8; Lk. 4.14-44). He also suggests that the Lukan travel narrative is similar to David's wandering with his followers (1 Kgdms 19–30; Lk. 9.51–19.28). Wright goes on to briefly establish an ongoing relationship between the story of David and Jesus in the passion, resurrection, exaltation and establishment of a true Davidic kingdom.[15]

While not everything Wright sees is certain, the vision cast is insightful and accords with Luke's emphasis on Jesus as the Davidic king and also his attention to the stories of Israel. Our aim in this chapter is to highlight and explore Wright's connection between the stories of Israel and Luke and ask how echoes from Kingdoms help the reader understand the shepherd setting of the birth narrative.

In support of the Davidic thread in Luke's Gospel, Scott Hahn has clearly but briefly traced the Davidic strand in Luke-Acts from both explicit and indirect references to David, showing how Davidic Christology is an important category

---

11. Ibid.

12. N. T. Wright, *The New Testament and the People of God* (Christian Origins and the Question of God, vol. 1; Minneapolis: Fortress Press, 1992), pp. 379–81.

13. Ibid., p. 380.

14. Wright says: 'Luke's Davidic theme is indeed typological – Jesus really is seen as the "true David" – but this is neither random nor arbitrary: it is held firmly *within a historical scheme*.' Ibid., p. 381.

15. Wright, *People of God,* pp. 380–1.

for Luke.[16] While he omits any reference to 19.10 as a Davidic king reference, his analysis of Luke's interest in the Davidic kingdom is persuasive. Hahn goes on to summarize the nature of OT Davidic monarchy to eight categories: (1) the Davidic monarchy was founded upon a divine covenant; (2) was the Son of God; (3) the Christ; (4) was linked to Jerusalem, particularly Mount Zion; (5) was bound to the temple; (6) ruled over the twelve tribes; (7) ruled over an international empire; and (8) was everlasting. As Hahn does not identify the Davidic monarchy as involved in a shepherding task, however, he overlooks 19.1-10 and its Davidic shepherd king allusion. Therefore, while this summary is excellent, it does not provide a fully comprehensive picture of the Davidic Jesus in Luke.

More recently, Yuzuru Miura provides a full examination of David in his monograph *David in Luke-Acts*.[17] He explores David in the OT, the Apocrypha and Pseudepigrapha, in the Qumran MSS, the writings of Philo and Josephus, early rabbinic writings, and early Jewish thought. His interest lies in whether there is a typological and genealogical aspect to Davidic Messianism, which he shows to be the case. This develops the work of Strauss who establishes Luke's interest in David to be primarily genealogical,[18] and of Wright who looks at the typological relationship. He supports Wright's typological proposal that Luke relates the story of Jesus in light of David's story in Samuel.[19] We shall confirm the relationship Miura finds between the story of David from the book of Kingdoms and Luke's portrayal of Jesus in the Gospel and support Miura's thought that 'in Luke 19, Jesus' earthly ministry is summarised with Davidic shepherd imagery'.[20] However, Miura's analysis of David in the OT does not identify David's role as a shepherd king to support his own statement. The categories of David for Miura are: (1) an ideal king; (2) a religious authority; (3) a Moses parallel; (4) a Solomon parallel; (5) a sinner; (6) a psalmist; (7) a model for the Jews; (8) a prophet; and (9) an indicator of the Messiah.[21] Although he upholds Marshall's view of the importance of 19.10,[22] and specifically identifies the *summative* nature of Jesus' earthly ministry as a *Davidic shepherd* in Luke 19, his analysis fails to show how his statement is supported in the Lukan narrative. I suggest Luke built his understanding of Jesus' ministry in a cumulative way which is summarized in 19.10. This study aims to add to Miura's apparent lacuna with respect to this feature of David.

---

16. Hahn, 'Kingdom and Church', pp. 294–326.
17. Yuzuru Miura, *David in Luke-Acts* (WUNT II/232; Tübingen: Mohr Siebeck, 2007).
18. Ibid., p. 137.
19. Ibid., pp. 238–9.
20. Ibid, p. 240.
21. Ibid., pp. 118–36.
22. Ibid., p. 225.

3.2 The beginning of the Lukan narrative

While Conzelmann largely ignored the infancy narrative in his significant work *Die Mitte der Zeit*,[23] the role his work plays in introducing key Lukan themes has been well noted since and accepted by scholars.[24] These themes include salvation, joy, temple, Jerusalem, prayer, the role of the Spirit, Gentile salvation and the early signs of Jewish rejection, the eschatological reversal paradigm, Jesus' role as Saviour and the long-awaited Davidic king who will reign with justice and righteousness.[25] These themes are introduced in the infancy narrative and can be traced throughout Luke-Acts – evidence of the *primacy effect* in action.

So how does Luke tell the beginning of his story? It is clearly different from Mark's Gospel where a quote from Malachi 3.1 and Isaiah 40.3 introduces John the Baptist, who has come to prepare the way for Jesus. Matthew opens his Gospel with the genealogy of Jesus which links Jesus to key events and people from Israel's history, providing credentials for him as Messiah. Luke's beginning is different. After his methodological prologue, Luke steps the reader back into the Septuagintal world with echoes of Israel's story. Rowe describes this as 'atmospheric resonance' where 'characters and events of the Old Testament are everywhere present and nowhere mentioned'.[26] Luke uses only two direct OT quotes in Luke 1–2 with the introductory ἐν τῷ νόμῳ κυρίου (2.23, 24), yet the Lukan narrative as a whole is richly allusive, drawing the reader back into OT characters and story.

Luke's focus on the continuing story of Israel has led some to see Luke's Gospel as the continuation of the biblical story,[27] yet as Talbert concludes, 'Luke and Acts tell the continuing story of salvation history ... [but] Let us remember, however, that salvation history narrows at the point of Jesus to the story of one individual. At that point, the history of salvation is best told by the literary genre biography',[28] and it is within this genre that Luke tells the story of Israel with Jesus as its pinnacle

---

23. Hans Conzelmann, *Die Mitte der Zeit: Studien zur Theologie des Lukas* (Beiträge zur historischen Theologie; Tübingen: Mohr, 1954).

24. H. H. Oliver, 'The Lucan Birth Stories and the Purpose of Luke-Acts', *NTS* 10 (1964): 202–26; Minear, 'Birth Stories', pp. 111–130; Tyson, 'Birth Narratives', pp. 103–20; Coleridge, *Birth*, pp. 28–9; Bock, *Proclamation*, p. 55; Green, *Gospel*, p. 49; Litwak, *Echoes*, p. 66.

25. Maxwell, *Hearing*, p. 132.

26. Rowe, *Early Narrative Christology*, p. 33. Bock aptly says of Luke's narrative: 'The Old Testament is not cited with exclamation points like Matthew, but it is woven into the fabric of the account.' Bock, *Proclamation*, p. 269.

27. Nils A. Dahl, 'The Story of Abraham in Luke-Acts', in *Studies in Luke-Acts* (eds Leander Keck and J. Louis Martyn; Philadelphia: Fortress, 1966), pp. 139–58 (153); Green, 'The Problem of a Beginning', pp. 61–86; Litwak, *Echoes*, p. 67.

28. Charles H. Talbert, 'The Acts of the Apostles: Monograph or "Bios"?' in *History, Literature, and Society in the Book of Acts* (ed. Ben Witherington III; Cambridge: Cambridge University Press, 1996), p. 70.

Table 1 Points of convergence between the book of Kingdoms and Luke's Gospel:

The story of Kingdoms	The Lukan infancy narrative
Hannah was barren (1.2).	Elizabeth was barren (1.6).
Set in Shiloh, the centre of worship (1.3).	Set in Jerusalem, the centre of worship (1.8).
Elkanah sacrificing to the Lord (1.3).	Zechariah, entered the sanctuary to offer incense (1.9).
Hannah and Elkanah shown as faithful (1.4-7).	Elizabeth and Zechariah are faithful and righteous (1.6).
Hannah says her son will be devoted, will not drink wine, and no razor will touch his head (1.11).	John will not drink wine and will prepare the way for the Lord (1.15-17).
The priest Eli speaks words of blessing to Hannah's prayer for a son (1.17).	The angel speaks of the blessing of a son to Zechariah (1.13-19).
Bore a son and called him Samuel (1.20).	Bore a son and called him John (1.13); bear a son and call him Jesus (1.31).
Hannah sings a song of individual praise (2.1-10).	Mary sings a song of individual praise (1.46-55).
Linguistic themes in Hannah's song: horn of salvation (2.1, 10), joy (2.1), holiness of God (2.2, 10), the theme of reversal (2.4-8).	Linguistic themes of Mary's song: salvation (1.46), joy (1.46), holiness (1.49), the theme of reversal (1.51-53).
	Linguistic themes of Zechariah's song: salvation (1.68, 71, 77), David (1.69, 76, 79), joy (1.68), faithfulness of God (1.72-73), peace (1.79).
On a literary level, Hannah's song is balanced by David's songs (2 Kingdoms 22, 23).	On a literary level, Mary's song is balanced by Zechariah's song (1.68-79).
Samuel kept going and became great and was in favour both with the Lord and people (2.26).	John grew and became strong in spirit (1.80). Jesus increased in wisdom and in years, in divine and human favour (2.52).
David is from Bethlehem (16.1).	Jesus is born in Bethlehem, πόλις Δαυίδ (2.4).
David is a shepherd (16.11).	Jesus is presented as the messianic shepherd recalling Micah 5.2-5 (2.1-20); his birth is announced first to faithful shepherds (2.8); he calls his disciples 'little flock' implying he is the shepherd (12.32); he is the faithful shepherd from the parable (15.3-7); Jesus is pictured as the Davidic shepherd king (19.10).
David is anointed and the spirit sprang upon him from that day and onward (16.13); from the Davidic covenant: 'I will be a father to him and he shall be a son to me' (2 Kgdms 7.14).	The Holy Spirit descends on Jesus at his baptism and words echoing the Davidic covenant are heard: 'You are my son, my beloved, with you I am well pleased' (3.22).
David, full of the Spirit (1 Kgdms 16.13), battles Goliath in the name of the Lord (17).	Jesus, full of the Spirit, battles Satan (4.1-13).
David is welcomed by the people (18.6-7), and then rejected by Saul (18.8).	Jesus is welcomed in Nazareth and then rejected by the people (4.16-30).
David travels with his followers as a fugitive from Saul (1 Kgdms 19–30).	Jesus travels with his followers (9.51–19.28).
David is anointed shepherd king over all Israel (2 Kgdms 5.2).	Jesus is hailed as 'king' by 'multitudes of disciples' (19.37); Jesus is Saviour, Messiah, and Lord of all (2.11).

or culmination (24.27, 44-45). For Luke, Jesus is the culmination of Israel's story, and Luke has created an 'echo chamber'[29] where he interacts with the many stories of Israel. Green and Litwak correctly note Luke's interest in Abraham in 1.55, 73, and they then go on to stress the points of congruence between Genesis 11–21 and Luke 1.5–2.52,[30] yet many of these also have parallels in the story of Kingdoms.[31]

I agree with Wright, who suggests Luke's beginning enters the reader into the book of Kingdoms with the story of Hannah and Samuel rather than entering the reader into Genesis and the story of Abraham, with the high point of the story 'the anointing of the young David'.[32] He deliberately sets the stage for Jesus' ministry as the Davidic shepherd king who seeks out and saves the lost sheep (19.10). This interest is first evident by the use of six explicit references to 'David', suggesting a *Leitwort* (1.27, 32, 69; 2.4 [twice], 11), and secondly by Luke's ongoing interest in echoes from 1 Kingdoms, and David's story in particular. This is demonstrated in Table 1.

3.3 Luke's Davidic references

3.3.1 Jesus' Davidic lineage (Lk. 1.27) and echoes of David in Isaiah

The first direct reference to David is in 1.27 where Jesus' legal lineage to the house of David is recorded; this will be affirmed in 2.4 and 3.31, establishing a clear connection between Jesus and the Davidic line. The reader's attention is also drawn to Mary as παρθένος; this information is recalled twice in 1.27,[33] signalling its importance for Luke.

Both Jesus' genealogical links to David's house and Mary's virginity suggest Luke is recalling Isaiah 7.14, where the house of David is given a sign that a virgin (παρθένος) will bear a son.[34] Isaiah 7.14 (LXX) translates עלמה as παρθένος. The Hebrew word suggests a young woman without the need for her to be a virgin.[35] Bock does not see anything particularly Isaianic in 1.27 and contrasts Luke's

---

29. Green, *Gospel,* p. 57. Wright also agrees that Luke does not limit himself to one parallel only while he does see the strength of the parallel between Kingdoms and Luke. Wright, *People of God,* p. 380.

30. Green, 'Problem of Beginning', pp. 68–71; *Gospel of Luke,* pp. 52–5; Litwak, *Echoes,* pp. 82–9.

31. See 'Appendix 1' in Harris dissertation.

32. Wright, *People of God,* pp. 379–80.

33. Luke confirms Mary's virgin status in 1.34. 'παρθένος', BDAG, p. 777.

34. Bovon, *Lukas 1,* p. 72; Green, *Gospel,* p. 85; I. Howard Marshall, *Gospel of Luke: A Commentary on the Greek Text* (NIGNTC; Exeter: Paternoster, 1978), p. 64; *Contra,* Fitzmyer, *Luke,* p. 336; Bock, *Luke,* p. 108; Raymond E. Brown, *The Birth of the Messiah: A Commentary on the Infancy Narratives in Matthew and Luke* (New York: Doubleday, 1997), pp. 299–300.

35. In the Jewish world there was no expectation of a virgin birth from the Messiah. Brown, *Birth,* p. 299; Fitzmyer, *Luke,* p. 338; Nolland, *Luke,* p. 47.

usage with Matthew's Gospel where he quotes Isaiah (Mt. 1.23).[36] Certainly Luke does not use a direct quote, but this is consistent with his highly allusive writing style, which Bock notes.[37] Brown argues that the step-parallelism between John and Jesus provides the reason for the attention to Mary as παρθένος[38] (although surely this would not account for the repeated mention), and that Jesus' connection to the house of David may be part of the pre-Gospel annunciation tradition.[39] He also notes the close wording of Genesis 16.11 and Isaiah 7.14 and concludes that there is no way to know if Luke was drawing on Isaiah. Fitzmyer and Brown also draw attention to Matthew's narrative where the tradition of Mary's virginity precedes the quote at Matthew 1.23, making his connection to Isaiah 7.14 clear.[40] There is no doubt that Matthew's intentions are clear, but that clarity need not preclude that Luke also wishes to make the same point.

Marshall, Bovon and Green, however, argue for a probable allusion,[41] with Bovon noting that there is an association between the themes of virginity and the fatherhood of God in Isaiah 7.14.[42] Matthew's use of Isaiah 7 demonstrates that the Isaianic passage was interpreted christologically in the Jewish Christian world,[43] and Luke may well have known this tradition. There is also considerable shared language between the two pericopae supporting the test for volume, as demonstrated in Table 2.

Table 2 The linguistic parallels between Isaiah 7.10-17 and Luke 1.26-38

	Isa. 7.10-17	Lk. 1.26-38
οἶκος, Δαυίδ	7.13	1.27
ὁ κύριος	7.10	1.28
παρθένος	7.14	1.27
ἐν γαστρί	7.14	1.31
τίκτω υἱόν	7.14	1.31
καλέσεις τὸ ὄνομα αὐτοῦ	7.14	1.31
ἐπὶ τὸν οἶκον	7.17	1.33

While the test for volume has some strong support in this explicit repetition of words, Luke does not allude to Isaiah 7.14 elsewhere in the Gospel and so the test for recurrence is not met. Yet we read that the shepherds are given a σημεῖον about the baby in the birth narrative (2.12) and a σημεῖον is given about the baby in Isaiah 7.11, 14. This primarily reflects Luke's Septuagintial style, as signs are

---

36. Bock, *Luke*, p. 108.
37. Bock, *Proclamation*, p. 55.
38. Brown, *Birth*, pp. 299–301.
39. Ibid., p. 300.
40. Fitzmyer, *Luke*, p. 336; Brown, *Birth*, p. 300.
41. Marshall, *Gospel*, p. 64; Bovon, *Lukas 1*, p. 66; Green, *Gospel*, p. 85.
42. Bovon, *Lukas 1*, p. 66.
43. Ibid.

common occurrences at significant narrative events in the LXX. However, there is a possibility that the sign of the baby (2.12) may refer back to Isaiah 7.14, linking the annunciation to Mary with the sign given to the shepherds. Furthermore, Luke also uses a preceding Isaianic passage (Isa. 6.9-10) in 8.10 in the parable of the sower and also at the end of Acts (Acts 28.26-27), showing his knowledge and interest in this early part of Isaiah and its relevance to the story of Jesus. Both Tannehill and Talbert have demonstrated the narrative links between the Gospel and Acts;[44] therefore, at the very least, we can assume with some confidence that Luke had the text of Isaiah 7.14 available to him.

Mallen has shown the importance of Isaiah in Luke-Acts,[45] noting that Luke includes more extended quotes from Isaiah than any other book,[46] that is, nine explicit quotations and more than one hundred allusions.[47] Further, Luke most likely alludes to Isaiah 9.1 in Zechariah's *Benedictus* (1.78-79), and Isaiah 49.6 and 42.6 in Simeon's *Nunc Dimittis* (2.32),[48] demonstrating that Isaiah plays an important role in the infancy narrative. Therefore, the volume of linguistic repetition between Isaiah 7.14 and the infancy narrative, coupled with Luke's prominent use of Isaiah's writing, means that the test of volume is met.

An echo also fits well within the thematic coherence of Luke's argument in which he is establishing deliberate links to the David tradition. Strauss and Bock both note that Davidic messiahship is the controlling Christology in Luke 1–2,[49] and Strauss, that this opening thematic concern is balanced by a return to this theme in the speeches in Acts where Jesus' Davidic enthronement is explicit (Acts 2.14-40; 13.16-41, 46-47; 15.13-21).

It is possible Luke's readers could have understood this echo with its repeated use of παρθένος within a Davidic context, as Matthew 1.23 demonstrates that early Jewish tradition had made the connection between Isaiah 7.14 and Mary's virgin birth. Therefore, it is historically plausible that Luke is drawing on Isaiah 7.14 in his narrative.

Furthermore, there is some precedent to accept the echo as we consider the history of interpretation. Bovon notes Matthew demonstrates a Jewish precedent for interpreting Isaiah 7 christologically, and concludes Luke has used the Immanuel prophecy.[50] Marshall comments that the probable allusion to Isaiah 7.14 strengthens the implication of virginity in παρθένος.[51] Finally, Green concludes, 'the conjunction of so many points of correspondence between the Gabriel-Mary encounter and Isa 7.10-17 cannot help but produce an echo effect … these

---

44. Talbert, *Literary Patterns*, pp. 15–23; Tannehill, *Narrative Unity*, p. 1:1–9.

45. Mallen, *Reading*, pp. 1–28.

46. He defines an extended quotation as more than one verse. Mallen, *Reading*, p. 2.

47. Mallen cites NA[27] list of allusions. Mallen, *Reading*, p. 3.

48. Marshall, *Gospel*, p. 121; Nolland, *Luke*, p. 120.

49. Strauss, *Davidic Messiah*, pp. 123–5; Bock, *Proclamation*, pp. 55–90. Bock further notes Jesus is also introduced as victorious Servant (2.29-32, 34-35).

50. Bovon, *Lukas 1*, p. 66.

51. Marshall, *Gospel*, p. 64.

reverberations establish an interpretive link emphasising how God is again inter-vening in history to bring his purpose to fruition.[52] Green is correct that this Isaianic echo helps to illuminate the surrounding text by bringing together the Davidic lineage of Jesus with Mary the virgin, the two key features of 1.27.

3.3.2 *The annunciation (1.28-38) and echoes of the Davidic covenant*

In 1.31-33 Gabriel announces to Mary that she is to have a baby. The angel says that her son who is to be called Jesus will be great and he will be called Son of the Most High. God will give him the throne of his ancestor David and his reign and this kingdom will be eternal. This is the second direct reference to David.

This passage confirms not only the Davidic descent of Jesus, but shows the father–son relationship between Jesus and God and that Jesus' birth stands in the Davidic covenant tradition (2 Kgdms 7.14; Pss. 2.7; 88.27-28; 4QFlor frag 10-13).[53] Bovon notes the clear basis for this when he says 'the foundation of this tradition is 2 Samuel 7'.[54]

The angel uses a high level of Davidic covenantal language (2 Kgdms 7), providing a strong intertextual link. The linguistic links are Jesus' description as υἱὸς ὑψίστου (1.32; 2 Kgdms 7.14), the use of μέγας (1.32; 2 Kgdms 7.9), θρόνος (1.32; 2 Kgdms 7.16), οἶκος (1.33; 2 Kgdms 7.13), βασιλεία (1.33; 2 Kgdms 7.12) and δοῦλος (1.38; 2 Kgdms 7.4, 8).

The father–son relationship which is so significant in the covenant is given preeminence in the annunciation;[55] in 1.32 υἱὸς ὑψίστου precedes the verb in the sentence, giving it an emphatic position where Jesus as *son* is prominent.[56] Marshall notes that this relationship is given prior to the Davidic genealogical relationship suggesting that Luke is showing something more than an adoptive relationship, and that the former interprets the latter.[57] Klein comments on the uniqueness of the child and the implication of his birth, saying: 'The son will be no ordinary child but "great", i.e. important for believers; moreover, he will be called "son of the Most High".'[58]

---

52. Green, *Gospel,* p. 85. Green, however, does not interpret Jesus as fulfilling the Isaiah 7 prophecy, but as suggesting God is once again acting in history to bring his purposes to fruition.

53. Scholars overwhelmingly support this echo and so it will not be analysed according to Hays' test for echoes, as this has been established conclusively. Bock, *Proclamation,* pp. 55–90; Fitzmyer, *Luke,* p. 338; Green, *Gospel,* p. 88; Marshall, *Gospel,* pp. 67–8; Nolland, *Luke,* p. 52; Miura, *David,* p. 200; Strauss, *Davidic Messiah,* pp. 76–125.

54. Bovon, *Lukas 1,* p. 75. Author's translation.

55. This father–son relationship continues with varying emphases in 1.68-79; 2.41-52; 10.21-22; 22.28-30.

56. Bock, *Luke,* p. 113.

57. Marshall, *Gospel,* p. 68.

58. Hans Klein, *Das Lukasevangelium* (KEK; Göttingen; Vandenhoeck and Ruprecht, 2006), p. 98. Author's translation.

The uses of ὁ ὕψιστος to describe God (1.32) is a common expression for God in the LXX[59] and the 'Son of the Most High' is synonymous with 'Son of God'.[60] This sonship expresses both the father's care of the son but also the responsibility of the son to the father. This is an ongoing feature of the Lukan Jesus' relationship with God where Jesus shows his dependence upon his father (1.35; 2.49; 3.22; 9.35; 10.21-22; 11.2, 13; 22.29, 42; 23.34, 46; 24.49; Acts 13.33).

Green argues that the emphasis of this father–son relationship in 1.31-33 demonstrates Luke is moving toward an understanding of Jesus' ontology whereby he is set apart for God's redemptive work from his conception.[61] Unlike Mark's Gospel which opens with John's ministry and Jesus' baptism (Mk 1.2-11), Luke shows that from conception Jesus is God's son who is a part of God's salvific plan. This plan of salvation is, however, thoroughly Davidic and is enacted by God in the divine conception (1.35). The repeated knowledge that Mary is παρθένος (1.27), which we noted Luke foregrounds, further suggests it is only God's actions which bring this plan about.[62] The father–son relationship is established early in the infancy narrative (1.31-33) but it also forms the centre of the final pericope in the infancy narrative when Jesus is at the Jerusalem temple (2.49).[63] As a result, there is a narrative link between the use of υἱὸς ὑψίστου (1.32) and Jesus as a boy in the temple when he says: οὐκ ᾔδειτε ὅτι ἐν τοῖς τοῦ πατρός μου δεῖ εἶναί με (2.49). This suggests the importance of the father–son relationship for the infancy narrative, and raises the possibility that the Davidic covenant is of particular importance for Luke as he establishes his key themes for the Gospel.

In reviewing the Davidic covenant, we noted that David is the shepherd leader of Israel when the covenant is established (2 Kgdms 5.2; 7.7-8), and the language of 'shepherd' is used twice to describe David as God's chosen shepherd ruler in 2 Kingdoms 7.7. As this forms such a prominent introduction to the Davidic covenant, there is the possibility that this shepherd king identity may also lie in the background of Luke's echo. While this point is yet unspoken by Luke, the transumed echo of David's story brings with it a causal chain whereby one thought is linked to another for the reader.[64] Hollander describes this causal chain in Henry Peacham's *The Garden of Eloquence*, where 'in speaking of darcknesse, we understand closenesse, by closenesse, blacknesse, by blacknesse, deepnesse'.[65]

---

59. For example, Gen. 14.18-22; Num. 24.16; Deut. 32.8; 1 Esd. 2.3; 6.30; 8.19; Pss. 7.18; 12.6; 17.14; 90.1; *Sir* 4.10; 2 Kgdms 22.14.

60. Green, *Gospel*, p. 89. Marshall suggests Luke may have chosen to use υἱὸς ὑψίστου so that there was no confusion with a similar pagan expression, and it also contrasts with the description of John in 1.76. Marshall, *Gospel*, p. 68.

61. Green notes that 'though Luke is not working with Johannine or later trinitarian categories, he is nonetheless moving toward a more ontological (and not only functional) understanding of Jesus' sonship'. Green, *Gospel*, p. 91.

62. Strauss, *Davidic Messiah*, pp. 90–1.

63. Green, *Gospel*, p. 156.

64. Hollander, *Figure of Echo*, pp. 133–49.

65. Ibid., p. 141.

As Luke will go on in the birth narrative to use a shepherd setting for Jesus' birth in the city of David, Bethlehem, there is the possibility that the reader will engage in the literary task of protention and retention to create new meaning. I suggest that the Davidic echo in 1.31-33 lays part of the platform for the birth of the Davidic shepherd king in 2.1-20.

Jesus is established as the fulfilment of the Davidic promise in the annunciation pericope. With this covenant story comes the background story of David whom God called from the sheepfolds of his father to shepherd the people of God (2 Kgdms 7.7, 8), and in which we find the close father–son relationship.

3.3.3 Mary's song (1.46-55) and echoes of Hannah's song

The song of Hannah and the song of Mary have many similar narrative features, and Hannah's song should be seen as the predominant model for the Magnificat.[66] As Bovon says, 'the author certainly knows Hannah's song after the birth of Samuel (1Sam [LXX 1Kgdms] 2:1-10)'.[67]

While this is a story of Hannah and not David, the story of Hannah's conception and the birth of Samuel is inextricably tied to the author's story of Israel's first two kings. We must remember that Samuel will go on to anoint David, which Campbell argues is the greatest purpose for Samuel in the narrative.[68] The inauguration of the monarchy and rejection of Saul are steps along the way to the major task of anointing David as shepherd king. As Brueggemann says, 'the first fifteen chapters are a preparation for him [David]'.[69]

The two songs come in a similar place in their respective books after an introduction to the characters and setting through narration and dialogue. They both function to provide a theological commentary on what is taking place providing a narrative pause through their hymn-like genre. Both songs are strophic and are personal songs of praise, lacking a communal call to praise reflected in the Psalms (Pss. 32, 46, 112, 116, 134, 135).

The theme of praise in Hannah's song comes out of a setting of prayer and worship (1 Kgdms 1.7-28) and the location is Shiloh (1.3) where the Israelites went to worship before the Jerusalem temple was built by Solomon (Josh. 18.1-10). Luke begins his narrative in the temple where Zechariah is offering incense, a

---

66. There is dispute about the source of Mary's song, and yet scholars agree it is rich with allusions to the LXX. Fitzmyer, Bock and Sanders note the strongest parallel comes from the song of Hannah, and Bovon concludes that Luke clearly makes use of the song. Bovon, *Lukas 1*, pp. 81–2; Miura, *David*, p. 204; Fitzmyer, *Luke*, p. 359; Bock, *Luke*, p. 148; James A. Sanders, 'Isaiah in Luke', in *Luke and Scripture: The Function of the Sacred Tradition in Luke-Acts* (eds Craig A. Evans and James A. Sanders; Minneapolis: Fortress Press, 1993), p. 17.

67. Bovon, *Lukas 1*, p. 82. Author's translation.

68. Campbell, *1 Samuel*, p. 2.

69. Brueggemann, *First and Second Samuel*, p. 2.

symbol of prayer (1.8-10), and he maintains a narrative focus on Jerusalem with its first reference coming in the infancy narrative (2.22).

Both women describe themselves as God's δούλη. Hannah uses this term frequently in her prayer to God (1 Kgdms 1.11, 16, 18) and Mary in her encounter with Gabriel and in her song (1.38, 48).

The content of the two songs shows points of similarity. Hannah's song centres on her thankfulness to God for the child she has prayed for in the opening chapter (1 Kgdms 2.1-2), and similarly, Mary's song focuses on her thankfulness to God and is a response to Elizabeth's words (1.45).

Both songs begin with praise of God and to God. Hannah praises the Lord with reference to her heart (καρδία), horn (κέρας) and mouth (στόμα), while Mary's does so with reference to her soul (ψυχή) and spirit (πνεῦμα). A horn is a symbol of power or strength,[70] and the raising of the horn is symbolic of the vertical patterns of elevation and descent in the narrative as a whole where the Lord's power reverses people's fortunes.[71] Hannah has been bowed down because she has been barren, but in the birth of her baby, God has saved her from her disgrace and lifted her up, bringing her salvation.

Hannah's song ends with a similar reference, ὑψώσει κέρας χριστοῦ αὐτοῦ (1 Kgdms 2.10), the horn functioning as an *inclusio* in the song.[72] This horn is related to the kingdom that is to come (1 Kgdms 2.10) and points to the monarchy. Hannah's words set the trajectory for the Davidic kingdom and the narrative will confirm this when David will say at the end of his life that God is the 'horn of my salvation' (2 Kgdms 22.3). Her song therefore introduces the theme of monarchy for the book of Kingdoms, giving the song an elevated role in the narrative even though it will be two generations until this will be accomplished.[73]

Mary's first statement of praise is to God her Saviour (1.47) and begins a Lukan emphasis on salvation, a theme that will be further established in the infancy narrative and beyond (1.69, 71, 77; 2.11).[74] Hannah's words speak prophetically of the monarchy which points to David, Mary's words speak of the Saviour which points to Jesus, the new Davidic king (1.32-33; 2.11).

The structures of the songs have similar features. Hannah's song has an introduction of praise for the Lord's sovereignty (1 Kgdms 2.1b-3), a focus on the reversal of human fortune beginning with her own reversal (2.4-5), a return to the Lord's sovereignty (2.6-10a) and finally a look ahead to the theme of kingship (2.10b). Mary's song has an introduction of praise (Lk. 1.46-47), a focus on the reversal of human fortune beginning with her own (1.48-49), an expression of

---

70. Firth, *Samuel*, p. 60; Werner Foerster, 'κέρας', TDNT 3, p. 669.

71. Alter, *David*, p. 9.

72. Tsumura, *Samuel*, p. 149.

73. Alter, *David*, p. 9.

74. Marshall, *Historian and Theologian*, pp. 94–102; Johnson, *Gospel*, p. 23; Nolland, *Luke*, p. 69; Douglas S. McComiskey, *Lukan Theology in the Light of the Gospel's Literary Structure* (PBM; Milton Keynes: Paternoster, 2004), p. 318; Maxwell, *Hearing*, p. 132.

God's sovereignty (1.50-53) and ends looking back to the promise to Abraham (1.54-55).

Both songs have a focus on God's holiness and of joy associated with the salvific events. Hannah talks of the holiness of the Lord (1 Kgdms 2.2, 10), and of the Lord's salvation which has brought her joy (2.1). Mary declares the name of the Lord is holy (1.49) and Elizabeth's baby leaps for joy in the womb (1.44), a passage which functions to introduce Mary's song. This linking of joy and salvation will come again in 2.10-11 when the angel announces Jesus' birth.

The central body of each hymn (1 Kgdms 2.4-8; Lk. 1.51-53) focuses on the reversal of the fortunes of the weak and begins with their own changed status. Both songs portray women who have seen God act powerfully in them not only to show God's favour to them, but also to bring about the salvation of God for others.

Mary is told she is favoured (Lk. 1.28, 30) and carrying the Davidic king, and so she is elevated from her lowly peasant status. She finds favour with God and with people (1.42-45; 2.34) and Jesus is increasingly portrayed as the one through whom salvation will come. While Mary praises God as Saviour in 1.47, Zechariah and the angels will give praise to God for Mary's baby who is the Davidic saviour (1.69; 2.11). It is through Jesus that Luke says all people will find salvation.

Therefore we can say that the reader can view Mary's song as closely related to Hannah's song given this level of interweaving of thematic material and similar structure. It is therefore likely that Luke intended an intertextual echo, making this another recollection of David's greater story.

3.3.4 The Benedictus (1.68-79) and echoes of David

Zechariah's *Benedictus* begins with a focus on what God is doing for Israel in Jesus as Davidic saviour (1.69-71), shifts to a focus on the Abrahamic covenant (1.72-75) and then returns to more Davidic imagery (1.76-79).[75] David's house is again specifically recalled in the *Benedictus* (1.69), showing Luke's ongoing interest in Jesus' lineage and the story of David.

In the *Benedictus* Zechariah praises God for raising up a redeemer to be a 'horn of salvation' or 'mighty saviour' for Israel ἐν οἴκῳ Δαυὶδ παιδός αὐτοῦ. However, it is not only that Jesus is specified as being from the house of David (1.69) that shows Luke's interest in the king at this point, it is the ongoing use of Davidic allusions in the hymn. David may be mentioned only once, but his presence is evident in various echoes.

Miura has recently found the language of the *Benedictus* as a whole reflects much of the language in 1 Kingdoms 2 (Hannah's song), 2 Kingdoms 22, 23 (David's songs), and *PssSol* 17, a late Davidic shepherd/warrior Psalm.[76] David or the covenant are central in each of these songs.

---

75. Strauss, *Davidic Messiah*, pp. 98–108.
76. Miura, *David*, p. 205.

The language of κέρας σωτηρίας (1.69) is Septuagintal language used sometimes to recall David (Ps. 17.3[77]; 2 Kgdms 22.3), and κέρας is also used in reference to David in the Psalms (Pss. 88.25; 131.17) and in Hannah's song in reference to God (1 Kgdms 2.1, 10).

Κέρας σωτηρία literally means 'a horn of salvation'[78] and in 1.69 refers to Jesus and not John, as there is nothing to suggest John is from the house of David. A horn represents a strong fighting animal such as a bull or ox (Deut. 33.17; Dan. 7.7; 1 Enoch 90.9),[79] and this expression fits with the Jewish expectation of a victorious Davidic messianic king.[80] The symbolism suggests Jesus is a powerful Davidic saviour who is able to save Israel from their enemies (1.71).

It is interesting that Luke qualifies κέρας σωτηρίας with ἐγείρω rather than ἐπαιρω (Ps. 74.6; Zech. 2.4) or ἐξανατελλω (Ps. 131.17) which are more common in the LXX. This verb ἐγείρω is more commonly used of raising up priests, kings and judges, and as Luke uses this in an early Christian hymn, Brown suggests the κέρας σωτηρίας 'has already been personified in Jesus the Saviour whom God had *raised up* (Lk. 7.16; Acts 4.10, 12)'.[81]

Hannah refers to κέρας at the beginning and end of her song (1 Kgdms 2.1, 10) as does David in his (2 Kgdms 22.3). For both Luke and the writer of Kingdoms, this horn is within the context of σωτηρία (Lk. 1.69; 1 Kgdms 2.1; 2 Kgdms 22.3, 36, 47, 51; 23.5), and the κέρας σωτηρία in 1.69 is clearly Davidic.

There is language used in the *Benedictus* that is also found in the Davidic covenant and *PssSol* 17. The language of παῖς in 1.69 is used in 2 Kingdoms 7.7 and *PssSol* 17.21. There is also shared language with αἰών (Lk. 1.70; 2 Kgdms 7.13, 16; *PssSol* 17.1, 3, 4, 35, 46)[82] and οἶκος (Lk. 1.69; 2 Kgdms 7.11, 13; *PssSol* 17.42).

The thematic links to *PssSol* 17 are especially relevant to this study, as the psalm ends with a picture of the Davidic shepherd king as the coming messianic figure. While there is no direct shepherd language in the *Benedictus*, Luke will move directly into his birth narrative after the *Benedictus*, where there is a remarkably clear shepherd setting. In *PssSol* 17.23-37 the psalmist's Davidic messianic figure is presented is as a shepherd king who brings righteousness through words rather than military might. This figure is the one who will restore justice to the people (*PssSol* 17.32). This is similar to the *Benedictus*, where the Davidic saviour brings salvation from enemies (1.71) and peace (1.79). The shared language with the Davidic covenant could also suggest a shepherd setting is not too far away from the *Benedictus* either.[83]

---

77. This is attributed to David in the superscription in Ps. 17.1.

78. Marshall, *Gospel*, p. 91.

79. Foerster, 'κέρας', *TDNT* 3, p. 669; Marshall, *Gospel*, p. 91; Nolland, *Luke*, p. 86; Strauss, *Davidic Messiah*, p. 99.

80. Brown, *Birth*, p. 371.

81. Ibid., italics original.

82. It is also found in David's prayer after the Davidic covenant (2 Kgdms 7.25) and in David's hymn (2 Kgdms 22.51).

83. This is the use of οἶκος (2 Kgdms 7.11, 13), παῖς (2 Kgdms 7.7), αἰών (2 Kgdms 7.13).

3.3.5 *The birth narrative (2.1-20)*

There are three further explicit references to David in the birth narrative: two occur in 2.4 in the context of the census and one in the message to the shepherds in 2.11. Mary and Joseph go up to Bethlehem, the city of David, and they do this because Joseph is ἐξ οἴκου καὶ πατριᾶς Δαυίδ (2.4). This information of the πόλις Δαυίδ (2.4) is repeated in 2.11 in the context of the angel's message to the shepherds. So, near the beginning of this new pericope, the lineage of Jesus to David is again established – narrative information that has become familiar to us throughout Luke 1.

First, we will discuss the shepherds who are foregrounded in 2.8-20 and who play a key narrative role in the pericope. With David's role as a shepherd woven throughout his story in Kingdoms, their narrative role in Luke's writing deserves to be evaluated. Why did the angels go to the shepherds? What narrative role do they play?

Secondly, another striking feature of the pericope is Augustus' census which is given prominence in the pericope. Luke takes five verses to describe the census (2.1-5), which contrasts the two verses given to the birth itself (2.6-7). We will examine the role the census plays in informing the reader's interpretation.

Thirdly, we will consider the narrative role of the 'city of David, Bethlehem' (2.4, 11). This phrase would have awakened the curiosity of first-century readers, as the city of David was historically known as Jerusalem, not Bethlehem. This study suggests that this is a deliberate gap or blank in the narrative which is left for the reader to fill.

These three features in the narrative all have strong Davidic shepherd king implications, and we will turn to these in order.

3.3.5.1 Why are there shepherds in the birth narrative?

Manson is correct in saying the shepherds form the centrepiece of the birth narrative.[84] While the setting is marked by Augustus' decree and the subsequent movement that this demanded (2.1-5), it is the shepherds who take centre stage in 2.8 and they maintain a prominent position until the end of the pericope at 2.20.

The reason for the inclusion of the shepherds, therefore, appears to be a question the text asks of the reader. Why did the angels go to the shepherds? Various answers have been given for this and these will be reviewed and evaluated.

This question has been answered in six main ways:

(I)　　They are regarded as sinners whom Jesus has come to save.

(II)　　They have been introduced in the style of Hellenistic Bucolic poetry.

(III)　　They are 'as angels'.[85]

(IV)　　They are examples of the lowly that Jesus has come to lift up (1.52).

---

84. William Manson, *The Gospel of Luke* (London: Hodder and Stoughton, 1955), p. 18.
85. Coleridge's description. Coleridge, *Birth*, p. 147.

(V)   They support the Davidic tradition.

(VI)   They point to the birth of the messianic shepherd.

These views will now be evaluated.

(I) The shepherds are sinners Godet in 1875 suggested that shepherds were regarded with 'contempt' and as 'heathen', and entitled this section in his commentary: 'The gospel is preached to the poor.'[86] He rests his case on the *b. Sanhedrin* and *m. Aboda Zara* but gives no references to either. A legacy of regarding shepherds as 'sinners' has since had an ongoing place in scholarly debate.

This position has been supported by Jeremias, especially in his book *Jerusalem in the Times of Jesus*,[87] and will be examined in detail here, even though Jeremias' own understanding of the shepherds in the birth narrative is primarily to support a 'stall tradition'.[88] This stall tradition explains why the shepherds knew where to find the baby whom the angels had announced was born in Bethlehem (2.12), for this tradition says they were the owners of the stall.[89] This is Jeremias' primary explanation for Luke's inclusion of the shepherds in 2.8-20, rather than that they were sinners, which he also supports.[90]

However, it is important to assess this view, as his underlying belief in shepherds as sinners, as expressed in *Jerusalem in the Times of Jesus* and also *The Parables of Jesus*, has been used by other scholars.[91] This has impacted scholars' views not only of the birth narrative's inclusion of shepherds, but also the interpretation in the parable of the lost sheep and the story of Zacchaeus where shepherd imagery is found and sinners are mentioned. Since this belief that shepherds were

86. F. Godet, *A Commentary on the Gospel of Luke, vol 1* (trans. M. D. Cusin; 2 vols; Edinburgh: T&T Clark, n.d.), p. 130.

87. Joachim Jeremias, *Jerusalem in the Times of Jesus: An Investigation into Economics and Social Conditions during the New Testament Period* (trans. F. H. and C. H. Cave; London: SCM, 1969), pp. 303–12.

88. J. Jeremias, 'ποιμήν', *TDNT* 6, p. 491.

89. Fitzmyer rightly comments that this goes well beyond what Luke suggests in the narrative. Fitzmyer, *Luke*, p. 395.

90. Jeremias does note that while shepherds are never judged adversely in the New Testament, this stands in contrast to the contempt of the Rabbis and so 'one is forced to conclude that it mirrors the actuality of the life of Jesus, who had fellowship with the despised and with sinners, and who shared sympathetically in their life'. Jeremias, 'ποιμήν', *TDNT* 6, p. 490.

91. William Hendriksen, *The Gospel of Luke* (Edinburgh: Banner of Truth Trust, 1984), p. 149; Charles H. Talbert, *Reading Luke: A Literary and Theological Commentary of the Third Gospel* (Macon, Georgia: Smyth and Helwys, 2002), p. 35; Craig L. Blomberg, *Interpreting the Parables* (Downers Grove: IVP, 1990), p. 180; Kenneth Ewing Bailey, *Poet and Peasant and Through Peasant Eyes: A Literary and Cultural Approach to the Parables of Jesus* (Grand Rapids: Eerdmans, 1983), p. 147.

sinners in first-century Palestine forms the backbone of many other scholars' interpretations, it will be dealt with in this discussion.

Jeremias' view of shepherds as sinners:
Jeremias equates first-century shepherds as ἁμαρτωλοί 'because they are suspected of driving their flocks into foreign fields, and of embezzling the produce of their flocks'.[92] He notes that being a herdsman is one of the long list of trades which were socially despised, including shopkeepers, physicians, butchers, sailors, tax collectors, publicans, and even dealers in produce of the sabbatical year (*m. Kidd.* iv.14; *b. Sanh.* 25b).[93] However, the *Babylonian Sanhedrin* 25b actually refers only to those shepherds with their own cattle, as they might be tempted to graze their cattle on another's land for gain, and it further limits this to herdsmen only in Palestine. This considerably qualifies Jeremias' list, and lessens his findings. The text says of herdsmen:

> 'Herdsmen': At first they thought that it was a question of mere chance; but when it was observed that they drove them there intentionally, they made the decree against them ... Raba said: The 'herdsmen' whom they [the Rabbis] refer to, include the herdsmen of both large and small cattle [i.e. both cowherds and shepherds]. But did Raba actually say so? Did he not say: Shepherds are disqualified only in Palestine, but elsewhere they are eligible ... Because they allowed cattle to graze on other people's lands. This law applies only to graziers of their own cattle, but not to hired herdsmen, for it is taken for granted that a man does not trespass unless material benefit accrues to him. (*b. Sanh.* 25b)

While the Babylonian Talmud is considered the single most important document of rabbinic literature,[94] it was not completed until 600 CE and so it cannot be fully relied upon to provide a definitive understanding of the attitudes of first-century Jews.[95] Marshall and Bock also note this late dating means this is not evidence that should determine how the shepherds are viewed in Luke's text.[96]

Jeremias, however, also gives evidence that shepherding was a despised trade from the earlier *m. Kidd.* iv.14, where there is a conversation between Jewish fathers about suitable occupations for their sons. It says:

> Abba Gurion of Sidon said, in name of Abba Gurya, 'A man should not teach his son to be an ass driver, a camel-driver, nor a barber, a sailor, *a herdsman*, or a shopkeeper. For their trade is the trade of thieves.' Rabbi Judah says in his name,

---

92. Joachim Jeremias, *The Parables of Jesus* (trans. S. H. Hooke; London: SCM, 1963), p. 133.

93. Jeremias, *Jerusalem in the Time of Jesus,* p. 304.

94. Jacob Neusner, *Introduction to Rabbinic Literature* (ABRL; New York: Doubleday, 1994), p. 187.

95. Neusner, *Introduction to Rabbinic Literature,* p.183.

96. Marshall, *Gospel,* 108; Bock, *Luke,* p. 213.

'Most ass drivers are evil; most camel drivers are decent, most sailors are saintly, the best physician is going to Gehenna, and the best of butchers is a partner of Amalek.' Rabbi Nehorai says, 'I should lay aside every trade in the world, and teach my son only Torah. For a man eats its fruit in this world, and the principal remains for the world to come. But other trades are not that way. When a man gets sick or old or has pains and cannot do his job, lo, he dies of starvation. But with Torah it is not that way. But it keeps him from all evil when he is young, and it gives him a future and a hope when he is old.' (*m. Kidd.* iv.14)[97]

The Mishnah was compiled by 200 CE,[98] so with an earlier dating than the Babylonian Talmud it may provide evidence closer to first-century Palestinian thought. It is unclear, however, whether this passage represents a normative historical prejudice against shepherds. In the text we first hear the advice of Abba Gurion about various professions including shepherds, while this is added to, both positively and negatively, by Rabbi Judah. While Rabbi Judah says no more about shepherds, clearly there are a variety of views about what professions are wise for sons to enter into. Ultimately, the conversation builds to Rabbi Nehorai, who states what they would have all agreed on – and where I suggest the conversation was always designed to head: that all trades are less than simply teaching your son the Torah. Indeed, as the Rabbi goes on to argue, the Torah is what keeps you whether you are young or old, and whether life is beginning in youth or nearing its end. This is surely the point of this passage rather than any real form of trade critique. To take this text and suggest it shows a sense of universal Jewish prejudice against shepherds, as Jeremias has done, is to misread the text.

It is also quite possible that there is a rhetorical element to the list of occupations. Abba Gurion of Sidon says of ass drivers, camel-drivers, barbers, sailors, herdsmen and shopkeepers that they are trades of *thieves*. Could it be that these occupations are thieves of time? That is, they are all occupations that steal time away from the study of Torah, the true occupation for a Jewish male. Furthermore, Rabbi Judah suggests his list of occupations will end up in Gehenna, the place of destruction for the wicked. This was originally known as the Valley of Hinnom (2 Chron. 28.3; 33.6; Jer. 7.31; 19.2-6; 2 Esd. 2.29; 7.36 [Latin only]) where apostate Israelites worshipped false gods and sacrificed their children in the fire. It was the place where the wicked suffered and atoned for their sins. In the Second Temple period, when an understanding of the afterlife developed, the Valley of Hinnom came to represent the place of eschatological judgement by the Jews (*1 Enoch* 26–27; 54.1-6; 56.1-4; 90.24-27).[99] In this Mishnah passage therefore, the reference

97. Italics are my emphasis.

98. Neusner, *Introduction to Rabbinic Literature*, p. 97. Günter Stemberger, *Introduction to the Talmud and Midrash* (trans. Markus Bockmuehl; Edinburgh: T&T Clark, 2nd edn, 1996), p. 109.

99. Duane F. Watson, 'Gehenna', *ABD* 2: p. 928.

to Gehenna may be a pictorial way to suggest these occupations too will ultimately end and be laid waste.

The same argument may hold for the reference to Amalek, who are known as God's antagonists and should be viewed pejoratively. Amalek fought with Israel at Raphidin (Exod. 17.8) after they had been delivered through the Red Sea and in the story of Saul and David, they are again viewed pejoratively (1 Kgdms 15).[100]

The reference to Amalek then, like the reference to Gehenna, appears to be strategically used to show God's displeasure. Overall, this passage from *m. Kidd.* iv.14 simply reinforces that the true occupation for a Jewish male is the study of Torah. Against this occupation, being a shepherd, a butcher, a shopkeeper, a physician, or any other occupation, cannot compare.

The Tosefta, as companion to the Mishnah and dated about 300 CE, has one further text regarding judicial procedures where shepherds are unreliable witnesses.[101] Jeremias does not cite this text. It reads: 'Among persons disqualified to act as judges or witnesses are also to be included robbers, herdsmen and extortioners, and all suspects concerning property. Their evidence is always invalid' (*T. Sanh.* II.2.5a).

The Tosefta is not, however, a free-standing document necessarily representing a 'primary view', but it is 'secondary, derivative and dependent',[102] and it does not sustain any commentary on the shepherds. Hence, a simple repetition without any amplification of the theme suggests that it should not be overemphasized.

Talbert similarly references *b. Sanh.* 25b to support a pejorative view of shepherds by Luke in the birth narrative saying that Luke's inclusion of the shepherds 'can only be regarded as a foreshadowing of the subsequent theme of God's grace shown to sinners that runs throughout Luke'.[103] This view, however, assumes Jeremias' conclusions about shepherds are correct, and as we have seen it is unlikely that is the case, although his identification of Luke's gospel as emphasizing the forgiveness of sin is correct. It is unlikely that Luke intends his readers to regard them as sinners while at the same time draw attention to the story of David (2.4, 11) when David is so widely understood as God's shepherd king.

Further, the *m.Bekhorot* 5.4 which discusses first-born animals as 'holy things' refers to 'Israelite shepherds' and 'priestly shepherds'. The texts says:

> [If] a firstling was running after him, and he kicked it and made a blemish in it – lo, this is slaughtered on that account. Any blemishes which are likely to happen at the hands of man – Israelite shepherds are believed [to testify that the blemishes came about unintentionally]. But priestly shepherds are not believed. Rabban Simeon b. Gamaliel says, 'He [a priest] is believed concerning another's [firstling] but not concerning his own.'

---

100. See also 1 Kgdms 28.18-19a.
101. Neusner, *Introduction to Rabbinic Literature*, p. 129.
102. Ibid., p. 152.
103. Talbert, *Reading Luke*, p. 35.

Shepherding later became a proscribed trade for Pharisees,[104] as this passage from the Mishnah suggests. This is consistent with Joshua 14.4, which says: 'For the people of Joseph were two tribes, Manassah and Ephraim; and no portion was given to the Levites in the land, but only towns to live in with their pastures lands for their flocks and herds.'

We cannot be sure when 'priestly shepherds' became so designated and if there were Pharisees who were known as this in the first-century Palestine, but it is unlikely that any religious leaders would become shepherds if they were known as ἁμαρτωλοί.

Another tradition which is informative in this discussion is that of Abel's sacrifice to the Lord as a shepherd which is compared favourably with Cain's grain offering (Gen. 4.2-4). While the biblical text does not provide the reason why the shepherd's offering found favour, traditions grew up to explain this event. One such tradition suggests shepherding was a more virtuous occupation.[105] Philo says: 'One of them labours and takes care of living beings … gladly undertaking the pastoral work which is preparatory to rulership and kingship. But the other occupies himself with earthly and inanimate things' (Philo, *Questions and Answers in Genesis* 1:59).[106]

Josephus also followed this tradition where Abel's profession was elevated over that of Cain's, stating:

Now the brothers took pleasure in different pursuits. Abel, the younger, has respect for justice [or righteousness], and, believing that God was with him in all his actions, paid heed to virtue: he led the life of a shepherd. Cain, on the contrary, was thoroughly depraved and had an eye only to gain: he was the first to think of plowing the soil. (Josephus, *Ant.* 1.53)

This tradition was followed by Ambrose of Milan, who later explained:

Plowing the earth … is inferior to pasturing sheep … Quite rightly then, when the brothers are born, the chronological order is preserved in Scripture [that is, Cain is mentioned before Abel, Gen. 4.1-2]. When however their way of life is mentioned, the younger comes before the older [that is, shepherding comes first, showing its superiority; Gen. 4.2]. (Ambrose of Milan, *Cain and Abel* 1.3.10)

---

104. Nolland, *Luke*, p. 771.

105. Other solutions to the problem are that Cain's sacrifice was defective and that Abel's 'firstborn' was superior, and Cain had a long history of sins and evil deeds and this is why his sacrifice was rejected. James L. Kugel, *Traditions of the Bible: A Guide to the Bible as it was at the Start of the Common Era* (Cambridge, MA: Harvard University Press, 1998), pp. 149-51.

106. This is also found in *The Sacrifices of Cain and Abel*, pp. 14, 51.

While Genesis 4.2-4 does not elevate shepherding or suggest Cain had an early history of wickedness, it is interesting that ancient interpreters tried to explain the story in light of a high view of shepherds.[107]

Pseudo-Philo LIX, writing in the Second Temple period, also tells the story of David's anointing and draws on the biblical texts of 1 Kingdoms 16.1-13; 17.34, and Psalms 61.2. In the *L.A.B.* LX-LXI he retells the story of David playing his harp to alleviate Saul's evil spirits, and David fighting Goliath. Unlike the biblical text, in Pseudo-Philo it is the Lord who says to Samuel: 'seek out the shepherd, the least of them all, and anoint him' (*L.A.B.* LIX.1). From a narrative perspective this focuses the readers' attention on God's voice, who chooses and anoints a *shepherd* as king.

The narrative begins with a conversation between God and Samuel, where God says to go and anoint the next king. This reflects the biblical text, while Pseudo-Philo adds the reason for the anointing, saying: 'because the time in which his kingdom will come to pass has been fulfilled' (*L.A.B.* LIX.1). As Murphy says, this stresses God's control and foreknowledge of the event, and that David's kingship was inaugurated at the proper time, unlike Saul's reign which was 'before the time'.[108] The psalm that is sung speaks of praising God, and gives an analogy from the story of Cain and Abel reinforcing the tradition of the superior shepherd sacrifice to support David's kingship. For Pseudo-Philo, God chose the offering from the shepherd in Genesis 4, and again he chooses the shepherd, David.

The story of David and Goliath begins with a short encounter of David and the Midianites who had come to take his sheep, and so David fights them and kills fifteen thousand. This establishes David as a successful warrior immediately prior to the Goliath challenge. Pseudo-Philo emphasizes David's faithful protection of his sheep, although the shepherd motif is then left aside.

Philo, another writer from the Second Temple period, has much to say about being a 'shepherd', and attributes them a role which is superior to a 'keeper of the sheep'. He defines a 'keeper of the sheep' as one who is 'indifferent to the flock', while a 'good and faithful one is called a shepherd'[109] (*Agr.* VI 29). He says: 'So full of dignity and benefit has the shepherd's task been held to be, that poets are wont to give to kings the title of "shepherds of peoples", a title which the lawgiver bestows on the wise' (Philo, *Agr.* X 41). He attributes being a shepherd positively to both Jacob (*Agr.* X 42) and Moses, whom he calls 'all-wise' (*Agr.* X 43). He also attributes the role of a shepherd to kings and to God. Philo writes:

> Indeed so good a thing is shepherding that it is justly ascribed not to kings only and wise men and perfectly cleansed souls, but also to God the All-Sovereign.

---

107. The writer of the first Gospel will call the blood of Abel δίκαιος (Mt. 23.35), and Luke will use Abel as one who died unjustly (Lk. 11.49-51).

108. Frederick J. Murphy, *Pseudo-Philo: Rewriting the Bible* (New York: Oxford University Press, 1993), p. 206.

109. This bears considerable resemblance to John's division of the hireling and the good shepherd (Jn 10.11-18).

The authority for this ascription is not any ordinary one but a prophet, whom we do well to trust. This is the way in which the Psalmist speaks: 'The Lord shepherds me and nothing shall be lacking to me (Ps. 23.1).' (Philo, *Agr.* XII 50)

He goes on to say: 'For land and water and air and fire, and all plants and animals which are in these, whether mortal or divine … are like some flock under the hand of God its King and Shepherd' (*Agr.* XII 51). He exhorts the world: 'Let therefore even the whole universe, the greatest and most perfect flock of God who IS say, "The Lord shepherds me and nothing shall fail me". Let each individual person too utter this same cry' (*Agr.* XII 51-52).

Commenting on Genesis 43, Philo says:

> Does it not seem as though they were more proud of being shepherds than is the king, than is the king who is talking to them, of all his sovereign power? They proclaim that not they only but their fathers also deliberately chose this course of life as worthy of entire and enthusiastic devotion. (*Agr.* XII 60)

Philo also says:

> Accordingly when the Mind, the ruler of the flock, taking the flock of the soul in hand with the law of nature as his instructor shews it the way with vigorous leadership, he renders it well worthy of praise and approval … With good reason, then, will the one take on him the name of king and be hailed as 'shepherd'. (*Agr.* XIV 66)

Philo's view of a faithful shepherd is positive and in no way pejorative. His views, current at the time of Jesus and much earlier than the later rabbinic Jeremias points to, help us see there was not a normative Jewish position which believed shepherds were all sinners.

On the balance of evidence, Jeremias seems to have overworked or even misread the late text of *b. Sanh.* 25b and the *m. Kidd.* iv. 14. The *T. Sanh.* II.2.5a, which scholars do not even refer to, is simply too little evidence for Jeremias, Bailey, Hendriksen and Talbert to suggest there is a 'Jewish' position that shepherds are sinners. The suggestion that Luke's understanding of shepherds was that they were sinners is therefore not to be considered likely and is set aside.[110]

(II) Shepherds represent Greco-Roman bucolic poetry Bultmann suggested Luke introduced the shepherds into the narrative as the most suitable representatives of a new humanity where the Saviour's goal is to restore a state of Paradise.[111] He

---

110. Marshall, Fitzmyer, Johnson and Bock also agree the shepherds are not examples of sinners. Marshall, *Gospel*, p. 107; Fitzmyer, *Luke*, p. 396; Johnson, *Gospel*, p. 52; Bock, *Luke*, p. 213.

111. Rudolf Karl Bultmann, *The History of the Synoptic Tradition* (trans. John Marsh; Oxford: Basil Blackwell, 1963), pp. 298–9. *Contra*, Fitzmyer, *Luke*, p. 395; Marshall, *Gospel*, p. 108.

perceives a shepherd's life constitutes this ideal image, as found in Bucolic poetry of the Greco-Roman world. Creed also notes how shepherds are found associated in legends with the birth and childhood of Romulus, Remus and Mithras, although he does not develop the idea.[112]

The main problem with this view is that Luke's narrative is firmly centred in the stories of the history of Israel rather than Greco-Roman allusions, so these former texts are most likely to be his interpretative field. Luke states his aim in the Gospel prologue (1.1-4) and says he wants Theophilus to be certain about the things in which he has been instructed (1.4). This most likely refers to some form of Christian instruction, though probably not the later structured Christian catechesis of the early church.[113] We can be confident anyway that the instruction would have been centred on locating Jesus in the Jewish scriptures, as Luke records Jesus explaining his story on the Emmaus road and for the disciples from the law, the prophets and the psalms (24.27, 44-45). We also note that Luke's writing is septuagintal in style and language after his initial prologue and his writing uses a high level of scriptural echoes, evidence that Luke's primary concern is to locate Jesus in the story of Israel. Furthermore, there is no other evidence for Hellenistic Bucolic ideas in Luke's birth narrative.[114] A Hellenistic interpretative basis therefore should not be considered likely.

(III) The shepherds 'as angels' Coleridge paints a vivid picture of the birth narrative where the shepherds are human players in a divine narrative, but he primarily suggests they are humans who become 'as angels' in delivering heaven's interpretation of the birth.[115] The beginning of the narrative suggests it is Caesar who is the prime mover in the plot, but the advent of the angels coming to the shepherds shows he is not the centre of the story, God is. Thus, the shepherds are strategic in the narrative by bringing together the realm of Caesar who brought the parents to Bethlehem, and the realm of God who revealed the message to the shepherds.

Coleridge also comments that the shepherds resonate with those sitting in darkness and the shadow of death (1.79) suggesting an echo of Isaiah 9.1;[116] while Isaiah 9.1-6 uses a military image, he concludes that Luke has abandoned the soldiers and military motif of Isaiah, in favour of shepherds. It is interesting that Coleridge does not develop or defend this echo, as this prophecy from Isaiah shows broader thematic features of Jesus from the infancy narrative. For example, we read in Isaiah that the child to be born will bring not only light to those in darkness (Isa. 9.1; Lk. 1.79), but joy (Isa. 9.2; Lk. 2.10), the release of oppression (Isa. 9.3-4; Lk. 1.51-55, 71-75), peace (Isa. 9.5-6; Lk. 1.79; 2.14), and will herald

112. J. M. Creed, *The Gospel According to St. Luke: The Greek Text with Introduction, Notes and Indices* (London: Macmillan, 1942), p. 31.

113. Marshall, *Gospel*, p. 43.

114. Fitzmyer, *Luke*, p. 395; Marshall, *Gospel*, p. 108.

115. Coleridge, *Birth*, p. 147.

116. Ibid., p. 153.

the Davidic kingdom which is characterized by judgement and righteousness (Isa. 9.6; Lk. 1.75). Coleridge remains content to simply imply that the shepherds are examples of ones who are sitting in darkness and who see a great light, as in Isaiah 9.1, and note that Luke exchanged shepherds for soldiers. It is possible Luke may be reversing the military motif of Isaiah 9, as when Luke quotes Isaiah 61.1-2 in Luke 4.18-19 he stops before the Isaianic reference to the vengeance of God, ending instead with a declaration of Jubilee, a picture of hope. This aligns well with the view presented here that Jesus comes as the Davidic shepherd king who binds up the injured and heals the sick (Ezek. 34.16) reversing the fortunes of God's flock. Thus a shepherd picture reverses the Jewish expectation of a military messiah and resonates with the Lukan Jesus who heals the sick, even the soldier who has his ear cut off (22.5-51); and a messiah who suffers (9.22; 18.31-33; 24.26, 46) and is silent before his oppressors (23.9).

Coleridge further describes the shepherds as examples of the marginalized who demonstrate belief, unlike the priest Zechariah, who does not believe the angel's message.[117] This, Coleridge explains, is shown when they become *as angels* by believing the message and delivering it to Mary and Joseph (1.17) and all who heard it (1.18). The story of Jesus' birth is reported briefly, while the narrative freight lies in the meaning of the birth. This knowledge is given to the shepherds, as it is they who put the facts and interpretation together for the parents and all who were present in the κατάλυμα.[118]

Coleridge notes the reaction of Mary in particular to the shepherds' message (1.18) which he suggests is astonishment to the point of incomprehension.[119] He posits that she is puzzled because of the unusual messengers and the circumstances of the birth, rather than the angel's message, as Mary has already heard the angel tell her who this child will be (1.26-38). From a literary point of view, Coleridge describes the inclusion of ὑπὸ τῶν ποιμένων and πρὸς αὐτούς (1.18) as literary redundancy which focuses on 'the extraordinary fact of such a message brought by such messengers who themselves have been visited by angels'.[120] The message is that the baby born in the city of David is the Saviour, the Messiah, and the Lord (2.11), and he is good news of great joy for all people (2.10). Coleridge stops short of making further narrative connections regarding the messengers themselves; however, could it be that the literary redundancy with regard to the *shepherd* messengers is an aid for the reader to reveal something embodied in their message of the Davidic Saviour, Messiah, and Lord born in the city of David?

The text goes on to narrate Mary's reaction, keeping the spotlight on her. Perhaps the reader is being led toward considering her perspective; Luke has already recounted Mary's encounter with Gabriel where we learn that the baby is the Son of the Most High and will be given the everlasting throne of David (1.31-33); she has already heard that her son will be the one to fulfil the Davidic

117. Ibid.
118. Ibid., p. 152.
119. Ibid., p. 148.
120. Ibid., p. 149.

covenant and so it is possible Mary might have made the link between the faithful shepherds in front of her with her baby's identity as Israel's new Davidic shepherd king. Luke has described Mary as a faithful servant of God when she responds to Gabriel (1.38) and Mary and Joseph are described as faithful Jews making pilgrimage to Jerusalem and the temple (2.22-24; 39, 41). Her song of praise echoes much of Hannah's song from Kingdoms, and so Luke presents her as knowledgeable of the stories of David and of scripture as a whole. It may be possible that Luke is suggesting that Mary pieces together something significant in the coming of the shepherds with the message of the Davidic saviour. Perhaps through the literary redundancy, Luke is highlighting the shepherds again as they are a part of the divine message. Could they be faithful shepherds coming to the Davidic shepherd?

When Coleridge's analysis is broken down, the shepherds' role *as angels* is really one of faithful human delivery of the message, rather than a more elevated role that 'angels' may suggest. He fails to suggest there is anything embodied in that message aside from the fact that they are marginalized people. In emphasizing the role of the angels and the divine in the narrative, however, Coleridge underplays the role of the shepherds. Commenting on 2.8, Coleridge says:

> From a narrative point of view, the prime question is not why God might choose the shepherds to receive the revelation, but why the narrator makes the sudden switch away from the birth scene when he might easily and more naturally have turned to the reaction of Mary and Joseph.[121]

This suggestion that the reader is not called to ask why God chose the shepherds as the recipients of the angel's message seems to overlook an important narrative feature. Why should the reader not ask this question? And why should we not ask why Luke chose to make the shepherd setting so prominent in the birth narrative?

These are questions this study seeks to examine, and are shortfalls of Coleridge's reading of the birth narrative. It appears that he has made a false choice by excluding an examination of the shepherds' involvement.

(IV) The shepherds as examples of the lowly The prevailing view of the shepherds in the birth narrative is that they are examples of people from a lowly status and so ideal recipients of God's grace. Creed says: 'the idea that revelation is made to the simple is thoroughly in harmony with the spirit of the Gospels in general, and with Luke in particular.'[122] He further notes that this is consistent with the pagan world where gods visited simple country folk rather than sophisticated city dwellers. Marshall comments that the motif of God announcing the birth to ordinary lowly people is 'undoubtedly present',[123] while Johnson describes

---

121. Ibid., p. 137.
122. Creed, *According to St. Luke*, p. 34.
123. Marshall, *Gospel*, p. 108.

the shepherds as 'low-esteemed labourers' and Mary and Joseph 'are transients, equivalent to the homeless of contemporary street people'.[124]

Fitzmyer supports this interpretation of the shepherds recalling 1.38, 52, while also recognizing the tradition that associates the birth of the messiah with Bethlehem and David.[125] He affirms that the shepherds are not sinners but also, contra Johnson, that they are not poor, since they are the implied owners of the flock.[126] Fitzmyer's reference to Mary's song at 1.52, where God brings down the powerful from their thrones and instead lifts up the lowly, is a reversal motif that is consistent with Luke's Gospel, while Fitzmyer's inclusion of 1.38 is confusing. In this verse Mary says to Gabriel: 'Here I am the servant of the Lord; let it be with me according to your word.' This does not necessarily imply she is a lowly member of society, rather that she is humble before God. Fitzmyer may suggest she is poor because she is a woman, although the focus here is on her words of submission to God and not her gender.

Bock also sides with this view that shepherds represent the lowly and humble who respond to God's message.[127] He cites Mary's humility at 1.38, the *Magnificat* at 1.52, and then appeals to the Nazareth manifesto at 4.16-18.[128] These verses highlight the eschatological reversal (or, I prefer, the language of realignment) whereby the lowly are lifted up and the poor have good news brought to them. This view stresses the work of God in bringing salvation to the poor, while it includes no recognition of a Jewish view of the divine shepherd from the OT. This is intriguing because Bock argues the view that shepherds are not sinners, based on the late dating of rabbinic evidence, and the positive view of shepherds from the OT and the NT.[129] He notes in particular that church leaders come to be known as shepherds, and 'in the OT, Abraham, Moses and David were all shepherds at some point in their lives',[130] while he does not identify God as a shepherd. He appears to have overlooked that God says he will be a shepherd for his people (Ezek. 34.11-16) and that David clearly knows God as shepherd (Ps. 22).

Green also sides with this predominant view of shepherds as lowly but he refers to the shepherds as 'outsiders'.[131] He views 'outsiders' in two ways. First, they are outsiders to the birth family showing not only how significant this birth is, but that it prefigures Luke's redefinition of 'family' in the Gospel. Secondly, they are outsiders because they are 'persons of low regard'.[132] He acknowledges that they

---

124. Johnson, *Gospel*, p. 52.

125. Fitzmyer, *Luke*, pp. 395–6.

126. Ibid., p. 396.

127. Bock, *Luke*, pp. 213–14.

128. The Nazareth sermon finishes at 4.19.

129. Bock wrongly positions Brown with this view of shepherds as sinners. Bock, *Luke*, 213. Talking of the view that shepherds are sinners from *b. Sahn* 25b., Brown states: 'This has led to the suggestion that for Luke they represented sinners whom Jesus came to save (see 5:32; 7:34; 15:1; 19:7); yet there is no hint of that in 2:8-20.' Brown, *Birth*, p. 420.

130. Bock, *Luke*, p. 213.

131. Green, *Gospel*, p. 132.

132. Ibid.

play a pivotal role in the narrative, and that they have been anticipated implicitly by the continued mention of David and the lowly in Luke 1.[133] He makes nothing further, however, of this connection between Luke's use of 'David' in the narrative and the shepherds.

Green does comment however, that the economic situation of shepherds sets them toward the bottom of the scale of power and privilege.[134] Bailey's research shows that

> the average family may have five to fifteen animals. A number of families get together and hire a shepherd. The shepherd may own some of the animals and be from one of the families. Thus, in the case of a small herd of about forty animals, the shepherd leading them may be their sole owner. In the case of a hundred sheep the shepherd is probably not their sole owner.[135]

Undoubtedly being a shepherd for someone else's sheep, or even being the owner of some of the sheep, suggests a low socio-economic status. Furthermore, the crippling taxation system would have meant that life was difficult economically. There is no doubt that shepherds can be identified as poor in first-century Palestine and Luke presents a reversal for the lowly in the Gospel. But I would question whether this is the primary function of the shepherds in the birth narrative and whether their historical economic situation is why Luke has given them such a central role in the birth narrative.

Green describes Luke 1–2 as an 'echo chamber' where many stories of Israel are heard.[136] Yet here, he and other scholars appear to underplay the role for the shepherds by only interpreting them in their literal setting, making no connection between them and the strong Davidic setting Luke has given in this narrative and the wider infancy narrative. While first-century Palestinian shepherds were economically poor, in Luke's narrative world, where Israel's stories abound, shepherds had a divine and noble heritage. It is therefore unlikely that their natural status as poor or marginalized is the only image they suggest.

(V) The shepherds support the Davidic tradition Fitzmyer, Nolland and Brown see varying degrees of resonance between the shepherds and the Davidic tradition, while the argument is only developed by Brown. Other scholars suggest an

133. Green, *Gospel,* p. 130.

134. Green references Lenski, who addresses the 'peasant class' over a broad geographical and historical domain from sixteenth-century Japan, modern Chinese peasants, Sukodhya Thailand, Hammurabi's Babylon, Christian Europe in the Middle Ages to thirteenth-century England. He does not directly address the economic situation of first-century Palestinian shepherds, although his analysis does provide a broad background for assessing the peasant class. See Green, *Gospel,* p. 130; Gerhard Lenski, *Power and Privilege: A Theory of Social Stratification* (New York: McGraw Hill, 1966), pp. 266–78.

135. Bailey, *Poet and Peasant,* p. 148.

136. Green, *Gospel,* p. 57.

allusion to the Davidic tradition from Micah 5.2, but they make this connection because of the mention of Bethlehem, and not the shepherds.

Fitzmyer's key rationale for the role of the shepherds is because they are examples of lowly members of society. He also attributes the introduction of the shepherds into the birth narrative to support the tradition which expects the Messiah to be born in Bethlehem. While Fitzmyer believes that Micah 5.2 lies in the background of Jesus' birth in Bethlehem, he is not willing to make the connection between the shepherds and the Davidic tradition.[137]

Nolland also briefly suggests the shepherds suit the pastoral roots of David, who was also from Bethlehem (1 Kgdms 16.11; 17.15; Ps. 77.70), although he fails to perceive any royal figure behind the shepherds in the Lukan drama.[138] Marshall does not find a connection between David and the shepherds in the birth narrative, since 'an allusion to the task of David as a shepherd ... is unlikely, since it should be the child who is a shepherd, not the witnesses of his birth'.[139] However, as Luke's readers are also presented with a strong Bethlehem setting (2.4, 15) and David's name occurs three times in the narrative, it might be wrong to assume Luke's readers would not make some level of connection here.

Nolland also considers the possibilities of a link between the shepherds and Migdal Eder, the 'Tower of the Flock' (Mic. 4.8), but with the key word 'tower' and 'dominion' missing in Luke's narrative, he sides with caution.[140] While it appears, therefore, that he may see possibilities within the David tradition, he does not make any connection between the shepherds in the birth narrative and David as the shepherd ruler of Israel.

Brown, on the other hand, perceives great symbolism in the shepherds, their point of origin from Bethlehem and the role of Micah 4.8.[141] He uses the word 'symbolism' frequently with regard to the shepherds, suggesting that there is something in them that implies something greater for the narrative. Brown proposes that there is a 'midrashic reflection' underlying Luke's narrative which is a key to the symbolism of the shepherds that attaches them to the Bethlehem area.[142] In this, he first states that it is likely there is a Jewish background to Luke's symbolism which is sound, as Luke draws so heavily on the stories of Israel in his Gospel.

He then notes that Jewish expectation was that the Messiah would come from Bethlehem. John 7.42 supports this when it says: 'has not the scripture said that the Messiah is descended from Bethlehem, the village where David lived?' This scripture John refers to is most likely Micah 5.2, a text Matthew cites (Mt. 2.5-6). While I do not suggest Luke knew Matthew's or John's Gospel, their Gospels do indicate that first-century Judaism did expect the Messiah to come from

---

137. Fitzmyer, *Luke*, p. 395.
138. Nolland, *Luke*, p. 106.
139. Marshall, *Gospel*, p. 108.
140. Nolland, *Luke*, p. 106.
141. Brown, *Birth*, pp. 420–4.
142. Ibid., p. 421.

Bethlehem, and we can expect that Luke also knew this tradition. This tradition is found in the prophet Micah's words.

In considering Micah 5:2, Brown looks to the broader historical picture of Micah 4–5. When the prophet was writing, the Northern Kingdom had fallen to Tiglath-pileser III and the Assyrian army (722 BCE) and Micah prophesies the fall of the Davidic monarchy and the Southern Kingdom. However, Micah says the Lord will rescue Jerusalem from her enemies through a ruler who will come from the small city where David was born, Bethlehem. First, he notes that Migdal Eder is called the 'tower of the flock' (Mic. 4.8) and Brown suggests that it is this that connects the shepherds and their flocks to the Bethlehem area.[143] He notes that both Genesis 35.21 and Micah 4.8 connect Migdal Eder with the Bethlehem area (Gen. 35.19; Mic. 5.1). He goes on to suggest that because the future victory for Jerusalem/Zion will come from Bethlehem's new ruler, Migdal Eder and Jerusalem are being identified together.[144]

Secondly, Brown notes that Luke describes Joseph going up to Bethlehem (ἀναβαίνω; 2.4) with the verb traditionally used for going up to Jerusalem, and also that Luke refers to the 'city of David' for Bethlehem and not Jerusalem.[145] He then suggests that, for Luke, 'Micah's reference to the "mountain of the house of the Lord" [Mic. 4.8] has been shifted from Jerusalem/Zion to Bethlehem, since it is there that one must go to see the Lord ([Lk.] 2:11-12)'.[146] This, he suggests, is possible if Luke, or a midrashic tradition available to him, read Micah 4.8 and 5.2 in parallel.[147]

Brown concludes that 'Luke's reference to shepherds pasturing their flock in the region of Bethlehem (2:8) may reflect his understanding that Migdal Eder, the Tower of the Flock of Mic 4:8, is in the environs of Bethlehem rather than at Jerusalem'.[148] However, Brown's midrash may be taking these parallels too far by equating one place (Migdal Eder/Jerusalem) with another (Bethlehem) and this seems an unlikely background for Luke's use of the city of David, Bethlehem.

The strength of Brown's analysis is the significance he places on the symbolism of the shepherds in Luke's narrative and identifying an echo of Micah's prophecy. This echo and the role of Bethlehem will be assessed later in the chapter, however we should note that Brown does not develop any tangible link between the messianic shepherd king of Micah 5.4 and the newborn Davidic baby. His focus is limited to narratively and geographically linking Micah 4.8 with Micah 5.2. It seems he may have limited his analysis of the shepherds in Luke too tightly by restricting his links to confirming the geographical setting and missing the fact

143. Brown, *Birth*, p. 421.
144. Ibid., p. 422.
145. Ibid., p. 423.
146. Ibid.
147. Brown quotes the MT, no doubt because a midrashic reflection would be a Jewish reading, while below is the LXX which Luke is more likely to have used.
148. Ibid, p. 423.

that Micah 5.2 is attached to a wider pericope of 5.2-5 where the shepherd ruler is described.

Nolland and Fitzmyer's reading of the shepherds in Luke 2 as drawing in some respects on the early story of David when he was in Bethlehem is sound and should be considered possible.

(VI) Shepherds signify Jesus as the messianic shepherd Bovon says that the overriding portrayal of shepherds in biblical literature is primarily positive, and that as a nation of shepherds, they used this image for God, for their king, and their expected messiah.[149] We have seen this at the beginning of Chapter 2. However, Bovon also notes that Ezekiel 34 shows the Jewish people were expecting an eschatological Davidic shepherd, and from Micah 5 that this messianic shepherd was going to be born in Bethlehem.

In his brief interpretation of the birth narrative, Bovon perceives Jesus as the *messianic shepherd*, and the role of the shepherds in the narrative as drawing the readers' attention to that fact. He rightly comments that 'what was expected from Micah 5 was, of course, not the birth of the Messiah among the shepherds, but the birth of the messianic shepherd'.[150] In this Bovon makes an interpretative link that combines resonant features of Davidic prophecy with the baby born to Mary. He cites not only the messianic shepherd from Micah 5 but also the Davidic shepherd king from Ezekiel 34. In Ezekiel 34 Bovon notes the criticism of the bad shepherds of Israel (34.1-10), the drawing together of Israel under God as shepherd (11-16), God's judgement of the people and leaders (16-22), the prophecy of the eschatological Davidic shepherd (23-24), and a description of the messianic age (25-31). In this echo, Bovon takes seriously the interplay of God as Israel's shepherd (11-16) and also the coming Davidic shepherd, his servant (23-31). This he develops no further.

The strength of Bovon's reading of the shepherds is that he assesses them in the context of the wider story of scripture. It appears from our analysis of the shepherds in Luke's narrative that there is a tendency for scholars to consider them as isolated characters in the narrative, and this limits how they are understood. Bovon, instead, reads them as a part of a wider connection to David, Bethlehem, and to God. This approach resonates with Luke's narrative writing style which assumes the narrative is a cohesive whole and one part of a narrative or one character works to complement the story as a unity. This is the view I will go on to develop.

3.3.5.2 The role of the census
This section will examine the narrative role of the census with respect to Augustus and the Greco-Roman background. Luke begins this pericope with news of Augustus' decree that all the world must be registered in their own towns.[151]

---

149. Bovon, *Lukas 1*, p. 122.

150. Ibid., p. 123. Author's translation.

151. For concerns around the census see Bock, *Luke*, pp. 903–9; Fitzmyer, *Luke*, pp. 399–405; Nolland, *Luke*, pp. 99–103.

Augustus' census dominates the first five verses by being recalled four times (2.1, 2, 3, 5). It therefore takes central stage in the setting of the birth narrative and it is against this backdrop that the reader learns of Mary and Joseph's movement to Bethlehem. As the census is located historically by Luke, first we will consider how mention of Augustus would have been perceived in the ancient world, and then what this may mean to the reader's interpretation.

Caesar Augustus, born Gaius Octavius Thurinus, was triumvir of Rome (43 BCE–31 BCE) in a shared military rule with Mark Antony and Marcus Lepidus, known as the Second Triumvirate. Octavian then held various autocratic positions of power over the Roman Senate until he came to rule the Roman world in supreme position from 27 BCE to 14 CE, when he was given the title *Augustus*.[152] His new name, Augustus, had semi-religious connotations and made claims of superior personal prestige and authority.[153] Augustus was the first Roman emperor to achieve 'worldwide' rule, so while other emperors before him had widened Roman rule, Octavius annexed Egypt in 30 BCE and achieved *Pax Augusta*. In a civil war that finally eliminated all his rivals, he declared: *per consensum universorum potius rerum omnium*, proclaiming his 'unchallenged and universal sovereignty'.[154] Further, the Mediterranean world believed imperial rule was underpinned by a god-like autocracy that was both religious and political.[155] The poet Horace summed up Roman thinking when he said: 'Because you show due reverence to the gods, you rule on earth.'[156] Virgil declared of Augustus: 'This is the man, this is the one whom you have long been promised, Augustus Caesar, offspring of a god, founder of the golden age.'[157]

By bringing temporal peace Augustus was viewed as the earthly prince of peace, and was looked upon in god-like terms. Dio Cassius records the occasion when the Romans formally conferred the title of 'Father' on Augustus,[158] when he was honoured as 'saviour of the citizens',[159] was given the title of Augustus

---

152. Crook notes how he gradually took over power in his position as consul when he gave gifts to soldiers and corn to the people while having a tight grip on Senate policy and the army. J. A. Crook, 'Augustus: Power, Authority and Achievement', in *The Cambridge Ancient History: The Augustan Empire 43 B.C.-A.D. 69*, Vol. 10 (ed. Alan K. Bowman, Edward Champlin and Andrew Lintott; Cambridge: Cambridge University Press, 2nd edn, 1996), pp. 113–14.

153. H. H. Scullard, *From the Gracchi to Nero: A History of Rome from 133BC to AD68* (London: Methuen, 1979), p. 219.

154. Scullard, *Gracchi to Nero*, p. 215.

155. S. R. F. Price, *Rituals and Power: the Roman Imperial Cult in Asia Minor* (Cambridge: Cambridge University Press, 1998), p. 25.

156. See Joseph Vogt's summary of the rule and reign of Augustus in, 'Augustus and Tiberius', *Jesus in His Time* (ed. Hans Jürgen Schultz; London: SPCK, 1971), p. 2.

157. Virgil, *Aeneid*, 6, pp. 791–2.

158. Dio Cassius, Book 55.10.

159. Dio Cassius, Book 53.16.

signifying that he was more than human,[160] and his power was described as that of a monarch.[161] Paulus Fabius Maximus, the proconsul of Asia decreed that 'in view of the distinctiveness of Augustus' birthdate as the beginning of a new era for humanity, it would be appropriate to adopt the natal day of Augustus as the beginning of the official year in the province'.[162] This document says:

> Whereas *Providence* ... has ... adorned our lives with the highest good: Augustus ... and has in her beneficence granted us and those who will come after us [*a Savior*] who has made war to cease and who shall put everything [in peaceful] order ... with the result that the *birthday of our God* signalled the beginning of *Good News for the world* because of him.[163]

Inscriptions talked about Augustus as 'the most divine Caesar', that he was 'the beginning of the breath of life for them', and in his birth was 'the beginning of all things'.[164] Many coins had images of his head in a temple and one of a sacrifice before the imperial temple.[165] The cult of the ruler as founder, saviour and benefactor was well established in the Greco-Roman world, and it served in the first instance as an 'ecumenical unifying force' for the empire, even though the 'divinity' of the emperor was constructed one way in the Latin West and another in the Greek East.[166] The seeds of the ruler's divinity were evident.

The language and images of *saviour, god, father, good news* and *lord* echo in the biblical text, and particularly in the infancy narrative where a new Davidic king was about to be born. In 2.1 Augustus issues a decree to literally the 'whole inhabited earth', and therefore Joseph and the heavily pregnant Mary go to Bethlehem. This powerful Roman figure, however, makes no further appearance on the Lukan stage. In the narrative he has fulfilled his function by bringing Mary and Joseph to the place where God needed them to be. The text tells us this is the city of David called Bethlehem.

The inclusion of Augustus and news of his census serves the narrative in three ways. First, it confirms Luke's interest in the historical world and his desire to connect his readers with their own culture and history. The Gospel could not simply be read by Theophilus and other first-century readers without their senses being alerted to this leading political figure. We have seen that Augustus'

160. Dio Cassius, Book 53.16.

161. Dio Cassius, Book 53.17.

162. Frederick W. Danker, *Benefactor: Epigraphical Study of a Graeco-Roman and New Testament Semantic Field* (St Louis: Clayton Publishing House, 1982), p. 215.

163. Danker, *Benefactor*, p. 217; Crossan, *Historical Jesus*, p. 31. Author's emphasis.

164. These are (translated) words from an ancient Roman statue where the Roman governor, who proposed starting the New Year on Augustus' birthday, expresses the crucial importance of the birth of Augustus. See Price, *Rituals and Power*, p. 55.

165. Ibid., pp. 200–1.

166. C. Kavin Rowe, 'Luke-Acts and the Imperial Cult: A Way Through the Conundrum?' *JSNT* 27 (2005), pp. 279–300 (280).

influence was pervasive in the Greco-Roman world and this study suggests any Christian writer who names him would have been doing so deliberately.[167] The mention of Augustus who is known to be *Saviour, Lord, the bringer of peace* and *good news*, in contrast to the angels who declare the baby has these roles, signals something of Luke's intention. As Bovon notes, the title of Saviour is comprehensible to everyone, both Jew and Greek, and it is especially salient to the Hellenistic rulership.[168] While Luke is positioning Jesus as fulfilling the promises to Israel, he is particularly showing how Jesus as Saviour and Lord impacts Theophilus' immediate context, the Greco-Roman world.

Secondly, the text demonstrates that God's power is greater than that of Augustus. Augustus issues the decree and all people must obey, and yet his actions lead to the fulfilment of ancient prophecy of Micah who said the messianic shepherd will be born in Bethlehem (Mic. 5.2). Caesar enters the narrative, fulfils his function to move Mary and Joseph to Bethlehem, and then exits. This suggests even Augustus, the Roman Emperor, is ultimately on God's timetable as God is the prime mover in the narrative. Augustus issues his decree when Herod is King in Judea (1.5), but God has issued his decree in the late eighth century BCE when Micah was prophet in the land of Judea. For Luke, real power resides in God and not in earthly rulers and their kingdoms.

Finally, Luke suggests an inherent contrast between the baby who is born in the 'city of (King) David' and Augustus. Both are rulers and so both are shepherds, but it is with respect to the type of rule they exercise that Luke draws a contrast. Augustus rules by political manoeuvring and imperial organization characterized by the census decree, while the baby's power comes from the divine throne characterized by the army (στρατιά) of angels who announce God's peace. It is God's power attributed to the baby which brings divine peace and therefore godly power to all the earth.

From this we can conclude that the mention of Augustus has a narrative role in the birth story which contrasts the power of imperial and divine worlds. For Luke, God is the one with true power as his decree was announced centuries before Augustus' reign, and this power now resides in the baby whose birth was announced by an army of angels.

---

167. There is no scholarly consensus regarding the role Augustus plays in the Lukan narrative. Marshall notes he functions to place Luke's account in the context of world history. Nolland, Fitzmyer, Brown, Bovon, Horsley and Green suggest that he is a deliberate contrast to the rule of Christ. Green comments that the issue of power takes centre stage, while Bovon takes one step further, claiming there is a political polemic. In contrast, Rowe does not believe Luke addresses the imperial cult directly, and thus reads no political critique. Marshall, *Gospel*, pp. 97–8; Nolland, *Luke*, p. 103; Fitzmyer, *Luke*, pp. 393–4; Brown, *Birth*, pp. 415–16; Bovon, *Lukas 1*, pp. 117–18; Richard A. Horsley, *The Liberation of Christmas: The Infancy Narratives in Social Context* (New York: Crossroad, 1989), pp. 23–38; Green, *Gospel*, p. 125; Rowe, 'A Way Through the Conundrum?' p. 282.

168. Bovon, *Lukas 1*, p. 125.

3.3.5.3 Bethlehem, the city of David

Luke's statement that Mary and Joseph go up to the πόλιν Δαυὶδ ἥτις καλεῖται Βηθλέεμ provides a possible echo of Micah 5.2-5, and also unexpected information that is important in understanding Luke's portrayal of Jesus as *Davidic shepherd king.*

Luke's focus on the city of David as Bethlehem is a signal of Luke's narrative interest. Bethlehem reminds the reader of the story of David as we first meet him at Bethlehem where he was anointed king by Samuel (1 Kgdms 16.1-13), and where he was a faithful shepherd for his father's flock. Bethlehem is also the place where Micah had said the messianic shepherd would be born (Mic. 5.2-5) which is the echo we will now evaluate.

Marshall, Nolland, Green and Strauss support a link to Micah's prophecy, while Bock assumes that it cannot be, for Luke does not cite the text while Matthew does (Mt. 2.6).[169] This hesitancy to attribute intertextuality here, based on a comparison to Matthew, shows undue caution and a lack of recognition of Luke's highly allusive writing. Luke has echoes of Micah 4.7 in Luke 1.33, Micah 7.6 in 12.53, and Micah 7.20 in 1.55,[170] so we know Luke knew and used the prophet's writing.

There are obvious parallels of vocabulary with references to Βηθλέεμ (Mic. 5.2; Lk. 2.4, 15), ποιμήν and cognates (Mic. 5.4; Lk. 2.8, 15, 18, 20) and talk of εἰρήνη (Mic. 5.5; Lk. 2.14). There is also the allusion to one giving birth in Micah (Mic. 5.2)[171] with Mary giving birth (2.7). The emphasis on one who is to rule is also shared between the texts while using different language; Micah talks of one to rule (ἄρχων; Mic. 5.2) while the wider text of Micah 4-5 uses βασιλεία (4.8) which is consistent with Luke's emphasis on Jesus being given the Davidic throne (1.32). There is also the possibility that the σήμερον in Luke 2.11, should be 'heard' as the fulfilment of the woman in labour in Micah (Mic. 5.2). This shows there is some evidence of volume through the repetition of language between the two passages.

On a thematic level we should not underestimate the use of some of this language. Peace is an aspect of salvation in Luke and is used as a common blessing (7.50; 8.48). Εἰρήνη has already been spoken by Zechariah in the context of salvation coming to Israel (1.79), it is in Simeon's hymn of praise (2.29) and is an echo of Isaiah 49.6 where salvation comes also to the Gentiles (2.32). It is mentioned in the context of the mission of the seventy (10.5, 6) and Jesus will bless the disciples with peace after the resurrection (24.36). It is sung of in the angels' hymn of praise before the shepherds in 2.14, where peace is tantamount to salvation. This is later recalled in a parallel hymn in 19.38 when multitudes of disciples sing of peace in heaven.

The use of μεγαλύνω (Mic. 5.4) in the context of the Bethlehemite ruler may also recall μέγας used in Luke 1.32 which, as we have seen, echoes the Davidic

---

169. Marshall, *Gospel*, p. 105; Nolland, *Luke*, p. 104; Green, *Gospel*, p. 127; Strauss, *Davidic Messiah*, p. 111. *Contra*, Bock, *Luke*, p. 205; Fitzmyer, *Luke*, p. 395.

170. See UBSGNT (rev. 4th edn), p. 900.

171. Brown also suggests Micah 4.10's birth pangs may resonate here. Brown, *Birth*, p. 422.

covenant (2 Kgdms 7.9). The description of Bethlehem being ὀλιγοστός (few in number; Mic. 5.2) also reflects the general thrust of Mary's song where it is the ones who are poor and lowly who are lifted up. There is an interesting use of ἔξοδος in Micah 5.2 which Luke uses uniquely in the transfiguration (9.31). This is understood as integral to Luke's exodus journey motif and so there may be wider Lukan cohesion here.[172] Finally, the description of being made great 'to the ends of the earth' (Mic. 5.4), has a Lukan flavour of the gospel going to the ends of the earth (Lk. 24.47; Acts 1.8), while the language used is different.

The thematic coherence of Micah 5.2-5 resonates very highly with identified Lukan themes. It comes with a strong base of scholarly support showing that many scholars using a range of methodological approaches have found an echo here, and it most certainly provides a satisfactory reading. In fact, combining the prominent shepherds in the Lukan narrative with this echo, we find support for Bovon's suggestion regarding the messianic shepherd; namely, the Davidic shepherd king.

Strauss rightly notes 'whereas Matthew emphasises Jesus' Bethlehem birth because it fulfils the prophecy of Micah 5.2, Luke wishes to stress the Davidic link'.[173] Matthew's concern is to show how Jesus fulfilled prophecy, while Luke's emphasis is to link Jesus' birthplace with his Davidic shepherd king identity. Therefore, Luke's unexpected reference to the city of David as Bethlehem, functions to recall the prophecy of Micah 5.2-5 of the Davidic shepherd ruler.

The juxtaposition of the city of David and Bethlehem In the birth narrative the reader's ears are alerted to the juxtaposition of the city of David with Bethlehem. The Jewish world knew the city of David was Jerusalem (2 Kgdms 5.7, 9; 6.10, 12, 16; 3 Kgdms 9.24; 14.31; 15.8) rather than Bethlehem. 2 Kingdoms 5.7-9 (cf. 1 Chron. 11.5-7) describes the taking of the Jebusite city and renaming it 'the city of David', otherwise known as 'Jebusite' Jerusalem, the holy city, or Zion.[174] The city of David was the place where the ark resided (2 Kgdms 6.12, 16; 1 Chron. 15.29) and where Solomon built his temple (3 Kgdms 3.1; 8.1; 2 Chron. 5.2), making it the key place of religious and divine power. It is also the place where the kings lived and were buried when they died,[175] suggesting a political interest. Luke's narrative interest in Jerusalem is well accepted,[176] and yet, at this point in the infancy narrative, it is Bethlehem and not Jerusalem to which Luke directs his readers. The question must be asked why Luke does this.

---

172. This will be discussed more fully in Chapter 5.

173. Strauss, *Davidic Messiah*, p. 111.

174. Philip J. King, 'Jerusalem', ABD 3, p. 751.

175. David (3 Kgdms 2.10), Solomon (3 Kgdms 11.43; 2 Chron. 9.31), Rehoboam (3 Kgdms 14.31; 2 Chron. 12:16), Abijam (3 Kgdms 15.8; 2 Chron. 13.23), Asa (3 Kgdms 15.24; 2 Chron. 16.14), Jehoshaphat (3 Kgdms 22.51; 2 Chron. 21.1), Jehoram (4 Kgdms 8.24; 2 Chron. 21.20), Joash (4 Kgdms 12.22; 2 Chron. 24.25) and Jotham (4 Kgdms 15.38; 2 Chron. 27.9).

176. For a clear summary see Peter W. L. Walker, *Jesus and the Holy City: New Testament Perspectives on Jerusalem* (Grand Rapids: Eerdmans, 1996), pp. 57–112.

I propose that Luke's use of Bethlehem in contrast to Jerusalem suggests king and kingdom are being redefined in Luke's Gospel. In the same way that Augustus, the leading Greco-Roman political figure, is sidelined in Luke's narrative, so too is the lineage of a Jewish political kingdom in Jerusalem. This suggests a kingdom that will have a different nuance to kings who conquered with armies and displays of power.

This proposal may be confirmed by Luke's genealogy (3.23-38). Luke has some clear differences to Matthew's record; notably, Luke shows David's son as Nathan (3.31) while Matthew has him as Solomon (Mt. 1.6).[177] Johnson notes that 'the most surprising aspect of Luke's genealogy is its rejection of the royal line of Judah'.[178] The kingly lineage in Matthew is from Solomon to Jechoniah (Mt. 1.6-12) while Luke's lineage is from Nathan to Neri in Luke (Lk. 3.27-31). Scholars have come to various positions regarding why Luke has done this. These views from least likely to most accepted are:

(1) Luke shows a tradition that traces Nathan the son of David to Nathan, the prophet.[179] The *Tg Zech* 12.12 links the family of the house of Nathan the prophet, to the Son of David, as does Africanus' *Letter to Aristides*, Eusebius,[180] and the *Apocalypse of Zerubbabel*. This position was suggested by Johnson in his earlier monograph where he argues this minority view was the tradition that Luke drew on.[181]

(2) Luke avoids the kingly line because of scandals associated with the kingly Davidic line.[182]

(3) The most widely accepted view is that Luke avoids the kingly line of Solomon to Jechoniah because he is aware of Jeremiah's prophecy to Jehoiakim that his son Jechoniah would not sit on the throne of David (Jer. 36.30), and that the line from Jechoniah would cease (Jer. 22.24-30).[183] Jeremiah says:

O land, land
Hear the word of the Lord:
Record this man as a banished person,

---

177. For a survey on the differences in the genealogies see Bock, *Luke,* pp. 918–23; Fitzmyer, *Luke,* pp. 495–6; Nolland, *Luke,* pp. 168–9. For a review of the differences from Neri to Nathan in Luke see Miura, *David,* p. 211.

178. Marshall D. Johnson, *The Purpose of the Biblical Genealogies with Special Reference to the Setting of the Genealogies of Jesus* (SNTSMS, 8; Cambridge: Cambridge University Press, 2nd edn, 1988), p. 240.

179. Johnson, *Genealogies,* 2nd edn, pp. 240–52; Ernest L. Abel, 'The Genealogy of Jesus: O XPICTOC', *NTS* 20 (1974): 203–10.

180. Eusebius, *Questiones Evangelicae ad Stephanum,* III. 2.

181. M. D. Johnson, *Purpose of the Biblical Genealogies* (SNTSMS, 8; London: Cambridge University Press, 1st edn, 1969), p. 246.

182. Johnson, *Genealogies,* 2nd edn, pp. 135–6.

183. Fitzmyer, *Luke,* p. 501; Strauss, *Davidic Messiah,* p. 215; Bock, *Luke,* pp. 356, 922; Miura, *David,* p. 212. Marshall notes this as a possibility: Marshall, *Gospel,* p. 161.

Because none of his offspring shall grow up
To sit on the throne of David,
As ruler again in Judah. (Jer. 22.30)

This position also acknowledges that Zechariah 12.10-14, and in particular vv. 12-14, describe the separate houses of David, Nathan, Levi and Shimeites, which are all a part of Luke's distinctive genealogy from Nathan to Neri. In this passage Zechariah makes no statement about the relationship of David and Nathan, but the four houses are each recorded in the pre-exilic section of Luke's genealogy (Lk. 3.30-31), making it very likely that Luke knew this tradition and was drawing upon it.[184]

Miura, in *David in Luke-Acts*, states that the reasons for Nathan's inclusion and the apparent rejection of the kingly line remains uncertain.[185] It is here this study wishes to add to the discussion.

The end of the kingly line and the rise of the Davidic shepherd king of Jeremiah Jeremiah's prophecy in Jeremiah 22.30 does not stop at v. 30 when he announces the cessation of the Jewish kingly line, but he continues with the announcement of a Davidic shepherd king. Jeremiah 23 follows immediately with a woe to the shepherds of Israel that they have not been caring for the flock and a declaration that the Lord will end their reign by replacing them with faithful shepherds (23.1-4). Then Jeremiah says God will raise up a Davidic shepherd king (5-6). Jeremiah first prophesies: καὶ ἀναστήσω αὐτοῖς ποιμένας, οἳ ποιμανοῦσιν αὐτούς. 'I will raise up shepherds for them who will shepherd them' (Jer. 23.4).

Then he prophesies a shepherd who will: (1) come from the house of David (23.5); (2) come as an ἀνατολή δίκαιαν (23.5); (3) be βασιλεύς (23.5); and (4) will bring Judah salvation (23.6). These four points are all reflected in Luke's infancy narrative.

First, Jeremiah's prophecy reflects Luke's interest that has already been established in Jesus' lineage through the house of David (Lk. 1.27, 32, 69; 2.4, 11). Secondly, the use of ἀνατολή δίκαιαν recalls ἀνατολή ἐξ ὕψους (1.78), where Jesus is the ἀνατολή, 'rising light', and which Strauss has shown has a Davidic basis stemming from Jeremiah 23.5; Zechariah 3.8; 6.12.[186] Luke also repeats δίκαιος in his narrative particularly to describe the covenant-keeping faithful (Lk. 1.6; 2.25; 23.50) who he shows are model respondents to God. However, most significant of all is Jesus, who is shown to be innocent in his trial by both Pilate and Herod, and then declared δίκαιος by the centurion (23.47). This use here of ἀνατολή δίκαιαν in Jeremiah therefore coheres with the Lukan Jesus who is both the Davidic 'rising light' and δίκαιος.

Thirdly, the status of Jesus as βασιλεύς and the resultant nature of that kingdom are of central interest to Luke. While Jesus' role as king is often implied in the

---

184. Johnson, *Genealogies*, 2nd edn, p. 241; Nolland, *Luke*, p. 170.
185. Miura, *David*, p. 212.
186. Strauss, *Davidic Messiah*, pp. 103–7.

narrative, the presentation of Jesus as king will be brought to the fore in 19.38 when Jesus enters Jerusalem. While Mark records 'Blessed is the *one* who comes in the name of the Lord' (Mk 11.9), Luke sharpens his focus to explicitly name Jesus as king. Furthermore, at his trial, Jesus is charged with forbidding people to give tribute to Caesar and saying ἑαυτὸν χριστὸν βασιλέα εἶναι (23.2). The initial setting for Jesus as king comes from the infancy narrative where Jesus is given τὸν θρόνον Δαυὶδ τοῦ πατρὸς αὐτοῦ (1.32), making clear for Luke that Jesus is king and specifically the *Davidic king*. However, as Luke's genealogy suggests, he has a particular type of king in view and this is not through Solomon's kingly line; Jeremiah 23 suggests that it is a king who will shepherd the people. The critique of the kings is specifically that they scattered the sheep, have driven them away and have not visited them (23.2). The shepherd king will instead receive sheep from every land and restore them to pasture where they can increase and multiply (23.3). The Davidic shepherd king will be characterized by righteousness and salvation (23.5-6). Ezekiel 34 will develop this further.

Finally, Jeremiah 23 uses the language of σῴζω, and salvation is a significant theme for Luke.[187] Luke's use of σῴζω and its cognates as a key indicator of Luke's interest cannot be overemphasized. The nature of salvation and who is the *Saviour* is the means by which Luke both sets and develops the boundaries of Jesus' mission to seek and save the lost in the Gospel, and where the Third Gospel stands in considerable contrast to Mark and Matthew. The use of the terms σωτήρ, σωτήριος and σωτηρία is almost uniquely Lukan among the Synoptics. Matthew does not use these words at all in his Gospel, and in Mark σωτηρία is only found once in 16.9 as part of the shorter ending, which is universally agreed not to be authentic.

Luke, in contrast, uses 'salvation' as a noun eight times in the Gospel (and seven times in Acts). God is clearly the Saviour who has sent John the Baptist to announce God's salvation has come (3.6) and Mary worships God, her Saviour (1.47). Zechariah declares God has raised up a Saviour (1.69) who will deliver them from their enemies (1.71) and that John will be the prophet of the Most High God and give 'knowledge of salvation' (1.77). The shepherds also hear that the baby born in the city of David is the Saviour (2.11), drawing the readers' attention to his role not only as *Saviour* but as *Davidic Saviour*. With six of these nouns occurring in the infancy narrative, it is likely that this establishes a *primacy effect*, whereby the nature of Jesus as Saviour and his role in bringing salvation functions programmatically throughout the remaining narrative.[188]

What we find therefore is that Luke's thematic interests cohere not only with Jeremiah 22.30, which has already been identified by many scholars and is evident in his genealogy, but also with the immediately following verses in Jeremiah where the Jewish kingly line centred in Jerusalem is replaced by the Davidic shepherd

187. Bock, *Luke*, pp. 29–33; Fitzmyer, *Luke*, pp. 179–92, 222–3; Green, *Gospel*, p. 23; Marshall, *Luke: Historian and Theologian*, pp. 94–102; McComiskey, *Lukan Theology*, p. 318.

188. See Minear, 'Use of the Birth Stories', pp. 111–30.

king. The volume and recurrence of words and themes strongly suggest that Luke perceives God is instituting a kingdom that does not follow the failed Jewish kingly line which was centred in Jerusalem, but is a kingdom where the faithful Davidic shepherd king reigns. Micah tells us he is from Bethlehem.

Luke's interest in tracing Jesus' lineage through Neri to Nathan is likely to be because: (1) he is intentionally presenting a kingdom which does not belong to the standard political line; and (2) he is pointing the reader to the Davidic *shepherd king* whose rule is characterized by righteousness and salvation.

The announcement in 2.4 of the πόλιν Δαυὶδ ἥτις καλεῖται Βηθλέεμ is an unexpected turn in the narrative which functions like a gap or blank. It suggests the reader is to recall the city of David's youth where, as a shepherd, he is anointed king by Samuel, and also the prophecy of Micah of the messianic shepherd. This suggests that Luke is presenting a specific picture of Jesus as king of Israel and also of the kingdom that he will reign over. While the readers expect to hear of the city of David called Jerusalem, they hear Bethlehem instead. Jerusalem's role as a Jewish political city has been subverted by Luke for the small city of Bethlehem where David the shepherd was born, and this is based on Micah's prophecy of the messianic shepherd ruler from Bethlehem. Through this reference the reader is expected to make an interpretative judgement in which lies an inherent critique of Jerusalem. This line of thinking is supported by the genealogy which shows Luke's interest does not lie in the Jewish kingly line, but in the Davidic shepherd king of Jeremiah 23.

3.3.6 Jesus in his father's house (2.41-52)

The final pericope we will consider is the single boyhood story of Jesus which comes at the very end of the unit (2.41-52), and where there is an echo of the Davidic covenant. The centre and climax of the story is 2.49 when Jesus says to his earthly parents: τί ὅτι ἐζητεῖτέ με; οὐκ ᾔδειτε ὅτι ἐν τοῖς τοῦ πατρός μου δεῖ εἶναί με; in these words the reader can hear an implicit echo of the Davidic covenant where the Lord is David's father and he is his son (2 Kgdms 7.14).

Many scholars have identified the significance of Jesus' reply to his mother at 2.49 as the centre of the pericope.[189] Bock calls it the high point of Luke 1–2 because Jesus speaks for the first time and reveals how he sees his own task.[190] Fitzmyer and Marshall conclude that the point of the passage is to show Jesus' unique relationship with his Father.[191] Green notes Jesus' reply to his mother is the 'dramatic nucleus' of the narrative,[192] and argues that Jesus' credentials (2.40, 52)

189. *Contra*, de Jonge and Strauss who place the climax at 46b-47. H. J. de Jonge, 'Sonship, Wisdom, Infancy: Luke 2:41-51a', *NTS* 24 (1978): 317–54 (339); Strauss, *Davidic Messiah*, pp. 120–3.

190. Bock, *Luke*, p. 259.

191. Fitzmyer, *Luke*, p. 437; Marshall, *Gospel*, pp. 128–9.

192. Green, *Gospel*, p. 156. Nolland also identifies 2.49 as the 'dramatic centre' of the pericope. Nolland, *Luke*, p. 128.

present him as having the hallmarks of someone with an extraordinary destiny in the Greco-Roman world.[193] Marshall and Green identify that *I*.49 confirms 1.32, 35.[194] Coleridge describes Jesus' words as the 'what' of Christology in Luke, where Luke's Jesus becomes prime interpreter of himself and where he shows he is the Son of God.[195] Bovon says the verse confirms Luke's understanding of the father–son relationship from a high christological perspective, while stopping short of identifying a Davidic covenant echo.[196] There is therefore considerable acceptance of the importance of *I*.49 as the centre of the pericope, and so we should expect this centre to be significant in interpreting the pericope.

Strauss, however, building on the analysis of Henk de Jonge, posits that the climax is *I*.46b-47 as a result of the 'concentric symmetry' in the text. As this centre ultimately produces a different Davidic echo, I will examine it in detail here. De Jonge's analysis shows:

A Mary, Joseph and Jesus go to Jerusalem (ἀναβαινόντων, 41-2)
  B Jesus stays in Jerusalem, which is not noticed (43)
    C His parents seek to find him (44-46a)
      D Jesus among the doctors (46b-47)
    C¹ His parents, annoyed, reproach him (48)
  B¹ Jesus' reaction which is not understood (49-50)
A¹ Jesus, Mary, and Joseph return to Nazareth (κατέβη, 51a)

In accepting de Jonge's analysis, Strauss then identifies the primary Davidic echo as stemming from Isaiah 11.1-3. Here he finds a Davidic wisdom passage which resonates with de Jonge's centre point D, while he also identifies a secondary echo coming from the father–son relationship.[197] Strauss' analysis from Isaiah 11.1-3 concludes that Luke is trying to show the Davidic Messiah who is endowed by God with wisdom and understanding (σοφία, v. 40; σύνεσις, v. 47). However, I note that the same Greek is used of David in 1 Kingdoms 16.18 to show he is qualified to enter Saul's kingly court, and may also echo David's early shepherd boy years. Furthermore it is used in *PssSol* 17.37 of the Davidic shepherd warrior king.

There are problems with this analysis of 2.41-51a by de Jonge. First, his analysis ends at 51a where the text says 'and he obeyed them', which excludes 51b where Mary 'treasured all these things in her heart' and v. 52, a summary statement that clearly balances 2.40. He argues that vv. 51b-52 are the summary ending for not only this pericope, but the whole childhood narrative.[198] His evidence comes

193. Green, *Gospel*, pp. 153–4.
194. Marshall, *Gospel*, p. 129; Green, *Gospel*, p. 153.
195. Coleridge, *Birth*, pp. 199–203.
196. Bovon, *Lukas 1*, p. 159.
197. Strauss, *Davidic Messiah*, p. 120.
198. He does not actually define what 'the childhood narrative' is. It may mean from 1.5, 2.1, or 2.22. De Jonge, 'Sonship, Wisdom, Infancy', p. 338.

partly from the Infancy Gospel of Thomas (in its first Greek form),[199] which he says ends with vv. 51b-52 as the last paragraph of the whole book. This may be flawed logic as the Infancy Gospel adds dialogue after v. 49 where the scribes and the Pharisees discuss Jesus' great wisdom with Mary, and then goes on to a version of vv. 51b and 52. Greek texts however did not include paragraphs and punctuation, and so this may build a case on modern logic as we cannot be sure where the original writer intended paragraphs to be. It is therefore a hypothesis that cannot be supported. Furthermore, the addition of the wisdom narration by the religious leaders in the Infancy Gospel of Thomas may support de Jonge's case for Luke's text having the central focus on Jesus' childhood wisdom, but it is likely to be a later conflation of the text, and the later dating rules it out as supporting Luke's pericope.

Secondly, it does not accept the rhetorical stress of the narrative when Jesus speaks for the first time in 1.49. In fact, de Jonge's analysis shows no recognition of the dialogue between Mary and Jesus, or of the way the reader is influenced by the main character's first words. Osborne notes that 'dialogue often carries much of the emphasis in characterization and theology'.[200] Alter similarly says: 'Everything in the world of biblical narrative ultimately gravitates toward dialogue – perhaps … by exercising the capacity of speech man demonstrated, however imperfectly, that he was made in the image of God.'[201] He further acknowledges that when a narrative event is considered to be important, this will come through dialogue rather than narration.

The reader listens for the interchange of characters knowing that important material is being overheard. Thus, we find in 2.48-49 and the interchange between mother and son, that Luke has balanced the conversation with each character asking a question and through the repetition of ζητέω. Mary and Joseph have been looking (ζητέω) for Jesus, and he replies: 'Why have you been looking (ζητέω) for me?' The stress then falls on Jesus' own answer: οὐκ ᾔδειτε ὅτι ἐν τοῖς τοῦ πατρός μου δεῖ εἶναί με. As Osborne suggests, it is here we find something of Luke's theology, and as Alter notes, here in speech we find the material Luke has deemed to be essential.[202] Using a narrative critical methodology therefore, we see that de Jonge's analysis falls short of giving adequate attention to the dialogue.

Thirdly, points B and B¹ do not appear to be well balanced. Point B shows simple narrative detail that sets up the story for later development, while B¹ contains key themes that will be developed in the wider narrative. These themes of redefining family[203] and the father–son relationship make v. 49 of much greater

---

199. The Second Greek form of the text does not even include the story but ends instead when Jesus is eight and miraculously lengthens wood to help Joseph.

200. Grant R. Osborne, *The Hermeneutical Spiral: A Comprehensive Introduction to Biblical Interpretation* (Downers Grove: IVP Academic, 2006), p. 209.

201. Alter, *Art*, p. 182.

202. Ibid.

203. Jesus redefines family most clearly when he says his mother, brothers and sisters are those who hear the word of God and do it (8.19-21).

narrative weight, outweighing de Jonge's point B. While there may be natural symmetry in any narrative we should not assume too quickly that a chiastic structure is present.

Fourthly, 2.49 contains Luke's first use of language of divine necessity (δεῖ), and as this is a significant Lukan motif of salvation-history,[204] de Jonge's analysis fails to reflect this. His point B[1] simply says 'Jesus' reaction, which is not understood (vv. 49–50), and this does not give any recognition to Luke's opening use of δεῖ. This is interesting, as de Jonge acknowledges the important role δεῖ plays in Luke's Gospel and how Luke uses it to describe divine laws being fulfilled,[205] and so this leads me to expect it would form a strategic part in a narrative structure. Under de Jonge's analysis it does not, and this is puzzling.

Finally, de Jonge makes too much of the wisdom motif which is only mentioned in Luke's secondary conclusion (2.52), and in vv. 46b–47, so is unlikely to be the main point of the episode.[206] He appears to rely too much on the *Infancy Gospel of Thomas* which is secondary to Luke's account and in which, as I have noted, there is an explicit wisdom motif. The *Infancy Gospel of Thomas* contains a conflated dialogue and should not be relied upon as evidence for Luke's own emphasis. The wisdom material does not constitute any part of the verbal exchange between Mary and Jesus, the only dialogue Luke records, and as we have seen, dialogue carries important theological weight. It certainly should be seen as more important than the narration of Jesus questioning the teachers (vv. 46-47).

As a result, de Jonge's analysis is flawed and Strauss' Davidic echo is unlikely to be the correct one, since in placing the interpretative stress within the wisdom tradition, he is searching for Davidic wisdom echoes only. In doing this, Strauss misses the force of Jesus' words at 2.49 that talk about the father–son relationship. Therefore, we will now consider the alternative view where v. 49 is at the heart of the message of the pericope and in which lies an echo of the Davidic covenant.

'Did you not know I must be in my Father's house?'
We note first that when Jesus speaks, he is in the temple at Jerusalem (2.46), the place where Zechariah first heard the angel's message of John's coming (1.8). This forms an *inclusio* in the infancy narrative around the beginning and ending of

---

204. Luke uses this motif: within the context of the good news being proclaimed (4.43); his suffering and death (9.22); criticism of the Pharisees who neglect the justice of God (11.42); the Holy Spirit's guidance; in the context of a saving encounter (13.14, 16); in predicting his death (13.33); in summarizing the need to celebrate the lost being found (15.32); in predicting his suffering and rejection (17.25); in a saving encounter with Zacchaeus (19.5); in an apocalyptic warning (21.9); with regard to the passover celebration which may hint at a salvific context and not only the actions of a faithful Jewish practice (22.7); when Isaiah 53.12 is said to be fulfilled (22.37); referring to Jesus' suffering and death (24.7, 22) and in the context of scripture being fulfilled (24.44). This usage is widely recognized by scholars. Bock, *Luke*, p. 28; Green, *Gospel*, p. 22.

205. De Jonge, 'Sonship, Wisdom, Infancy', pp. 350–1.

206. Fitzmyer, *Luke*, p. 437.

the unit, as both are in the temple.[207] Luke's ongoing interest in the temple and in Jerusalem suggests that this pericope has been carefully chosen and placed in the Gospel. In this we find another internal parallel that strengthens the literary unity of Luke 1–2 and shows the boyhood story is a part of a wider unit and is not merely a transition story.[208]

The words that Jesus speaks when he identifies himself as God's son, by saying 'Did you not know I must be in my Father's house?', form a *literary inclusio*.[209] I suggest these words recall the annunciation story near the beginning of the infancy narrative where Gabriel says Jesus will be called the Son of the Most High, and has been given the throne of David to reign over an everlasting kingdom (1.31-33). Alter notes that 'the reading of any literary text requires us to perform all sorts of operations of linkage, both small and large, and at the same time to make constant discriminations among related but different words'.[210] This is one such occasion, when the reader should link the father–son relationship in 1.32 with Jesus' reference to his father (2.49) when he is in the Jerusalem temple. In one sense this is not a difficult link to make, as Green and Marshall indicate,[211] and it is made easier to do so, as Luke has foregrounded the words by using dialogue at this point; however, it also requires the reader to recall the wider story of Israel and draw on echoes of scripture. In 2.49 we have Jesus speaking of his relationship with his father, calling the temple his father's house, and saying there is a divine necessity in his being there. These are all key ideas to the Lukan narrative, but also recall 2 Kingdoms 7 where the Davidic covenant is established.

In 2 Kingdoms 7 David wants to build a house for the Lord (2 Kgdms 7.13, 16), but he is told instead the Lord will build him a house. Thus, the nature of a house is inherently about a lineage. The covenant goes on to establish the very close father–son relationship David and his descendants will have with God. These two features are evident in Jesus' words to Mary, and overheard by the reader, although Luke does not use οἶκος in 2.49. The two similar features are that Jesus is God's son and God is his father (2.49; 2 Kgdms 7.14), and there is the possibility that even at this early stage of the Gospel, the house of God is being redefined around the person of Jesus, a descendant of David, rather than the temple building.

In evaluating a Davidic covenant echo in 2.49, in terms of volume it is the language of πατήρ coupled with the setting in God's house (ἱερόν; v. 46) that leads

207. Ibid., p. 438.

208. Ibid., p. 435; Strauss, *Davidic Messiah*, p. 120.

209. There is debate around the 'father's house' as this is an implied reading stemming out of the Greek phrase, ἐν τοῖς τοῦ πατρός μου δεῖ εἶναί με. Is he among those of his father's house, the teachers of the law (2.46)? Is he about his father's business? Is he in his father's house? The final view is the prevailing view and the one this study supports. This view reads the neuter plural article (τοῖς) followed by the genitive as implying a house, and in this case the temple (v. 46), the house of God. For a survey see Bock, *Luke*, pp. 269–70; Fitzmyer, *Luke*, pp. 443–4.

210. Alter, *Art*, p. 188.

211. Green, *Gospel*, p. 153; Marshall, *Gospel*, p. 129.

the reader back to both 1.31-33, 35 and 2 Kingdoms 7. Because Luke foregrounds this echo in 1.31-33, 35, we see some movement toward the test for recurrence. Gabriel says the Davidic role is the central identity for Jesus in his declaration, and in his narration in 1.27 Luke stresses the lineage of Joseph to qualify him as the successor of the covenant promise. We have seen an ongoing recollection of David and the book of Kingdoms in Luke 1 and the birth narrative also has many Davidic statements and echoes as we have seen. Here in the final event in the infancy narrative, Luke takes the reader back to the earliest stage of the infancy narrative by recalling the father–son relationship spoken of by Gabriel. This provides substantial evidence for the test of thematic coherence where the story of Jesus is told repeatedly in terms of David's story.

While there is not a history of identifying the Davidic covenant here, there are scholars who have identified the link to 1.31-33. I would suggest that, in light of the Davidic material we have seen, particularly in recovering the role of the shepherds and the recollection of an echo to Micah 5.2-5 in the birth narrative, the logical step is to view 2.49 as not only recalling the annunciation, but also the Davidic covenant. This echo gives a high level of satisfaction in reading the surrounding discourse as it forms an *inclusio* in which Jesus is firmly established as the Davidic Saviour, the Davidic Shepherd and the Davidic King.

3.4 Summary

As we come to the end of this chapter's analysis of the beginning of the Lukan Gospel, it is helpful to recall Sternberg and Perry's work on the *primacy effect*. We know this is a carefully used rhetorical device in literature, and functions to set parameters for interpretation and to show the author's interests. Therefore we must agree with Coleridge that 'there is never anything inevitable about the way a narrative begins: a narrator may start anywhere, and where to begin is therefore a matter of choice'.[212] Luke has clearly chosen to highlight Jesus as being given the throne of David and thereby fulfilling the Davidic promise, and we can anticipate that this will have an ongoing resonance in Luke-Acts. From Luke's opening in 1.5 the reader hears echoes of the LXX, and we have noted the many echoes of David's story. As a result we hear not only of Jesus' genealogical relationship with David, but in support of Chae and Wright, we are presented with a typological portrayal where we find the Davidic covenant fulfilled in Jesus.

Further to this, given the way we have heard and reheard of David both explicitly and implicitly, we should consider the role of David as a *Leitwort* that reveals Luke's interest in Jesus in the light of David's story. The sheer volume of repetitions of David's name and features from his life demonstrate this is a key primary lens for the Lukan Jesus. He is not only Saviour, he is the Davidic Saviour. He is not only Messiah, he is the Davidic Messiah. Jesus is consistently clothed in shades of David's story that point the reader to ways he fulfils these roles. He is

212. Coleridge, *Birth*, p. 28.

the Davidic Messiah who will bring God's salvific peace to earth. Unlike Strauss, who says that 'how Jesus will fulfill the Davidic promise is barely suggested',[213] the birth narrative suggests that Jesus is the Davidic shepherd king coming from the city of David.

The Davidic covenant is the opening motif which interprets Jesus' birth (1.31-33), and yet we find the same echo, perhaps a little fainter, in the final story of the unit (2.49). As a result we have the Davidic covenant forming an *inclusio* around the infancy narrative giving light to what is in its midst.

At the very core is the birth narrative where we have found Jesus stands in contrast to Augustus, and in the same way that Jesus is superior to John, Jesus is superior to Augustus. This is evident through the use of Hellenistic claims of *saviour, lord, bringer of peace,* and *good news* which Luke attributes to Jesus while the ancient world attributed them to Caesar (2.1-20). We also see a contrast between God's power and Augustus' power. For Luke, Augustus moves on God's timetable when his census brings Mary and Joseph to Bethlehem to fulfil Micah's prophecy. What is at stake here is the nature of leadership and power, and while Augustus' might is found in decrees and imperial rule, an important aspect of Jesus' identity is found in him as the shepherd king. The shepherd king is Davidic, he is righteous, and he brings peace. Furthermore, for Luke, the prominent shepherds in the narrative are not to be viewed as sinners or even necessarily as only humble and lowly, they are indicators of the messianic shepherd.

Luke appears to have made very clear that the primary motif for interpreting Jesus' birth is as the promised Davidic king (1.31-33) and in light of his birth narrative, we see that an important aspect of this is that he is the long-awaited Davidic *shepherd* king. The shepherd nature of this promised king is a feature of the Davidic covenant from 2 Kingdoms 7, but is also suggested in the transumed echo of David which cannot be separated from his narrative role as Israel's chosen shepherd king. I consider that Luke's choice to echo the Davidic covenant in the annunciation should be considered deliberate and a key area of interest for Lukan theology. To find this same echo, although more faintly in the final story of the unit supports seeing this as a guiding paradigm in the story of the Lukan Jesus. This gives some light to Miura's undeveloped thought, and that we signalled in the outset in Chapter 1, that the motif of Davidic shepherd does have a role to play in summing up Jesus' earthly ministry.

---

213. Strauss, *Davidic Messiah*, p. 124.

4

THE FAITHFUL SHEPHERD

In the previous chapter, we saw how Luke uses the motif of David and the Davidic shepherd king to highlight an important aspect of the nature of Jesus and his identity. Now we turn to the ministry years of Jesus and will consider how this motif is used in three pericopae. First, we will consider the shepherd saying in the household mission, where Jesus is implicitly the shepherd who sends the disciples into households with salvific peace (10.3). Secondly, we will look at Luke 12.32, where the motif is used by Jesus when he is addressing his disciples regarding what they will eat and wear (12.22-32). Thirdly, we will consider the parable of the lost sheep in Luke 15.1-7. Then we will turn to Acts and note the return of the motif in the Miletus Speech (Acts 20.28-29). In these four pericopae we will see that Ezekiel 34 is a text which Luke drew upon when talking of the role of the shepherd. It is significant that the motif, while not prominent, does not disappear from the narrative and is relevant for early church leaders. This chapter will end with a consideration of Luke's shepherd omissions (Mk 6.34; 14.27).

4.1 Jesus, the shepherd in the mission mandate (10.3)

Go, I am sending you like lambs in the midst of wolves.
In the mission mandate near the beginning of the travel narrative, Jesus sends out seventy[1] disciples into households to cure the sick and to say that the kingdom of God has come near (10.9). The shepherd saying falls within the household mission mandate (10.1-24). The pericope is unique to Luke, while the shepherd saying shares some aspects of the Matthaean command when Jesus sends out the twelve (Mt. 10.7-8).[2] The uniqueness, placement and the sheer size of the pericope reveal its narrative importance,[3] as do the Gentile territories that are recalled in 10.13-14, for this is another way Luke's universal mission grows in visibility.[4]

---

1. For textual matters see Metzger, *Textual Commentary*, p. 151.

2. For a summary see Bock, *Luke*, pp. 986–91.

3. Bock, *Luke*, p. 986.

4. Marshall, *Gospel*, p. 424; 'Political and Eschatological Language in Luke', in *Reading Luke: Interpretation, Reflection, Formation* (eds Craig G. Bartholomew, Joel B. Green and

Simeon has foretold the universal mission (2.32) and Jesus and the disciples have already journeyed into Samaritan territory as the travel narrative begins (9.52).[5] Now Jesus sends the seventy out in pairs, which was the local custom for travel, although it may also relate to the double witness requirement and its wilderness journey context (Deut. 19.15).[6] As the mission is placed so close to the beginning of the travel narrative, there is a level of priority being afforded it by Luke. The degree and importance of household mission grows as Jesus ventures into Zacchaeus' house at the end of the travel narrative, and the household becomes central to the Gentile mission in Acts. This, therefore, suggests the motif is setting a trajectory for narrative units that comes after it, and it is being used strategically by Luke to prefigure Gentile mission making the inclusion of the shepherd significant.

The key thrust of the mission is that peace, which is more than an ancient greeting for Luke, is spoken to the household (10.5); peace is a metaphor for salvation,[7] and is also a feature of the Davidic shepherd king in Micah and Ezekiel (Mic. 5.4; Ezek. 34.25). In the household mission the greeting of peace is either received or rejected (10.7-11), and it is this acceptance or rejection which signifies the reception of the message. The salvific mission is framed by the command to stay in one house eating and drinking whatever is given, suggesting the ritual purity code was no longer the determining factor for where the message could be proclaimed. This is consistent with Jesus' prior actions in eating and drinking with sinners (5.29-39; 7.33, 36-50), many of whom had already found salvation. We will go on to see that this resonates with the 'lost' parables, the story of Zacchaeus, and further, it will form the heart of the Gentile mission in Acts where matters of table fellowship will be finally settled in the Jerusalem Council (Acts 15). This characteristic 'eating and drinking' also resonates with the Davidic shepherd king from Ezekiel who seems particularly concerned with the flock being fed (Ezek. 34.2, 3, 5, 10, 13, 14, 15, 16).

This mission to possibly unclean households is of considerable relevance for the wider vision Luke casts. Inclusive table-fellowship inaugurates a new opportunity for a 'sacred space',[8] a space centred on fellowship, a feature of the early church (Acts 2.42-47). This may go as far as to point beyond the temple as the primary 'sacred space', as salvation is now found in the house.

The disciples are sent ahead of Jesus (9.52; 10.1) to places Jesus intended to go. We do not know why the Lukan Jesus sent them ahead, but in doing so he places great confidence in their ability to carry out the task. Luke 10.2 describes that the harvest is plentiful and so the call is made for labourers to be sent out

Anthony C. Thiselton; Scripture and Hermeneutics Series 6; Grand Rapids: Zondervan, 2005), p. 173; Talbert, *Literary Patterns*, p. 20.

5. Matson, *Household*, p. 27.

6. Bock, *Luke*, p. 994.

7. 1.79; 2.14, 29; 7.50; 8.48; 19.38, 42; 24.36. Ibid, p. 45; Green, *Gospel*, p. 413; Fitzmyer, *Luke*, p. 847.

8. Matson, *Household*, p. 48.

(ἐκβάλλω) into the harvest. The use of ἐκβάλλω suggests the seventy are sent out with some level of force (Mt. 9.38; Acts 16.37),[9] and the reference to wolves in 10.3 confirms the strength of this idea. As Bovon says, 'in spite of fear, lack of preparation and limited resources they should now go'.[10] The mission task is one that involves risk and danger, and so in v. 3 Jesus forewarns the disciples of the dangers, demonstrating that he knows ahead of time what perils his followers will encounter. This knowledge appears to be of divine origin, but it may also suggest that Jesus is offering some protection in this forewarning.[11] This protection also falls within the role of a faithful shepherd who is to protect the sheep (Isa. 40.11; Ezek. 34.4-6, 16).[12]

Jesus says to the seventy, ὑπάγετε· ἰδοὺ ἀποστέλλω ὑμᾶς ὡς ἄρνας ἐν μέσῳ λύκων (10.3), whereas the shepherd motif is not used in Luke's sending of the twelve (9.1-6). Bock describes the significance of the motif where the 'Great Shepherd, [is] God himself'.[13] This is supported by *b.Toledot* 32b where God is the Great Shepherd.[14] Hendriksen notes that in this pericope Jesus, 'is no one less than their Shepherd'.[15] Bock in particular believes Ezekiel 34 is behind the usage, giving some level of recognition and strength under Hays' test for the history of interpretation.[16]

With Jesus cast as a shepherd in 10.3 and the seventy sent to carry out his mission, this suggests that even though he sends them as 'lambs', he is also sending them as shepherds like himself to bring salvific peace to the scattered flock; perhaps 'as lambs' he is addressing their vulnerability in the task. The mission they carry out is that of the shepherd who seeks his lost sheep. There is evidence for this in the text. Luke has a double use of ἀποστέλλω where Jesus *sends* the disciples (10.3) and God *sends* Jesus (10.16). Fitzmyer notes with regard to 10.16:

> The saying lends authority to the preaching of the disciples. The principle implied in it is that of representation ... The one sent is to be regarded as the sender himself. The disciples, therefore, speak and act in the name of Jesus, just as he speaks and acts in the name of the one who sent him.[17]

9. 'ἐκβάλλω', *BDAG*, p. 299.

10. François Bovon, *Das Evangelium nach Lukas 2. Teilband Lk 9,51-14,35* (Evangelisch-Katholischer Kommentar zum Neuen Testament; Zürich: Benziger, 2008), p. 50. Author's translation.

11. Marshall, *Gospel*, p. 417.

12. Bock, *Luke*, p. 996.

13. Ibid.

14. *b. Toledot* 32b., the sixth weekly Torah portion in the annual Jewish cycle of Torah reading, says: 'There is something great about the sheep (Israel) that can persist among the seventy wolves (the nations). He replied, 'Great is the Shepherd who delivers it and watches over it and destroys them (the wolves) before them (Israel)'.

15. Hendriksen, *Luke*, p. 573.

16. Bock, *Luke*, p. 996.

17. Fitzmyer, *Luke*, p. 857.

As representatives of God, who is known to the Israelites as their shepherd, and Jesus, who is implied in this passage as a shepherd, we have the disciples: (1) going as representatives of Jesus who is a shepherd; and (2) carrying out his mission to households where eating and salvific peace are preeminent. These are character-istics of Ezekiel's Davidic shepherd king (Ezek. 34.13, 14, 15, 25), features that may have led Bock to identify Ezekiel 34 behind this passage.

Thus, the seventy are sent out as Jesus' representatives to speak and act in his name. Their mission is a shepherding task, and they come into households to share the kingdom proclamation as faithful shepherds who are seeking the lost sheep. This 'shepherd mission' is for the wider group rather than the twelve (9.1-6) as the 'shepherd mission' is a task that will characterize more than a few individuals. This resonates with the Miletus speech where the church leaders are named as shepherds (Acts 20.28), but the roots of the shepherd motif for leaders seem to lie in 10.1-24. The Acts passage also makes clear that feeding the sheep relates to teaching. It is also possible that when the shepherds from the birth narrative return to their workplace and community glorifying and praising God for all they have seen and heard (2.20), they also take on the role of early proclaimers of the message of salvific peace, which was what the angels declare (2.14).

The disciples are called 'lambs', which are characteristically vulnerable animals, especially among wolves. Matthew refers to πρόβατον in his sending narrative (10.16) rather than Luke's ἀρήν, with Luke's designation stressing the precariousness of the task.[18] Bock and Hendriksen suggest Luke may be drawing on Isaiah 40.11 where God is the shepherd who cares for the ποιμήν, ἀρνός, and the γαστήρ,[19] and this is quite possible. Isaiah 40.1-11 shows God as a victorious warrior shepherd, classifications that suit this Lukan passage where the mission task is reflected on in the context of a cosmic battle (10.17-20). Both Isaiah 40 and Luke 10.1-24 convey the double use of battle and shepherd, and both come at the beginning of a new narrative section. Isaiah 40, although read within the whole book of Isaiah at the time of Luke, does convey a new historical period, while Luke's narrative setting is equally new with Jesus' journey to Jerusalem having just begun (9.51). Therefore under Hays' tests for echoes, there is some resonance shown by the tests for volume, thematic recurrence, history of inter-pretation, and certainly satisfaction, making this a possible backdrop to Luke's use of ἀρήν.

The reference to the ἀρήν in 10.3 may also resonate with the Jewish use of the lamb representing God's people. *Psalms of Solomon* 8.23 describes the devout of God as righteous lambs,[20] and *PssSol* 8.30 describes the 'devouring' of the people where the use of καταπίνω[21] also suggests the motif of the vulnerable lambs.

18. ἀρήν is a NT *hapex legomenon*.

19. Bock, *Luke*, p. 996; Hendriksen, *Luke*, p. 573.

20. Michael Wolter, *Das Lukasevangelium* (Handbuch zum Neuen Testament, 5; Tübingen: Mohr Siebeck, 2008), p. 378.

21. BDAG notes this can refer to animals that devour (their prey). 'καταπίνω', BDAG, p. 524.

In *1 Enoch* 89.14, 18-20 we also find the image of vulnerable sheep and the wolves, and at this time it is the *Lord of the Sheep* who protects his flock (*1 Enoch* 89.16). Wolter notes that the use of wolf and lamb in *1 Enoch* recalls that 'the Israelites lived in Egypt as sheep amongst wolves'.[22] Evans notes it is hard to identify who the wolves are in Luke 10.3, although in Acts 20.29 the wolves are false teachers,[23] which is not the idea behind the Gospel passage.

Luke's household mission pericope comes immediately after three discipleship sayings where the pattern for following Jesus is one of considerable cost (9.57-62), and so this picture of vulnerable lambs is consistent with the Lukan Jesus' journey. Jesus has recently predicted his passion (9.21-22), and called for the disciples to deny themselves and take up their cross daily and follow (9.23-27). This saying coheres with the Lukan Jesus' own journey, so that 'the vulnerability of those sent is a mirror of Jesus' own vulnerability'.[24] The combined image of the lambs and wolves suggests this vulnerability.[25] This verse is followed by the call to take no purse, bag or sandals and to greet no one on the road (10.4), leaving the disciples exposed and unprotected.[26]

In Ezekiel 34, God is the faithful shepherd of his flock, unlike the shepherd rulers of Israel who have neglected the sheep and instead pursued their own comfort. The result of this neglect is that sheep are scattered on the mountains and hills and have become food for animals of the plain (Ezek. 34.6-8). While Ezekiel does not refer to wolves (λύκος) in ch. 34, he does in Ezekiel 22.27 where he explains that Israel's rulers in its midst were like wolves catching prey to shed blood so that they gain through greed. This is the situation we find in Luke's Gospel where the religious leaders have neglected people who they considered ritually impure, and this has hindered God's salvific plan (5.29-32; 7.36-50; 15.1-32; 19.1-10). Luke shows Jesus instead going to the borders of society and seeking out the sinner (5.32) and the lost sheep (19.10), demonstrating he is God's faithful shepherd. In doing this he places the needs of the flock ahead of his own, even at great personal cost. This is seen when Jesus is criticized for eating with toll collectors and sinners (5.30; 15.2; 19.7), and he lays himself open for criticism when he touches and heals the leper (5.12-16). We note that it is after this occasion when the religious leaders come down from Jerusalem to hear him speak (5.17). His ministry causes him to pray all night (6.12) and he always attends to the needs of the crowd (4.42; 5.17; 6.18-19; 7.17; 8.4, 19). Ultimately, Jesus' mission will cost him his life, a motif Luke will pick up in Acts 8.32-33 where Jesus is said to be like a sheep led to slaughter (Acts 8.2).

In 10.3, Jesus is the faithful shepherd who sends the disciples to carry out a shepherding task, and this will be costly for them. They are vulnerable like lambs in the midst of wolves (10.3), for some will reject their message (10.10-11, 16) and

22. Wolter, *Das Lukasevangelium*, p. 378. Author's translation.
23. Evans, *Saint Luke*, p. 447.
24. Nolland, *Luke*, p. 551.
25. Wolter, *Das Lukasevangelium*, p. 378.
26. Wolf and lamb imagery is also found in 2 Clem. 5.2-4.

they will contend with demons (10.17). Yet this is a significant sending of a large group of disciples who enact his mission and start to count the cost of following the shepherd to the margins of society.

4.2 Jesus, the faithful shepherd (12.32)

This verse is a shepherd saying that is attached to a Q passage (Lk. 12.22-32;[27] Mt. 6.25-34), and is located in the travel narrative which has begun at 9.51 when Jesus sets his face to Jerusalem. The verse has no parallel in Matthew and is unique to Luke. With Luke's writing demonstrating a high level of allusion and echo, it is very possible that the expression τὸ μικρὸν ποίμνιον has its roots in Israel's history where the Lord is shepherd of his people. The phrase is spoken by Jesus to his disciples, and while Jesus only calls the disciples *little flock* once, the metaphor does recur in Acts 20.28 in the context of Paul speaking to the Ephesian elders.

This pericope is part of the wider section of 12.1–13.9 where the focus is on being ready for the coming judgement of God. The preceding parable of the rich fool (12.13-21), turns the eschatological focus to the theme of material wealth. In 12.22-32 Jesus explains to his disciples that God is the provider for their daily needs, adding commentary to the preceding parable's discussion on wealth. That is, the disciples do not need to have bigger barns to store their wealth, not only because this stored wealth will not make them rich toward God, but because they can rely on God as their daily provider.

Marshall suggests the teaching is similar to wisdom literature, with an emphasis on encouraging the disciples to 'sit lightly to material possessions and help the poor',[28] and Fitzmyer notes the key idea as the priority of values for the disciples.[29] Bock takes a plain reading of the text where the disciples can trust God for their provision, noting how 'a kingdom focus prevents excessive anxiety about one's earthly possessions'.[30]

The unit opens with Jesus speaking to *his* disciples (12.22). A minor textual variant shows a few significant manuscripts omit the αὐτοῦ,[31] while there is strong support from other witnesses.[32] The pericope emphasizes that God will provide food and clothing for the disciples. It encourages them not to worry, as to do so

27. Fitzmyer ends the unit at 12.32, while Marshall, Bock, Green and Nolland end the unit at 12.34. However, it is possible to see 12.33-34 as a separate short unit as in Matthew's Gospel, who places it separately earlier in his Gospel (Mt. 6.19-21). See Fitzmyer, *Luke*, p. 975; Marshall, *Gospel*, p. 525; Bock, *Luke*, p. 1156; Green, *Gospel*, p. 485; Nolland, *Luke*, p. 689.

28. Marshall, *Gospel*, p. 525.

29. Fitzmyer, *Luke*, p. 977.

30. Bock, *Luke*, p. 1156.

31. These are P[75] B 1241 it[c. e]

32. These are ℵ A D L W Δ Θ Ψ 070 0233 *f*[1] *f*[13] it[a. aur. b. d.] vg syr[c. s. p. h] cop arm. For a full consideration, see Harris dissertation.

characterizes those who do not know God, and instead to prioritize seeking the kingdom of God. In doing this, Jesus states God will provide for the disciples' daily needs and the kingdom will be given to them. There are two statements made about the kingdom; the disciples are to seek the kingdom and the kingdom is given to them. The rationale for trusting God is centred in two metaphors. First, God is their father and he will care for his children (12.30, 32). Secondly, God is a shepherd who feeds and cares for his sheep (12.32) and so as a vulnerable *little flock*, they can rely on a faithful shepherd. This resonates with what we have seen in 10.3.

The phrase τὸ μικρὸν ποίμνιον could be a simple term of endearment, and yet the internal evidence from the Gospel, Acts and the LXX suggests that there may be more in this simple saying.[33] There are many reasons why the term may carry significance in this saying and these will be discussed below: (1) we have already seen how the infancy narrative has used the reference to shepherds to reveal an aspect of Jesus' identity as the Davidic shepherd king, and how Jesus is the shepherd in 10.3; (2) the shepherd saying in 10.3 positions Jesus as the disciples' shepherd; (3) the same word recurs in Acts 20.28; (4) the parable of the lost sheep speaks of Jesus as shepherd; (5) 19.10 has a well-recognized allusion to Ezekiel 34 which is a noted shepherd passage; (6) it is a well-known OT description for God's people; and (7) the thrust of the unit's message is on practical provision and especially on the disciples being fed by God. This theme echoes Ezekiel 34's emphasis on βόσκω and Green suggests an allusion here.[34]

Points (3) and (4) above will be addressed in detail later in this chapter, and (5) will form the focus of Chapter 5 and so will not be addressed here. Their presence in this argument however is important; this is not an isolated use of the term ποίμνιον. Notably, in Acts, the church is called ποίμνιον and elders are called 'to act as shepherds' (ποιμαίνω). Furthermore, in Acts it is the Holy Spirit who has chosen them for this task, and the role of the Spirit is well known in Luke's writing.[35] It seems unlikely that Luke would use τὸ μικρὸν ποίμνιον simply as a term of endearment if he uses it so strategically in another part of his writing. Similarly, the parable of the lost sheep, which is yet to be told in the Lukan narrative, suggests Jesus is positioned as a faithful shepherd (15.4-7), which strengthens the possibility that the term here means Jesus is likening himself to the disciples' shepherd. Further, Luke 19.10 is a well-established allusion to Ezekiel 34, making it a passage we know that Luke drew upon and a metaphor

---

33. Green notes that 'in spite of their seeming diminutive presence ("little flock"), the disciples are nonetheless the recipients of God's dominion'. Green, *Gospel*, p. 495.

34. Ibid.

35. Bovon says: 'The Holy Spirit plays a preeminent role in Luke's writings. In fact, the Third Gospel mentions the Spirit more frequently than the other two synoptics, and chapters 1–12 of Acts constitute the portion of the NT in which the πνεῦμα appears with the most insistence'. Bovon, *Luke the Theologian*, p. 228; Joseph A. Fitzmyer, 'The Role of the Spirit in Luke-Acts', in *The Unity of Luke-Acts* (ed. J. Verheyden; BETL, 142; Leuven: Leuven University Press, 1999), pp. 165–83.

he identifies with Jesus. These passages in Luke's writing suggest the term should not be overlooked here, but is rather a recollection and development of the shepherd motif.

'God's flock' is an ongoing metaphor in the LXX and at this point in the narrative Jesus' disciples are all Israelites (6.13-16), and so we can suppose they might have perceived some OT resonance when Jesus spoke. Scholars agree there is an OT source for this expression. Nolland notes this is a stock image for Israel and Judah, and refers to Jeremiah 13.17, Ezekiel 34, and Zechariah 10.3,[36] while Bock also points to various shepherd or flock passages as support (Pss. 22.1; 27.9; 73.1; 76.21; Isa. 40.11; Jer. 13.17; Zech. 11.11; 13.7).[37] Neither scholar develops these ideas.

Fitzmyer and Marshall point to other shepherd allusions, making this almost certainly a significant shepherd expression. Fitzmyer suggests that Isaiah 41.14 may reflect the τὸ μικρὸν ποίμνιον as the LXX says, Ιακωβ, ὀλιγοστὸς Ισραηλ, ἐγὼ ἐβοήθησά σοι (O Jacob, O small Israel, I have helped you). This allusion is possible as Isaiah 40 begins with shepherd imagery and the notion of Israel as God's flock is a well established metaphor. However, this seems less likely as Isaiah is not discussing God feeding his flock but their protection from Babylon (Isa. 41.12).

Marshall considers if Zechariah 13.7 and the scattering of the sheep may lie behind the saying.[38] Nolland and Bock also refer to this verse, while producing no argument for this possibility. However, an echo of Zechariah is worthy of consideration as Luke draws on Zechariah 12.12-14 in his genealogy, therefore making another echo more likely.

Zechariah 13.7 stresses that bad shepherds will be judged by the Lord if they do not care for the vulnerable sheep, taking up Luke's idea of τὸ μικρὸν ποίμνιον. However, the LXX does not contain the notion of *little* sheep, and alters the MT which uses צער, meaning 'small'.[39] In the wider context of Zechariah 9–14 the predominant metaphor is that of an eschatological shepherd, and while Luke's wider unit (12.1–13.9) relates to coming judgement, the focus in this unit is on God as provider. While earlier in Zechariah the prophet recalls God's care for the physical needs of the flock (Zech. 10.1-12),[40] the focus in Zechariah 13 is on eschatological judgement where idols, unclean spirits, and unfaithful shepherds will be removed.

As we have seen, Luke's focus is on the practical provision for the disciples by God, albeit within a broader eschatological picture of wealth, which is at variance with Zechariah's focus. An allusion to Zechariah in Luke 12.32 is unlikely therefore for this particular unit, as the main foci of Luke and Zechariah vary too greatly

---

36. Nolland, *Luke*, p. 694.

37. Bock, *Luke*, p. 1165.

38. Marshall also suggests Daniel 7.27 may be behind the combined use of βασιλεία and πατήρ. Marshall, *Gospel*, p. 530.

39. Smith, *Micah-Malachi*, p. 282.

40. This includes rain for vegetation, healing for sickness, and the protection of a warrior shepherd king (Zech. 10.1-12).

to make this a strong link. What is of interest to this study is that scholars agree there is a scriptural echo of some description in the phrase τὸ μικρὸν ποίμνιον.

I suggest the particular echo Luke would be drawing on is most likely to centre not only in shepherd imagery of God's flock, but it would occur in the context of God as provider of material needs, as this is Luke's narrative context. It is more likely that Luke has chosen this shepherd saying as his unique ending because it is most informative or resonant with Jesus' teaching to the disciples which began at 12.22.

This leads me to consider Green's and Johnson's suggestion that Ezekiel 34 is behind this shepherd saying.[41] Luke's emphasis on material provision in the unit and especially on what the disciples will eat, coupled with the shepherd metaphor, echoes Ezekiel 34's marked emphasis on God's desire that his sheep are fed. Green goes so far as to suggest that τὸ μικρὸν ποίμνιον is present in 12.32 to remind the disciples of Ezekiel 34 where God is the shepherd of the flock, and suggests that this is the primary echo here. Johnson similarly gives this as the sole allusion, while Nolland suggests it as one possible echo.[42] This provides a significant history of interpretation.

With Ezekiel's repeated stress that the shepherds feed the flock, we find a thematic coherence with this passage's discussion of practical discipleship matters. It is historically plausible that Luke used τὸ μικρὸν ποίμνιον as an allusion to Ezekiel 34 and did indeed see the correlation between God as a shepherd feeding the sheep, as this not only reflects Ezekiel's shepherd theme, but it is also how Israel had understood God from the time of the wilderness (Exod. 16.4-21).

We know Ezekiel 34 was available to Luke as it recurs as an established echo in 19.10 and later in this chapter we will note that Luke makes further use of the passage. Both texts show an emphasis on God's concern for his people's practical provision which satisfies the test for thematic coherence. Three scholars suggest this is the likely echo, and two exclusively so, which lends support to the test for the history of interpretation. As Hays says, this is the least reliable of the guides, but on the level of satisfaction this echo scores highly. This is the most logical of the echoes as it illuminates the surrounding discourse with clear resonance to the thematic focus of 12.16-21, 22-32 of God as provider of material needs and especially food. Hence, we find valuable evidence that Ezekiel 34 is the text behind Luke's shepherd saying in 12.32.

This gives us evidence that Jesus adopted the shepherd motif as he taught *his disciples*, which presents him as their Davidic shepherd, and as a unique saying, it points to a Lukan special interest. As a result, we find the expression *little flock* is more than just a term of endearment and is a narrative reminder that Jesus' ministry is as a faithful shepherd who looks after God's sheep. On a narrative level, we find a repetition of the motif of Jesus as a shepherd which suggests Luke sees

---

41. While other commentators posit many possible OT passages that Luke is drawing on, Green and Johnson suggest Ezek. 34 exclusively as Luke's allusion here. Green, *Gospel*, p. 495; Johnson, *Gospel*, p. 200.

42. Johnson, *Gospel*, p. 200; Nolland, *Luke*, p. 694.

an ongoing role for the motif. Jesus as a *shepherd* who is talking of the faithful care of God is very relevant to the picture of the Lukan Jesus to this point who is gathering in the lost sheep (5.29; 7.1-10, 36-50; 8.26-39) and healing the sick (5.12-16, 17-26; 6.6-11, 18).

4.3 *The parable of the faithful shepherd (15.1-7)*

The significance of Luke's three 'lost parables' in ch. 15 have been consistently noted by scholars. Ramaroson describes these parables as 'the heart of the Third Gospel';[43] Bovon suggests they are at the midpoint of the Gospel and they foreground God's magnanimity to the lost,[44] and Manson that they are Luke's 'Gospel for the outcast'.[45] All agree on the parables' significance and that there is something of Luke's essential theology tied up in them. To understand Luke's gospel, scholars agree, one must grapple with their message.

In attempting to understand parables, scholars have journeyed from rejecting allegory to accepting there is some allegory inherent in a parable.[46] While the extent of allegory is not settled, as we consider Luke 15.1-7 we will seek to recover echoes in the text which will help support a sound interpretation. As we have seen, Luke appears to have a particular interest in David and the motif of shepherd established in the infancy narratives, in 10.3 in the mission mandate, and in the echo of Ezekiel 34 in 12.32. Now, at approximately the half way point of the Gospel narrative we find three 'lost parables', the first of which is the 'lost sheep'. This is of great interest to this study due to its shepherd content.

First, we will look in depth at the setting which provides an interpretative key for the parables. Secondly, we will examine the parable's text, and thirdly, we will establish the LXX echoes within the text. Finally, we will review what we have learnt about the shepherd in the parable.[47]

4.3.1 *The setting (15.1-3)*

The parable of the lost sheep is part of three parables, popularly known as the *lost* parables, which have the central theme of salvation at their core. They are primarily theologically motivated and speak of what God does as the one who

43. Léonard Ramaroson, 'Le coeur du Troisième Évangile: Lc 15,' *Bib* 60 (1979): 338-60. Author's translation.

44. In Acts he identifies the Jerusalem Council (Acts 15). Bovon, *Lukas 1*, p. 16.

45. Manson, *Sayings*, p. 282.

46. Jeremias, *Parables*, pp. 66–89; Bailey, *Poet and Peasant*, pp. 15–26; Blomberg, *Parables*, pp. 29–69; Klyne R. Snodgrass, 'From Allegorizing to Allegorizing: A History of the Interpretation of the Parables of Jesus', in *The Challenge of Jesus' Parables* (ed. Richard N. Longenecker; Grand Rapids: Eerdmans, 2000), pp. 3–29.

47. For a comparison with Mt. 18.12-14 and Gospel of Thomas §107 and a discussion on unity see Harris' dissertation.

seeks the lost rather than focusing on the lost themselves; that which is lost is of concern, but this is not the primary message. The sheep who is lost is, for Luke, the setting within which the agent (the shepherd) comes and finds the sheep and joyfully restores it to the fold. The narrative deals foremost with the actions of the shepherd. Léonard Ramaroson expresses it well when he says: 'The centre of interest in the three parables is neither the object which is lost nor the object which is found, but the owner of the object, or more precisely, the owner's joy when he finds the lost.'[48]

Because the parables are theologically centered, I have renamed the parables to reflect this: the Faithful Shepherd, the Good Woman, and the Gracious Father.

Luke provides the setting for the three parables in his introduction in vv. 1-3, and scholars rightly suggest the setting is the interpretive key for the three parables.[49] As a result, establishing what Luke is saying in the setting and how this informs the parables is essential for the reader to understand the parable of the faithful shepherd.

Verse 3 informs the reader to whom the parables are spoken when it says, Εἶπεν δὲ πρὸς αὐτοὺς τὴν παραβολὴν ταύτην λέγων. Here the text's use of αὐτοί refers to the Pharisees and scribes who are the named audience, although 14.25 notes the large crowds that are travelling with Jesus. Therefore, this is told for the benefit of the Pharisees and scribes who were known as shepherds of God's flock. With the context of the first parable focused on a faithful shepherd, the parable is directly clearly at them and it is almost certain they would have heard this as a critique of their leadership.[50] Neale notes this is twofold as the parables justify Jesus' action in eating with the sinners, but he also critiques the religious leaders whose behaviour is not welcoming.[51] But it is Bailey, Green, Klein and Blomberg who see most clearly the link between the leaders as *shepherds* and the faithful shepherd of the first parable.[52] Bailey shows this clearly when he says:

The *original* audience of the Pharisees and scribes is pressed to make something of the following decision/response: We, the shepherds of Israel, have 'lost our

48. Ramaroson, 'Le Coeur', p. 349. Author's translation.

49. David A. Neale, *None But the Sinners: Religious Categories in the Gospel of Luke* (JSNTSS, 58; Sheffield: JSOT Press, 1991), p. 154; Tannehill, *Narrative Unity*, 1, p. 106; Johnson, *Gospel*, p. 239; Steven Curkpatrick, 'Parable Metonymy and Luke's Kerygmatic Framing', *JSNT* 25 (2003): 289–307.

50. Kenneth Ewing Bailey, *Finding the Lost: Cultural Keys to Luke 15* (St. Louis: Concordia, 1992), p. 91; Neale, *None but the Sinners*, p. 159; *Contra*, Adams who says, 'The emphasis is not an attack against the Pharisees' failure to seek the lost but a rebuke against their failure, like the elder brother, to rejoice over Jesus' mission to rescue them'. Adams, *Sinner*, p. 166.

51. Neale, *None but the Sinners*, p. 155.

52. Bailey, *Finding the Lost*, p. 91; Green, *Gospel*, p. 575; Klein, *Das Lukasevangelium*, p. 523; Blomberg, *Parables*, p. 180.

sheep' and Jesus, acting in God's place, at great cost has found them. Rather than attack him we should rejoice at the restoration of these lost even if Jesus in the process radically redefines repentance.[53]

Wolter further notes that this setting shows a clear comparison to the story of Levi.[54] However, not every scholar believes the shepherd character in this parable is directly referring to the religious leaders. Nolland finds it unusual that the parable would suggest a first century Pharisee or scribe would own any sheep, let alone one hundred of them, and so does not make the connection between religious leaders and shepherds.[55] He takes the use of the hundred and the ninety-nine sheep as a literary device to show the disproportionate investment in time and effort to find one sheep, and suggests it has its roots in the rabbinic text of *m.Peah* 4.1-2. This position however only views the shepherds in the text as literal first century shepherds, and does not take into account the way scripture repeatedly refers to leaders as shepherds of God's people. The Pharisees and scribes were so highly trained in the scriptures it is to be expected that they would have made connections to passages like Jeremiah 23 and Ezekiel 34 where the shepherds were also criticized for not seeking out the lost sheep.

Jeremias equates first century shepherds as ἁμαρτωλοί, 'because they are suspected of driving their flocks into foreign fields, and of embezzling the produce of their flocks',[56] however, as we have seen, Luke is not portraying shepherds as sinners. As we have seen, although there are a few rabbinic texts that portray shepherds unfavourably, this is the opposite of Philo's perspective which views shepherds as respectable, noble, and for whom God is the preeminent example of a shepherd.

It appears that the Lukan setting (vv. 1–3) suggests that these three parables are directed specifically for the purpose of challenging the religious leaders as to their non-acceptance and welcome of toll collectors and sinners. The use of αὐτοί in 15.3 implies Luke's intention to challenge their attitudes and behaviour. Luke also challenges the Pharisees and scribes for grumbling (διαγογγύζω), for their charge of people as ἁμαρτωλοί, for their lack of welcome (προσδέχομαι), and Jesus defends the notion of eating with (συνεσθίω) sinners. We will explore these key ideas before looking at the parable.

What does the 'grumbling' imply?
The introductory verses state that πάντες the toll collectors and sinners are drawing near to listen to Jesus while the Pharisees and scribes are grumbling (διαγογγύζω) and that Jesus is both welcoming and eating with sinners. The use of πάντες is hyperbole for the sake of emphasis,[57] and functions to highlight the

---

53. Bailey, *Finding the Lost*, p. 91.
54. Wolter, *Das Lukasevangelium*, p. 523.
55. Nolland, *Luke*, p. 771.
56. Jeremias, *Parables*, p. 133.
57. Neale, *None but the Sinners*, p. 155.

positive portrayal of the toll collectors and sinners. Luke's use of ἀκούω in 15.1 recalls 14.35 where the conclusion of the parable of salt says, ὁ ἔχων ὦτα ἀκούειν ἀκουέτω. Immediately, in 15.1 we see that it is the toll collectors and sinners who have been positioned in the narrative to be the model responders to Jesus by them listening (ἀκούω) to Jesus. Johnson suggests 'hearing' is a sign of conversion,[58] although this may be overstating the point but with Nolland, 'It is certainly a move in the direction of that possibility'.[59]

The Pharisees and scribes are set up to be viewed pejoratively. Luke never uses διαγογγύζω (15.2; 19.7) or its simple form γογγύζω (5.30) in a positive light. In all three of these pericopae those who are grumbling are characterized negatively, and all use the imperfect tense giving the sense of the ongoing nature of their attitude. Both points lead the reader to conclude that those grumbling are the antagonists in the narratives.

Gowler notes that in 15.2 the Pharisees are indirectly attacking Jesus' honour in their murmuring, and this would have been perceived as offensive.[60] It has been suggested that the grumbling of the scribes and the Pharisees echoes the Israelites who were grumbling at Aaron and Moses in the wilderness.[61] Evans originally proposed that the travel narrative modelled the exodus journey, and this view has gained general support with varying emphases in the works of Moessner,[62] Green,[63] O'Toole,[64] Strauss,[65] Scobie[66] and Turner,[67] with Pao exploring this in Acts.[68] As scholars have analysed Luke's travel narrative they have noticed that

---

58. Johnson, *Gospel*, p. 235.

59. Nolland, *Luke*, p. 770.

60. David B. Gowler, *Host, Guest, Enemy and Friend: Portrait of Pharisees in Luke and Acts* (Eugene: Wipf and Stock, 1991), p. 254.

61. John O'Hanlon, 'The Story of Zacchaeus and the Lukan Ethic', *JSNT* 12 (1981): 16; Johnson, *Gospel*, p. 235; Dwayne H. Adams, *The Sinner in Luke* (Eugene: Pickwick, 2008), pp. 155–6.

62. C. F. Evans, 'The Central Section of St. Luke's Gospel', in *Studies in the Gospels: Essays in Memory of R. H. Lightfoot* (ed. D. E. Nineham; Oxford: Basil Blackwell, 1955), pp. 37–53; D. P. Moessner, *Lord of the Banquet: The Literary and Theological Significance of the Lukan Travel Narrative* (Harrisburg: Trinity Press International, 1989).

63. Green, *Gospel*, pp. 353–4.

64. O'Toole, 'Parallels Between Jesus and Moses', pp. 22–9.

65. Strauss, *Davidic Messiah*, pp. 261–336.

66. Charles H. H. Scobie, 'A Canonical Approach to Interpreting Luke', in *Reading Luke: Interpretation, Reflection, Formation* (ed. Craig G. Bartholomew, Joel B. Green and Anthony C. Thiselton; Scripture and Hermeneutics Series 6; Grand Rapids: Zondervan, 2005), pp. 327–49.

67. Max Turner, *Power From On High: The Spirit in Israel's Restoration and Witness in Luke-Acts* (JPTSS, 9; Sheffield: Sheffield Academic, 2000), pp. 244–50.

68. D. W. Pao, *Acts and the New Isaianic New Exodus* (WUNT II/130; Grand Rapids: Baker Books, 2000).

the transfiguration sets the scene for the journey by its unique shaping of Jesus' mission as an exodus. There is considerable evidence for this.

Luke uniquely uses the word ἔξοδος in the transfiguration narrative (9.31); he uses νεφέλη three times (9.34 [twice], 35) which may recall the pillar of cloud that led the Israelites (Exod. 13.21, 22; 14.19, 24; 33.9, 10; Num. 12.5; 14.14; Deut. 31.15),[69] and uniquely speaks of the δόξα (9.31, 32)[70] which may recall the glory mentioned in Exod. 24.16-17 and Deuteronomy 5.24. Other exodus indicators are given when Luke presents Jesus in a prophet-like-Moses role fulfilling Deuteronomy 18.15 – for example, Luke's use of the *Shema* in 10.27 (Deut. 6.5), and the sending out of the seventy (10.1), which may look back to the seventy elders who assisted Moses (Num. 11.16-17, 24-25).[71] The focus in Luke on the Spirit's presence in Jesus (4.1, 14; 5.17) may also be equated with the presence of God who led the Israelites (Exod. 33.14), and Moessner suggests the teaching from 10.1–18.14 largely parallels Deuteronomy 1–26.[72] Watts explored the idea of the Isaianic new exodus in Mark, and Strauss has tested this motif in Luke's writing finding the exodus motif is not limited to the travel narrative, but begins with John the Baptist in the wilderness.[73]

The high level of scholarly support for the Lukan Jesus travelling on an exodus journey does suggest that the grumbling of the religious leaders in 15.2 may well recall the exodus. This reinforces a pejorative view of the grumbling leaders, and may even go so far as to indicate the religious leaders' unfaithfulness to God and God's mission to bring salvation to sinners. However, as Hollander points out, an echo brings with it a causal chain that links an idea to the wider picture.[74] That is, one significant word or idea suggests something greater. With the Lukan Jesus on his exodus journey therefore, this mention of grumbling leaders may bring into view a picture of the exodus where the reader can perceive the grumbling Israelites who are God's flock and God who is their shepherd (Pss. 76.21; 77.52-53; 79.2). This is made more likely as the first parable in the unit of three is that of a shepherd. As this study agrees with scholars such as Bailey, Neale, Johnson and Curkpatrick that this Lukan setting of 15.1-3 is the interpretative key of the chapter,[75] then this echo of the exodus is particularly informative for the reader.

---

69. The other synoptics only use this twice each (Mk 9.7 [2x]; Mt. 17.5 [2x]).

70. This also recalls Luke 9.26-27.

71. Scobie, 'A Canonical Approach', pp. 337–8.

72. Moessner, *Lord of the Banquet*, pp. 45–79. Moessner suggests a fourfold exodus typology as a heuristic principle for the travel narrative of Luke, which he ends at Luke 19.44.

73. Rikki E. Watts, *Isaiah's New Exodus in Mark* (Biblical Studies Library; Grand Rapids: Baker Books, 2000); Strauss, *Davidic Messiah*, pp. 261–336.

74. Hollander, *Figure of Echo*, pp. 131–49.

75. Bailey, *Finding the Lost*, p. 91; Neale, *None But the Sinners*, p. 154; Johnson, *Gospel*, p. 239; Curkpatrick, 'Parable Metonymy', pp. 289–307.

The use of ἁμαρτωλός and what it may imply

In the setting the Pharisees and scribes grumble that Jesus is dining with and welcoming *sinners*. This notion of ἁμαρτωλός is significant in this text and the wider Lukan narrative. Luke uses the term eighteen times in comparison with Mark, who uses it only six times, and Matthew, five times.[76] However, this volume of recurrence is heightened by Luke's unique use of the word which suggests this is a significant concept for Lukan theology. Luke uses the term four times where there are synoptic parallel passages (Lk. 5.30, Mk 2.15, Mt. 9.10; Lk. 5.32, Mk 2.16, Mt. 9.13; Lk. 7.34, Mt. 11.9; Lk. 24.7, Mk 14.14, Mt. 26.45),[77] yet he also uses ἁμαρτωλός in fourteen unique passages. These are in the Sermon on the Plain (6.32, 33, 34 [twice]), and six pericopae where the focus is on Jesus' relationship with ἁμαρτωλοί (5.8; 7.37, 39; 13.2; 15.1, 2, 7, 10; 18.13; 19.7). However, key mission statements in the Gospel (5.32; 19.10) are in 'sinner' pericopae,[78] therefore, this use of ἁμαρτωλοί at the midpoint of the Gospel may also be of particular note.

Luke's basic understanding is that all people are sinners and in need of repentance. This is most clearly seen in two no fault stories (13.1-5) showing that none are worse sinners than any other. Adams says: 'In Luke 13:1-9, the term "sinner" broadens out to include the entire listening audience of Jesus, and by implication, all Israel and even the reader.'[79] In our context this includes the religious leaders, the shepherds.

In the Gospel neither being ἁμαρτωλός (or its antonym δίκαιος) is tied to gender,[80] race[81] or class.[82] The defining feature is whether one's life is humbled before God. Simon shows humility when he declares he is ἁμαρτωλός (5.8) and falls down at Jesus' knees. This action is repeated by the γυνή ἁμαρτωλός (7.36-50) who is saved by her faith and demonstrates her gratefulness for the forgiveness Jesus has offered her by bending down to kiss and anoint his feet. A repentant and grateful heart, a sign of forgiveness (7.47), now makes the woman δίκαιος rather than Simon the Pharisee. Thus, the reader finds the model respondent is not only a woman, but she is favourably contrasted to a man of status in the community. Similarly, in the parable of the Pharisee and the toll collector, it is the toll collector

76. The word is notably absent in Acts. Adams has most recently suggested Luke 24.7 provides a 'conceptual bridge into Acts in which the rejection of Jesus or opposition to the preaching about Jesus is described as opposing God and placing one under his wrath'. See Adams, *Sinner*, p. 196.

77. Luke 24.7 is in Luke's resurrection narrative, while Mark 14.14 and Matthew 26.45 are in Gethsemane.

78. Adams, *Sinner*, p. 190.

79. Ibid., p. 152.

80. Elizabeth is described as δίκαιος (1.6), so are Zechariah (1.6), Simeon (2.25) and Joseph of Arimathea (23.50).

81. Gentiles such as Cornelius (Acts 10.22) are δίκαιοι, while the Jewish rulers are called ἁμαρτωλοί (Lk. 24.7).

82. Elizabeth as δίκαιός would have been considered poor, while Cornelius would have been comparatively wealthy.

who names himself as the sinner and in doing so, the reader learns he is 'justified' (18.14). Again the reader finds the protagonist is the one least expected, for Luke subverts the roles society has attached to them.

These two groups are also visible in the parable of the faithful shepherd for they are represented in the two groups in 15.1-2; the Jewish religious elite who believe they are δίκαιοι, and those they claim are ἁμαρτωλοί. The implication that they are not righteous but sinners adds to the interpretative framework of the parable.

The significance of Jesus eating with and welcoming sinners

In 15.2 Jesus welcomes and eats with toll collectors and sinners and this brings criticism from the religious leaders. The Lukan Jesus is often at meals in the Gospel;[83] there are many parables that centre on eating and drinking,[84] and we find Jesus teaching at meals.[85]

In the ANE hospitality was an essential part of daily life, and for the Pharisees of Jesus' time, purity of the meal table was an important concern as it set them apart as *faithful* Jews.[86] Borg notes that it also pointed to their destiny as an eschatological kingdom of priests which would be inaugurated at a banquet.[87] Certainly the dominance of table fellowship *halakhic* practices is a central defining feature of their sect in later rabbinic literature.[88] Josephus describes the Pharisees as the party of ἀκρίβεια, a term which describes those Jews who apply the laws for daily life with strictness and precision.[89] This development stemmed from the Jews' post-exilic past where holiness was defined through separation, and thus this was not a matter of etiquette but a visible act where loyalty to Yahweh was enacted.[90]

The relationship between pre-70 CE Pharisees and later rabbinic texts is of course not certain, and we cannot assume a first-century practice from later rabbinic texts. Yet, the strictness around matters of table fellowship suggested by rabbinic texts is similar to the separation between the religious leaders and the

83. Jesus eats with the Pharisees (7.36-50; 11.37-53; 14.1-24), toll collectors and sinners (5.29-32; 7.34; 19.5-7), disciples (6.1-5; 22.7-23; 24.28-32, 42-43), and the crowds (9.12-17).

84. See 10.30-37; 11.5-8; 12.16-21; 14.7-11, 15-24; 15.11-32; 16.19-31.

85. See 5.29-39; 7.36-50; 10.38-42; 11.37-52; 14.1-24; 22.14-38.

86. Neusner goes so far as to describe them as a 'table fellowship sect' and Borg that table fellowship was their 'survival symbol'. See Jacob Neusner, *From Politics to Piety: The Emergence of Pharisaic Judaism* (New York: Ktav Publishing House, 1979), p. 80; Marcus J. Borg, *Conflict, Holiness and Politics in the Teachings of Jesus* (SBC, 5; Harrisburg: Trinity Press International, 1998), p. 96.

87. Borg describes this as both *praxis* and *telos*. Marcus J. Borg, *Conflict, Holiness and Politics*, p. 96.

88. See Jacob Neusner, *The Rabbinic Traditions about the Pharisees before 70*, (3 vols; Leiden: Brill, 1971), vol. 1, pp. 303-4. See also Neale, *None But the Sinners*, pp. 40-67; Borg, *Conflict, Holiness and Politics*, pp. 93-134.

89. Josephus, *War*, 1, p. 110; 2, p. 126; *Ant.* 17.41; *Life*, p. 191. For a discussion see Dunn, 'Pharisees, Sinners and Jesus', pp. 266-8.

90. Borg, *Conflict, Holiness and Politics*, p. 96.

ritually impure in Luke-Acts, and it is a central concern for Luke's 'gospel to the ends of the earth', where the issue of table fellowship would ultimately need to be resolved in the Jerusalem Council (Acts 15).

It is not, however, simply that table fellowship separated people; eating together was an act of intimacy that demonstrated one's acceptance of another, and conversely to not share table fellowship expressed disapproval and rejection. Bailey notes that 'in the East today, a nobleman may feed any number of lesser needy persons as a sign of his generosity, but he does *not* eat with them'.[91] When Jesus had table fellowship with such people, he not only defied social barriers which kept the Pharisees separate, more importantly, he expressed a welcome that implied acceptance and forgiveness. Luke 15.1-3 heightens the drama as Jesus is the *host* of the meal.[92] This appears to be a deliberate symbolic act where Jesus is fighting the prevailing norms.[93] The use of προσδέχομαι (a synonym of δέχομαι in Luke's writing)[94] is particularly important as it is a salvific term which is often tied to waiting for and welcoming the kingdom; Many model respondents such as Simeon (2.28), Anna (2.38), the children (18.17), Zacchaeus (19.6) and Joseph of Arimathea (23.51) are shown as welcoming Jesus and/or the message. Furthermore, the parable of the sower talks of μετὰ χαρᾶς δέχονται τὸν λόγον (8.13), an image that will become established in Acts (Acts 8.14; 11.1; 17.11). Therefore, when Jesus welcomes and eats with the sinners, the narrative suggests there is an implied salvific function at the meal table.

4.3.2 The parable (15.4-7)

As we have found from the setting, v. 3 informs the reader that Jesus is speaking the parable primarily to the shepherd leaders whose negative words and actions suggest they are sinners and in need of repentance.

The parable itself begins with a protracted question (vv. 4–6) where the listeners are encouraged to identify themselves as shepherds.[95] Verse 4 begins τίς ἄνθρωπος ἐξ ὑμῶν (which one of you... ?); a direct question to the religious leaders.[96] The parable itself is simple; a shepherd has lost one of his one hundred sheep, and so leaves them in the wilderness to look for the lost sheep. He searches for it until he finds it. When he finds it, he lays the sheep on his shoulders and carries it home rejoicing. This costs the shepherd considerably to carry the sheep back to the community, but this 'burden of restoration'[97] is presented as the task of a faithful

---

91. Bailey, *Poet and Peasant*, p. 143. Emphasis original.

92. Ibid. *Contra*, Craig L. Blomberg *Contagious Holiness: Jesus' Meals with Sinners* (NSBT, 19; Downers Grove: IVP/Leicester: Apollos, 2005), p. 150.

93. Borg, *Conflict, Holiness and Politics*, p. 97.

94. Bailey, *Poet and Peasant*, p. 143.

95. Blomberg, *Parables*, p. 180; Green, *Gospel*, p. 573.

96. Klein, *Das Lukasevangelium*, p. 523.

97. Bailey, *Poet and Peasant*, p. 148.

shepherd. The parable ends with a comment that there is more joy in heaven over one sinner who repents than ninety-nine who do not need repentance.

The opening question is rhetorical, as there is an implied understanding that a shepherd would certainly look for a lost sheep. Sheep were valuable commodities and the response of the shepherd is taken for granted.[98] As Klein notes, 'because he knows that the sheep cannot find its way to the flock alone, he sets out after the lost'.[99]

Jeremias comments that 'when a sheep has strayed from the flock, it usually lies down helplessly, and will not move, stand up or run'.[100] With the weight of an average sheep estimated to be about 32 kilograms,[101] and rural countryside likely to be undulating if not rocky, carrying the sheep home to the community would be a costly task. Luke describes the terrain as the wilderness (ἔρημος) where the shepherd leaves the other sheep, suggesting harsh conditions.

The shepherd's rejoicing is of interest. Rejoicing is a favoured response in Lukan stories, and in this parable it is the response of the shepherd (χαίρω; 15.5), the friends and neighbours (συγχαίρω; 15.6), and also the angels in heaven (χαρά; 15.7). This repetition functions as a literary highlighting tool which, if combined with the idea of joyful restoration, forms part of the centrepiece of the parable.

Luke often uses χαίρω or χαρά when in salvation stories and it is an attribute of a model respondent in the Gospel (1.14; 2.10; 8.13; 10.17, 20; 13.17; 15.5, 7, 10, 32; 19.6, 37; 24.52; Acts 5.41; 8.39; 11.23; 13.48, 52). Four of these examples are from Luke 15, giving some weight to Ramaroson's view that it is the owner's joy at finding the lost object which is the central focus in the parables.[102] Indeed, this is 'the heart of the Third Gospel'. This joy is found, as Luke 15.7 shows, when a sinner repents. This central interest in the joy of the shepherd is visible in Bailey's analysis of the parable below in point C and C¹:

> 1 Which man of you (a direct address to the audience)
>> 2 one
>> 3 ninety-nine
>>> A the lost
>>>> B find
>>>>> **C joy**
>>>>>> D restoration
>>>>> **C¹ joy**
>>>> B¹ find
>>> A¹ the lost
>> 1¹ I say to you (a direct address to the audience)
>> 2¹ one
> 3¹ ninety-nine[103]

---

98. Fitzmyer, *Luke*, p. 1077; Green, *Gospel*, p. 574.

99. Klein, *Das Lukasevangelium*, p. 523.

100. Jeremias, *Parables*, p. 134; also Snodgrass, *Stories With Intent*, p. 102.

101. Imperial measurement is 70 pounds. Bailey, *Finding the Lost*, p. 74.

102. Ramaroson, 'Le Coeur', p. 349.

103. Bailey, *Poet and Peasant*, pp. 144–5.

For Bailey the mid-point (D) is the calling of friends and neighbours together in his house and his theological analysis focuses on the 'joy at the restoration'. He says:

> This brings us to a consideration of the centre stanza ... we have a long, somewhat unnatural statement which is clearly constructed to provide the inversion of the ideas that will fill out the parallelistic form and climax on 'joy at the restoration' in the centre of the parable. [104]

Here Bailey links his points C and D, the joy and the restoration; however, he also engages the idea of the 'burden of restoration', which describes the shepherd's actions in carrying home the sheep and their christological implications. I agree that the burden of restoration is a key idea in the parable as it charges the religious leaders with the costly task of seeking out the lost sheep, but I note that it also contains two ideas: the burden of carrying the sheep *and* the restoration to the community. Bailey seems to have overworked his analysis by dividing up points C and D which for him theologically are the heart of the parable. I suggest the centre is the *joyfully enacted burden* where the shepherd at great personal cost carries the sheep home to the community. To divide it more than this is to over-analyse the parable.

Bovon optimistically notes: 'All the shepherd's exertion fails to exhaust or extinguish his joy';[105] however, this overlooks the personal cost for the shepherd. Some commentators cast the picture of the shepherd with a sheep on his shoulders as an idyllic pastoral picture from Isaiah 40.11.[106] Isaiah 40.11, however, is linked to the image of the warrior in v. 10 who comes with strength and authority bringing all flesh σωτήριον (Isa. 40.5). Historically this was Cyrus who brought Israel deliverance (σωτήριον) from Babylon in 539 BCE, while Luke says God is now bringing his σωτήριον through Jesus the Saviour, Messiah, and Lord (2.11) to all people. In Luke's parable, the picture in 15.5 is not primarily of an idyllic pastoral scene, but a picture of a joyfully enacted *burden*. The narrative location of these parables should also be noted. Jesus has turned his face to Jerusalem in 9.51 having made clear that he will suffer and die (9.21-22 and again 13.33; 17.25; 18.31-33). Jesus is clearly on the journey to his suffering and death as he travels to Jerusalem.

Bailey develops the idea and makes a soteriological interpretation of the parable where the faithful shepherd carrying the sheep back to the community on his shoulders describes Jesus' work on the cross, and posits that the doctrine of the atonement originates in the parables.[107] Snodgrass notes that this was a medieval understanding of the parable,[108] although he and other major commentators

---

104. Ibid., p. 146.

105. Bovon, *Lukas 3*, p. 27. Author's translation.

106. Marshall, *Gospel*, p. 601; Bock, *Luke*, p. 1301.

107. Bailey, *Finding the Lost*, pp. 75–80; Bailey, *Jacob and the Prodigal*, p. 78.

108. Snodgrass, *Stories with Intent*, pp. 103, 106–7; Steven L. Wailes, *Medieval Allegories of Jesus' Parables* (Berkeley: University of California Press, 1987), pp. 128–30.

doubt there is any vicarious dimension at work in this parable. Bock directs us to the care of the shepherd (Isa. 40.11; 49.11), Johnson adds it reflects Hellenistic pastoral tradition, Nolland maintains that the sheep is most quickly returned to the flock in this manner, Green fails to make any comment, and Marshall says that it shows the care of the shepherd (Isa. 40.11) and perhaps a 'triumphant air'.[109] Fitzmyer is the only commentator who gives anything other than an idyllic picture of the shepherd carrying the sheep. He notes that the figure is consistent with statues in the catacombs, but he makes no suggestion as to what this might mean.[110]

There is no doubt that Bailey's idea of the burden of restoration resonates with the Lukan journey, and the early church used the picture, but is Luke suggesting a proleptic picture of the atonement?

First, Luke shows that this restoration is costly to the shepherd; it was a back-breaking task. This resonates with the Lukan Jesus who talks repeatedly of his own suffering as he travels to Jerusalem while also visible is the critique Jesus receives from the religious elite; befriending sinners is also a costly task.

Secondly, we have noted that Luke's parable is primarily theological and points to God as the shepherd who searches for the lost sheep. Every sheep is valuable and should not be lost, and if even one goes missing a faithful shepherd will search for it until he finds it. Jesus' action of welcome demonstrates Jesus enacting the parable, making a christological reading appropriate. Green tentatively asks, 'Is it possible to understand the parable not only *theologically* but also *christologically*? If so, Jesus would be portrayed as fulfilling the role of Yahweh in caring for the lost sheep.'[111] Snodgrass agrees, saying:

> If Jesus defends his eating with sinners by pointing to God's character and saying God is like a shepherd searching for the lost, then he implicitly claims he is doing God's work. At least with respect to Luke, the analogy of the shepherd refers to both the character of God and the activity of Jesus.[112]

Jesus is doing the work of God here, but whether this is an atonement picture needs to be tested out. Certainly the parable comes in the travel narrative where Jesus is on his way to Jerusalem to suffer and die, but how much Luke intended the reader to understand this as a picture of the cross is uncertain. As with 12.32, one way the verse's interpretation may be tested is by the LXX echo behind the text. This we will do, but first we will examine the last key idea in the parable.

The reference to the ninety-nine who need no repentance (15.7) is another important feature in the parable. Some have taken this literally to mean that Jesus is saying some have no need of repentance as they are already righteous. Neale,

---

109. Bock, *Luke*, p. 1301; Nolland, *Luke*, p. 772; Marshall, *Gospel*, p. 601; Johnson, *Gospel*, p. 240; Green, *Gospel*, p. 574.

110. Fitzmyer, *Luke*, p. 1077.

111. Green, *Gospel*, p. 575. n. 215.

112. Snodgrass, *Stories With Intent*, p. 107.

even though he believes Luke attributes a negative stance toward the religious leaders' grumbling, holds this position. He says: 'In this parable Jesus clearly thinks some indeed are "righteous" in the sense of being in the fold and this includes, by analogy, the Pharisees.'[113] Similarly Johnson notes the religious leaders, like the elder son, have stayed within the covenant but that 'Luke's compositional frame makes it unmistakable: he told these stories to the *righteous ones* who complained about the prophet accepting sinners (15.1-2)'.[114] Others rightly query how Jesus could refer to the religious leaders as righteous when the setting suggests he is criticizing them. Bailey posits an ironic tone with the idea of self-righteousness in view,[115] yet, as Blomberg points out, Luke uses δίκαιος positively elsewhere in the Gospel and the thrust of the verse is toward repentance.[116] Blomberg suggests that as in the parable of the gracious father, Luke appears to be using a carrot rather than a stick to encourage the religious leaders to turn again to God.[117] However, we have noted that the setting paints a pejorative picture of the leaders and the protracted rhetorical question suggests these shepherds of Israel are in need of repentance.[118] For Luke, all are sinners and need to live lives in humility before God – attributes not of these leaders but the toll collectors and sinners who drew near to Jesus.

We will now examine the primary echo behind the parable which Green, Johnson, Adams, DeConick, Barton and Bailey suggest is Ezekiel 34.[119] This will enable us to evaluate Bailey's suggestion that there is an atonement image in the parable.

4.3.3 Ezekiel 34 in Luke 15.4-7

There are many linguistic and thematic ties between Ezekiel's shepherd chapter and Luke's parable of the faithful shepherd. First, Ezekiel begins with a warning to the shepherds that they are not fulfilling their role as shepherds of God's flock.

---

113. Neale, *None But the Sinners*, p. 163.

114. Johnson, *Gospel*, p. 242. Emphasis is mine.

115. Bailey, *Poet and Peasant*, p. 155.

116. Blomberg, *Parables*, p. 182.

117. Blomberg, *Parables*, p. 183.

118. Green, *Gospel*, p. 575. *Contra*, Bock, *Luke*, p. 1302.

119. Green, *Gospel*, p. 574; Johnson, *Gospel*, p. 240; Adams, *Sinner*, p. 159; Bailey, *Jacob and the Prodigal*, pp. 68–85; DeConick, *Gospel of Thomas*, p. 286; Steven C. Barton, 'Parables on God's Love and Forgiveness (Luke 15:1-32)', in *The Challenge of Jesus' Parables* (ed. Richard N. Longenecker; Grand Rapids: Eerdmans, 2000), p. 204. Bailey suggests Ps. 23, Jer. 23.1-8, and Ezek. 34 are behind the parable. Bailey includes Jeremiah 23.7-8 which do not appear in the LXX, Luke's accepted scriptural base. In *Finding the Lost* Bailey makes a more developed case for Ps. 23 as the echo in the parable. Snodgrass says the connections to Psalm 23 are 'imaginative and none too convincing' (p. 106), when Bailey creates too much out of the idea of 'bringing back' to mean repentance in Psalms 23.3. Bailey, *Finding the Lost*, pp. 68–92; *Jacob and the Prodigal*, pp. 66–72; Snodgrass, *Stories With Intent*, p. 106.

They have become preoccupied instead with their own needs and have neglected their responsibility to the sheep, and so the sheep have become scattered across every mountain and hill (Ezek. 34.1-10). The critique upon them is sustained and judgement follows. Luke's parable and its setting clearly mirrors this critique; the sustained question in vv. 4-6 is directed toward the shepherd leaders who are not seeking out the lost sheep.

Secondly, the idea of sinners needing to repent is present in both passages. Ezekiel 34 is preceded by Ezekiel 33.8, 19 where the prophet uses the notion of ἁμαρτωλός, and particularly of sinners who need to turn back to the Lord. This thinking then underpins the prophet's woe in ch. 34.[120] In Ezekiel 33 the reader finds the Lord showing the repentant sinner forgiveness, in the same way as the repentant sinner finds forgiveness in Luke's parable (15.7).

Thirdly, feeding is at the centre of both pericopae. Luke shows Jesus in the midst of toll collectors and sinners and sharing food with them. The idea that συνεσθίω (15.2) suggests Jesus is hosting sinners is entirely consistent with the picture in Ezekiel 34 where the Lord will feed his sheep. Ezekiel 34 makes much of the call for the shepherds of Israel to *feed* the sheep as we have seen. The practical action of the Lord's people being fed seems to resonate in Luke 15 with Jesus eating with sinners, but also in the wider narrative where Jesus is often at meals.

Fourthly, it should be noted that Ezekiel refers to sheep being safe *in the wilderness* (Ezek. 34.25), as this is Luke's setting (15.4).[121] In Luke's parable the sheep are safe in the wilderness because the shepherd is with them, and even when one sheep is lost the faithful shepherd will look for it, most likely leaving another shepherd with the ninety-nine.[122] This suggests a picture of safety for the sheep. In Ezekiel's prophecy it is after the Lord has made a covenant of peace with his shepherd David, that the sheep are safe in the wilderness. With so many other linguistic echoes of Ezekiel 34 in Luke 15, this reference to the wilderness, though not a strong link, should not be discounted.

Fifthly, both passages have a theological focus on God as shepherd, and also Ezekiel has a clear role for the Davidic shepherd king who will be the Lord's servant (Ezek. 34.23-24). While the Lord is ultimately the shepherd for the prophet, his hands and feet in the task of shepherding are his servant David. This appears to be the role that Luke shows Jesus to be fulfilling in the parable;[123] he is the faithful shepherd of the parable who has sought out the lost sheep (the toll collectors and sinners) who have drawn near to listen to him. While the religious leaders deride his actions, Jesus' welcome demonstrates the message of the parable in action. This also resonates with Jesus' Davidic shepherd identity that Luke has painted in the infancy narrative and in the genealogy, where leadership is characterized by a faithful shepherd leading them. The link with Ezekiel 34 is also quite

---

120. Adams, *Sinner*, p. 160.

121. Ezek. 34.6 notes the sheep are scattered on the mountain and also they find safety around my mountain.

122. Bailey, *Poet and Peasant*, p. 149, n. 34.

123. Green, *Gospel*, p. 575, n. 215.

possible, since Luke has already used Ezekiel 34 in 12.32, showing his knowledge and use of the passage.

Furthermore, Jesus' ministry is characterized by ministry to the sick, poor, and marginalized; Jesus helps the weak, heals the sick, and searches for the lost. Indeed, the programmatic statement where Jesus is identified as the anointed one who brings good news and freedom to the poor, captive, blind and oppressed resonates with the Davidic shepherd who faithfully shepherds God's flock. Luke 15.1-7 can thus be read as not only a reflection of God's care for the lost, but Jesus' care as the faithful shepherd. Ezekiel shows both are shepherds, and it appears so too does Luke.

What Ezekiel 34 does not support is any sense of a vicarious suffering of the shepherd. The shepherd goes to great lengths to seek out and gather in the sheep. He is charged with feeding, binding up the injured, and providing places of rest for the sheep. He is also required to guard the strong, but there is no picture of him carrying or suffering on behalf of the sheep. While the tasks described are strenuous and time consuming, Ezekiel does not develop this or even allude to a burden for the shepherd. Rather, he expects that a faithful leader will simply carry out these tasks as they are responsibilities of the faithful shepherd.

The many linguistic ties, the setting of each passage, and the theological thrust all suggest that an echo of Ezekiel 34 is the echo behind Luke's parable. The volume and recurrence cohere, as do the thematic concerns. Furthermore, there is a growing body of scholars who find this echo most likely.[124] I would suggest this history of interpretation makes this the most satisfactory reading of the parable. The Pharisees and scribes had a duty of care for God's flock, and yet the parabolic unit situates them pejoratively, suggesting they are shepherds who are not caring for God's flock. Jesus is the example of the faithful shepherd by enacting the message of the parable, but this does not press toward Bailey's proleptic picture of the cross.

4.4 The faithful shepherds in Ephesus (Acts 20.28-29)

In the Miletus speech in Acts 20.17-38, the motif of shepherd and flock reappears. The motif comes in a unique passage where Paul speaks to Christian leaders, and which Walton describes as 'an island in the sea of Acts'.[125] The return of shepherd and flock language at such a significant and distinctive speech in Acts makes it of particular relevance to this study as this may demonstrate that as the church progressed this motif held currency for Luke.

Paul addresses the leaders of the church of Ephesus at Miletus on his way to Jerusalem where, according to Luke, he was hurrying to be for Pentecost (Acts 20.16). Miletus is a short distance of about 48 kilometres from Ephesus and there

124. Green, *Gospel*, p. 574; Johnson, *Gospel*, p. 240; Adams, *Sinner*, p. 159; Bailey, *Jacob and the Prodigal*, pp. 68–85; Barton, 'Parables on God's Love', p. 204.

125. Steve Walton, *Leadership and Lifestyle: The Portrait of Paul in the Miletus Speech and 1 Thessalonians* (SNTSMS, 108; Cambridge: Cambridge University Press, 2000), p. 99.

are conflicting suggestions about why he did not simply go to Ephesus to speak to the church leaders.[126] Notably, it is the only speech we have of Paul where his audience is exclusively Christian, and in the speech he calls for the leaders to look to God for their future wellbeing.[127] I accept the 'we' passages are most likely suggesting that the author is present and functioning as an eyewitness to the speech.[128] While there is considerable suggestion that the 'we' passages are a literary device or are from someone else's diary,[129] I agree with a large body of scholars who note that the literary style and perspective cohere with the larger narrative and suggest Luke is not heavily reliant on another source here, and is not trying to assert an authority in the use of 'we' to gain the confidence of the reader. Therefore, when Acts 20.15 says that 'we' came to Miletus, I assume the author is present for Paul's speech in Miletus as he goes on to use 'we' when the leaders depart from Miletus (Acts 21.1). The speech itself uses the third person which is appropriate as Paul is the one giving the speech. This ensures that the narrative maintains a clear focus on Paul rather than the body of travelling companions.

The passage falls into two basic sections with the first centering on introductory remarks (vv. 18-27) including an announcement of his departure and future suffering (vv. 22-25), while the second section contains exhortations and farewell material (vv. 28-35). Verse 28 opens the second half of the speech where Paul calls the leaders to faithfulness, diligence and wisdom. He starts this call with the central motif of the leader as shepherd of the flock, the church of God.

The speech is Paul's *Abschiedsrede* and it shows similarities to Jacob's farewell speech in Genesis 49, Joshua's in Joshua 23–24 and, as Witherington notes, especially that of Samuel in 1 Samuel 12. There are also some shared parallels with

126. See Paul Trebilco, *The Early Christians in Ephesus from Paul to Ignatius* (WUNT, 166; Tübingen: Mohr Siebeck, 2004), pp. 172-6.

127. Beverly Roberts Gaventa, *The Acts of the Apostles* (ANTC; Nashville: Abington Press, 2003), p. 291.

128. Darrell L. Bock, *Acts* (BECNT; Grand Rapids: Baker Academic, 2007), p. 15; F. F. Bruce, *The Book of Acts* (Grand Rapids: Eerdmans, rev. ed, 1988), p. 388; Walton, *Leadership*, p. 12; Ben Witherington III, *The Acts of the Apostles: A Socio-Rhetorical Commentary* (Grand Rapids: Eerdmans, 1998), pp. 52-4; Gaventa, *Acts*, p. 57; Colin J. Hemer, *The Book of Acts in the Setting of Hellenistic History* (ed. Conrad H. Gempf; WUNT, 49; Tübingen: Mohr [Paul Siebeck], 1989), pp. 312-34; David Wenham, 'The Purpose of Luke-Acts: Israel's Story in the Context of the Roman Empire', in *Reading Luke: Interpretation, Reflection, Formation* (eds Craig G. Bartholomew, Joel B. Green and Anthony C. Thiselton; Scripture and Hermeneutics Series 6; Grand Rapids: Zondervan, 2005), pp. 81-2.

129. See E. Haenchen, *The Acts of the Apostles: A Commentary* (trans. B. Noble et al.; Oxford: Basil Blackwell, 1971), p. 85; Richard I. Pervo, *Acts: A Commentary* (Hermeneia; Minneapolis: Fortress Press, 2009), pp. 5-7; Mikeal C. Parsons, *Acts* (ΠΑΙΔΕΙΑ; Grand Rapids: Baker Academic, 2008), pp. 238-40; Hemer, *Book of Acts*, p. 319; Joseph A. Fitzmyer, *The Acts of the Apostles: A New Translation with Introduction and Commentary* (AB, 31; New York: Doubleday, 1998), pp. 98-103.

Jesus' speech to his disciples in Luke 22.14-38 which give some credence to the Gospel–Acts parallels Tannehill and Talbert have found.[130] Most farewell speeches come close to one's death, and yet Paul is still far from death at this point. As Trebilco points out, in 1 Samuel 12, Samuel's speech is not close to his death either, making a classification of farewell speech still the most likely.[131]

The speech is addressed to the Christian community and is more epistle-like than apologetic or evangelistic. While the speech is to the *Ephesian* church leaders, it is believed that the content is of a universal nature for the church. Witherington views the speech as a Lukan summary of the Pauline message to Christians, and Trebilco that, 'the Ephesian elders are almost certainly representatives of the whole church and in particular of its leaders'.[132] In agreement with Walton and more latterly Holmås, we note that here Paul passes on the model of Christian discipleship and leadership taught and loved by Jesus.[133]

While this *Abschiedsrede* is accepted to be predominantly Lukan in language and style,[134] Luke's text uses many words and phrases of Paul's teaching as recorded in his epistles.[135] Our concern therefore is whether the shepherd language is Lukan or Pauline. In these verses the church is called ποίμνιον (vv. 28, 29), and the ἐπίσκοποι are called to shepherd (ποιμαίνειν) the church or gathering of God (v. 28).[136] Paul continues by warning the ἐπίσκοπους of savage wolves, probably false teachers who will try and hurt the flock from within (v. 29). As he concludes

130. Talbert, *Literary Patterns*, pp. 15–23, 58–63; Tannehill, *Narrative Unity*, 1: 1–9.

131. See Witherington, *Acts*, pp. 612–16; Trebilco, *Early Christians*, pp. 176–7.

132. Witherington, *Acts*, p. 615; Trebilco, *Early Christians*, p. 177.

133. Walton, *Leadership*, pp. 134–6; Holmås, *Prayer and Vindication*, p. 237.

134. Lambrecht lists forty-six examples of Lukan language and style. J. Lambrecht, 'Paul's Farewell Address at Miletus (Acts 20:17-38)', in *Les actes des apôtres. Traditions redactions, théologie* (ed. J. Kremer; Gembloux: J. Duculot, 1979), p. 325; Witherington, *Acts*, p. 611; Trebilco, *Early Christians*, p. 177.

135. Many scholars agree that there are distinctively Pauline language and themes. Bruce, *Acts*, p. 387; Luke Timothy Johnson, *The Acts of the Apostles* (SP, 5; Collegeville: Liturgical Press, 1992), p. 367; Parsons, *Acts*, p. 290; Witherington, *Acts of the Apostles*, p. 610; Trebilco, *Early Christians*, p. 177.

136. The ἐπίσκοπος in this passage is some form of leader in the church, while Luke uses πρεσβύτερος in v. 17 as he calls for the Ephesian leaders to come to Miletus. The terms appear to be used interchangeably alongside ποιμαίνειν, and functionally means the same. Ehrman notes that there is no mention of plural ἐπίσκοποι in 1, 2 Clement or the Shepherd of Hermas. Hans Conzelmann, *The Acts of the Apostles* (Hermeneia; Philadelphia, Fortress, 1987), p. 173; Bruce, *Acts*, p. 392; Trebilco, *Early Christians*, p. 187; Gaventa, *Acts*, p. 284; Paul W. Walaskay, *Acts* (WBC; Louisville: Westminster John Knox Press, 1998), p. 189; Bart D. Ehrman (ed.) (trans.), *The Apostolic Fathers Vol. 1: 1 Clement, 2 Clement, Ignatius, Polycarp, Didache* (LCL; Cambridge, Mass: Harvard University Press, 2003), pp. 27, 159; Bart D. Ehrman (ed.) (trans.) *The Apostolic Fathers Vol. 2: Epistle of Barnabas, Papias and Quadratus, Epistle to Diognetus, The Shepherd of Hermas* (LCL; Cambridge, Mass: Harvard University Press, 2003), p. 27.

the speech, Paul specifies that the leaders should use him as an example and support the weak (v. 35). This is not direct shepherd language, but in the context of the speech describes the responsibility of the shepherd to the most vulnerable of the community, the weak. Therefore the motif is not restricted to vv. 28–29 but extends to v. 35, underpinning Paul's final words to the leaders.

Furthermore, Luke seems to be using the image carefully and with some theological weight in v. 28 as he draws attention to the Holy Spirit who has given these individuals their leadership role, and also that in some way Jesus' blood has purchased or obtained the church. The role of the Holy Spirit in birthing the church in Acts is pervasive beginning in Acts 1.8 and on the day of Pentecost and this speech presents the Spirit's role in appointing leaders.[137] The use of περιποιέω (preserve, obtain, acquire)[138] carries with it an echo of Israel as the elect people from 2 Kingdoms 12.3, Isaiah 43.12 and Malachi 3.17, and so gives an elevated theological sense to Paul's words.[139] Barrett describes the verse as 'both the practical and theological centre of the speech'.[140] It is noteworthy that this statement also reflects the three members of the Godhead,[141] and while not yet a formula, we find the efficacy of the cross (the Son), the work of the Holy Spirit, and the church of God. Therefore within a single statement where the speech moves from Paul's suffering and ministry into a hortatory plea by Paul to the leaders, Luke provides a vignette of the Godhead at work. The shepherd motif in this verse is therefore of all the more relevance and significance. But whose language are we hearing? Luke is recording a speech of Paul's, and as a probable eyewitness to this event, we need to consider if this is simply Pauline language or if this is a Lukan redaction.

This shepherding language has not been a major focus of any particular study in this speech, and it is generally considered that the shepherd language in the Miletus speech is neither Pauline nor Lukan.[142] However, Lambrecht's analysis of this text finds forty-six words or phrases reflecting Luke's hand and includes ποίμνιον (vv. 28, 29),[143] and Walton also notes ποίμνιον as one of the Lukan linguistic features which point to 'substantial parallels in Luke 12, 21 and especially 22'.[144]

Luke uses ποίμνιον in Luke 12.32 with an echo of Ezekiel 34. Paul, on the other

---

137. This should not be understood as invalidating Paul and Barnabas who selected leaders in Acts 14.23 through prayer and fasting, and so were drawing on the guidance of the Spirit.

138. 'περιποιέω', BDAG, p. 804.

139. Johnson, *Acts*, p. 363.

140. C. K. Barrett, *A Critical and Exegetical Commentary on the Acts of the Apostles* (ICC; Edinburgh: T&T Clark, 1998), 2, p. 974.

141. The language of trinity was not known by Luke or Paul.

142. Trebilco, *Early Christians*, p. 189.

143. Lambrecht, 'Paul's Farewell Address', p. 325. A foundational study on the language in Acts is Jacques Dupont, *Études sur les actes des apôtres* (Lectio Divina, 45; Paris: Éditions du Cerf, 1967).

144. Walton, *Leadership*, pp. 126, 135.

hand, does not use ποίμνιον or cognates except in 1 Corinthians 9.7 and Ephesians 4.11. The passage in 1 Corinthians is a simple visual metaphor and not theological, while the writer of Ephesians does express the role of pastor (ποιμήν) in a list of ministries in the body of Christ showing his acceptance of the term in the church.[145] The word is also used in 1 Peter 5.2, 3, reflecting 1 Peter closely,[146] and by Clement in *1 Clement* 16.1; 57.2, where he appeals at length to Isaiah 53, where there is a pastoral metaphor which he uses in his plea for unity. While the motif therefore was seen as relevant by Paul, he did not use it often and others used it more.

It is further likely that ποίμνιον should be considered an emphasis of Luke, as there are parallels between Luke 12.1-53 and the Miletus speech that extend well beyond this pastoral motif. In Walton's examination he notes the shared themes of leadership, suffering, and money and also other verbal parallels including the use of ποίμνιον.[147] He concludes that while one or two parallels could be considered coincidental, the 'several clear-cut verbal parallels' clustered together lead us to take seriously the likelihood of conceptual parallels'.[148]

Scholars have pointed out the deliberate parallels between Jesus and Paul in the Gospel and Acts respectively, and these appear to be evident in the Miletus speech. In the speech, we find Paul is the suffering servant who is heading to Jerusalem (Acts 20.24), and whom the Holy Spirit says will be imprisoned and persecuted. The link is often made between the ministry of Jesus in the Gospel and Paul in Acts, and therefore this *Abschiedsrede* is compared to Luke 22.14-38 when Jesus farewells and warns his disciples before his death.[149] Both Jesus' and Paul's journeys are to Jerusalem; their speeches talk of coming suffering/death (Lk. 22.15-16, 21-22; Acts 20.22-25, 38), contain warnings of coming temptations (Lk. 22.31-34; Acts 20.29-30), exhortation to lead well (Lk. 22.26-30, 32; Acts 20.28, 35), talk of the kingdom (Lk. 22.29-30; Acts 20.25), and note the compassionate care shown by Jesus and Paul to their community (Lk. 22.19, 27, 32; Acts 20.35).[150] These Jesus–Paul parallels further suggest that the shepherding language in the Miletus speech may be an emphasis of Luke.

Furthermore, in Jesus' *Abschiedsrede* Luke quotes Isaiah 53.12 in Luke 22.37, stating that this scripture informs Jesus' death. The wider passage of Isaiah 53 uses a pastoral motif (Isa. 53.6-8) and if this wider passage is in some way in view, then

---

145. Pauline authorship of Ephesians is in doubt. Charles H. Talbert, *Ephesians and Colossians* (ΠΑΙΔΕΙΑ; Grand Rapids: Baker Academic, 2007), pp. 7–11; Andrew T. Lincoln, *Ephesians* (WBC, 42; Dallas: Word, 1990), pp. ix–xxiii.

146. Johnson, *Acts*, pp. 362–3.

147. Walton, *Leadership*, pp. 118–27.

148. Ibid., p. 127.

149. Witherington, *Acts*, p. 612; Walton, *Lifestyle*, p. 134; Tannehill, *Narrative Unity*, 1: 253; Talbert, *Literary Patterns*, pp. 15–23.

150. Walton notes four themes paralleled: (1) suffering to come (Lk. 22.15, 28, 31f, 37; Acts 20.22-24); (2) efficacy of the death of Jesus (Lk. 22.19f; Acts 20.28); (3) leadership (Lk. 22.24-30; Acts 20.28); and (4) money (Lk. 22.35f; Acts 20.33-35). Walton, *Leadership*, p. 100.

we have a link, albeit not a very close one, where both Acts 20.28 and the farewell speech use a similar motif.

These factors add to a body of evidence that suggests the use of the shepherd motif can be considered Lukan; and in the Miletus speech, Luke, as an eyewitness, is translating what Paul actually said with pastoral language. Luke has used the shepherd motif for Jesus and now for the leaders of the church who seek to proclaim him. While this is the only use of the motif in Acts, it is also the only time we have a formal address to the church leaders.

Luke appears to use the motif of shepherd because of its relevance for the church and its leaders. With our understanding of Luke's significant use of allusions and echoes of scripture, this should come as no surprise, as we know how pervasive the motif is in the OT for leaders of Israel. In particular, we know the value Luke places on Jesus as the Davidic shepherd king from the infancy narrative, and we are coming to see how Luke works this motif into his presentation of Jesus' life as the seeking and saving shepherd of the lost sheep.

There also seems to be a particular level of resonance with Ezekiel 34's call to the leaders of Israel to shepherd the flock of God. In this chapter the prophet shows the faithful shepherd to be the one who provides not only for the needs of the sheep, but also protects them from wild animals (Ezek. 34.6, 8, 22, 25, 28, 29). This echoes the warning of the Lukan Paul regarding the savage wolves who will come in among the flock (Acts 20.29), and that some from even their own group will distort the truth (Acts 20.30). While Luke 10.3 has implied wolves come from outside the disciples' group, Acts 20.29 is clear that people from among them will threaten the safety of the flock. In the Pastoral Epistles and Revelation we learn that such problems did take hold in the church at Ephesus (1 Tim. 1.19-20; 4.1-3; 2 Tim. 2.17-18; 3.1-9; Rev. 2.4), although in Ignatius' letter to the church a short time later the church was doing well.[151] The ongoing relevance of this shepherd motif for the church is evident in other writers including Peter and Clement, bishop of Rome.

Paul says in the speech that he is an example for the leaders to follow and in particular calls them to support the weak (Acts 20.35). Walton has demonstrated Luke's presentation of Paul who embodies and personifies a Christian leadership model taught and lived by Jesus,[152] to which we add being a faithful shepherd as described in Ezekiel 34.16. We have seen Jesus in this role, so too we find Paul imitating Jesus.

(1) Luke shows Paul feeding the sheep through preaching and teaching in Perga (Acts 13.16-41), Iconium (14.1-3), Derbe (14.21-22), Antioch (15.35), Thessalonica (17.1-4), Ephesus (19.8-10), Beroea (17.10-12), Corinth (18.11), Jerusalem (21.17-20) and Rome (28.17-31).

(2) He shows Paul gathering the scattered sheep through Paul's mission to

---

151. Ignatius, *To The Ephesians* 1, pp. 1-2, p. 1.
152. Walton, *Leadership*, pp. 134–6.

the Gentiles (Acts 13.46), his encounter with Lydia at Philippi (16.14-15), the Philippian jailer (16.25-34), and with the Athenian idol worshippers (17.16-34). In this we see that there is now clearly a gospel for all people and it has broadened out from the Gospel narrative where we saw the mission prefigured (2.32; 10.1-24). The lost sheep are not simply from Israel but all nations.

(3) Paul binds up the crushed when he heals the crippled man at Lystra (Acts 14.8-10), the sick in Ephesus and Malta (19.11-12; 28.7-9), and brings Eutychus back to life (20.8-10).

(4) Paul supports the weak when he has Timothy circumcised because of the Jews (Acts 16.3), he responds to the Macedonian call (16.9), undergoes the rite of purification in Jerusalem (21.24-26), and speaks Hebrew to the Jews (22.2).

(5) Luke shows Paul watching the strong when he encounters the magician Elymas (Acts 13.8-12), engages with the council at Jerusalem (15.1-5), the slave girl (16.16-18) and the seven sons of Sceva (19.11-20).

(6) We see Paul going to the Jews even after he turns to the Gentiles (Acts 14.1; 16.13; 17.1; 18.4; 19.8; 21.15-26) so that at the end of the narrative Paul is still engaging with the Jews (28.17), trying to gather in the scattered sheep.

Therefore, Paul can say with confidence to the Ephesian elders that he has been an example to them in the ministry he has faithfully carried out. This faithfulness is best described as a shepherd of the flock. The call to the elders is then endorsed by a quote of Jesus, adding an authoritative stamp to Paul's plea (Acts 20.35). Having established the church, his desire is for it to be strengthened and kept safe from wolves that would come among the flock and scatter it.

4.5 Luke's omissions

Mark uses two shepherd sayings which Luke omits (Mk 6.34; 14.27). If the shepherd motif is so important to Luke, why has he done this?

Mark 6.34

Mark 6.34 says that Jesus, seeing a great crowd, 'had compassion for them, because they were like sheep without a shepherd', and so he began to teach them. The context for this saying is the feeding of the five thousand and the teaching Jesus refers to is the object lesson in the five loaves and two fish. This immediately precedes Luke's 'great omission' of 6.45–8.27.

Luke also records Jesus feeding the five thousand, while his setting says 'he welcomed them, and spoke to them about the kingdom of God, and healed those who needed to be cured' (Lk. 9.11). Thus Luke's account draws attention to his well-known interests of welcome and hospitality, the kingdom of God and healing,[153] while it does not use the 'sheep without a shepherd' reference which draws on Numbers 27.17; 1 Kings 22.17 and possibly Ezekiel 34.5.[154] Why did Luke not use this shepherd reference?

First, it is intriguing that with access to Mark's Gospel and an interest in the shepherd motif, Luke has not chosen to make use of this saying. Undoubtedly it would have been helpful to this study if he had done so; however, I will go on to argue that the shepherd motif is not far from the surface of Luke's text, that this omission does not downplay his later use of the motif in the travel narrative (10.3, 12.32; 15.1-7, 19.10), and that this saying which expresses concern over the lack of a shepherd was not relevant for Luke, as Jesus functions as the faithful shepherd by carrying out shepherding tasks. What this also confirms is that, as we suggested at the outset of the argument, Luke presents a range of christologies rather than a single christology, and it appears that in the Lukan Jesus' Galilaean ministry, it is not a motif Luke specifically used.

It is also helpful to note that the relationship between Mark and Luke in these passages 'is complicated',[155] and there is the possibility that Mark and Luke had access to different sources, while we acknowledge that even if this is a Lukan redaction, Luke has made choices which reflect his own special interests.[156] This is true of Mark as well as Luke. Stein concludes that Mark's reference to teaching (6.30) and its use to introduce a miracle story (6.34) show his redactional work as illustrated in Mark 1.21-22,[157] while Bovon notes that Luke replaces the shepherd allusion with the introduction of healings.[158]

The content of Luke's feeding story is set within the context of welcome (ἀποδέχομαι), healing, and the kingdom of God, which are actions of the Davidic shepherd. For example, Jesus' welcome is often salvific and in the context of this feeding story (9.10-17), it is helpful to remember that Ezekiel's Davidic shepherd had a distinct call to feed the sheep. We have seen that Ezekiel 34 lies behind Luke 12.32 and 15.1-7, which are also both feeding stories, and this will be reinforced with Zacchaeus dining with Jesus in 19.1-10. Therefore, while Luke does not use Mk 6.34 in his feeding story, he does cast Jesus as the Davidic shepherd who compassionately feeds people.

Further, it is quite possible that the reference to Jesus healing in Luke 9.11 indirectly points to the Davidic shepherd whose charge is to heal the sick sheep (Ezek. 34.4, 16). As Bovon has suggested, Luke replaces the shepherd motif of Mark with the motif of Jesus healing,[159] perhaps because by his actions in healing the people, he perceives Jesus as the faithful shepherd who is diligently

153. Bock, *Luke*, p. 829.

154. Robert A. Guelich, *Mark* (WBC, 34A; Dallas: Word, 1998), p. 340.

155. Fitzmyer, *Luke*, p. 762.

156. Bock, *Luke*, p. 829; Fitzmyer, *Luke*, pp. 762–4.

157. Robert H. Stein, *Mark* (BECNT; Grand Rapids: Baker Academic, 2008), p. 309.

158. Bovon, *Lukas 1*, p. 467.

159. Ibid.

caring for the needs of the sheep. Thus Mark's sentiment that the crowd are without a shepherd is not true for Luke. The people had a faithful shepherd leader in Jesus.

Similarly Luke's setting tells us that Jesus is speaking about the kingdom of God. The kingdom is of primary importance for Luke with the first reference to it coming in relation to the Davidic throne (1.33) and with the ongoing knowledge that it is not a kingdom of this world (4.5) but a Davidic kingdom of peace and salvation (2.8-14). The term ἡ βασιλεία τοῦ θεοῦ is used repeatedly by Luke; it is the purpose of Jesus' ministry (4.43) and in the forty days between Jesus' resurrection and ascension, it is singled out as the topic of Jesus' teaching (Acts 1.3). We have seen that Luke presents a particular perspective on the nature of the kingdom in Luke 1–2, and particularly in the birth narrative and genealogy; the kingdom which the Davidic baby represents is heralded by an army of heavenly beings rather than the military might of Rome, and is marked by its repetitive use of the language of shepherd and points to a kingdom of divine peace supported by a Micah echo. Therefore, any discussion of kingdom, even in Luke's feeding story, is coloured by this Davidic shading.

Finally, the question of omission must be balanced with the acknowledgement that while Luke has not employed the shepherd motif in the Galilaean ministry, he uses it repeatedly and at key places in the travel narrative where we find the bulk of Luke's own material. Perhaps Luke considered this motif as most helpful in his journey section where Jesus the Shepherd, like Moses the shepherd, led God's people in the exodus.

Mark 14.27

In 14.27 Mark quotes Zechariah 13.7, in which Jesus warns his disciples that they will desert him, saying: 'I will strike the shepherd, and the sheep will be scattered.' This is another direct shepherd saying which Luke omits. We know that Luke favours echoes and allusions over quotes, and so including a quote is less likely, yet on the occasion of his passion narrative, Luke breaks with his predominant pattern and quotes Isaiah 53.12 in Luke 22.37. In Acts 8.32-33 we will find another extended quotation from Isaiah 53.7-8 which Philip uses to point to Jesus.

I suggest that instead of using Zechariah 13.7, Luke has chosen to form part of his passion story around the servant passage in Isaiah, a prophet he turns to at significant narrative junctures. For example, John the Baptist's ministry is qualified through Isaiah 40.3-5 (Lk. 3.3-6), Jesus' ministry is described in Isaianic terms (Lk. 4.18-19; Isa. 61.1-2), and one way Jesus' death is interpreted is through Isaiah 53's suffering servant figure (Lk. 22.37; Acts 8.32-33). There are three quotations in Acts,[160] with Luke quoting Isaiah's own call narrative (Isa. 6.9-10) at the conclusion of Acts (Acts 28.26-27). Mallen has recently demonstrated the

---

160. Acts 7.49-50 (Isa. 66.1-2); Acts 8.32-33 (Isa. 53.7-8); Acts 28.26-27 (Isa. 6.9-10).

pervasive force of Isaiah in Luke-Acts and especially in Jesus' ministry,[161] and it is likely that Luke has turned to Isaiah rather than Jeremiah in his passion account.

In Isaiah 53 we also find pastoral language, as we do in Zechariah. We find the sheep that is led to slaughter and the lamb which is silent before his shearers (Isa. 53.7; Acts 8.7). This resonates with Luke's travel narrative where Jesus, on God's mission, journeys (or is led) to Jerusalem, and it certainly typifies Jesus who is silent before Herod (Lk. 23.9). In Chapter 6, I signal this as an area for further study, since the pastoral language in this servant song is related to this shepherd study, while outside its parameters. Isaiah 53 pictures the servant through the motif of a sheep who becomes a sinless offering on behalf of the sinful. This thematic link correlates with Luke's gospel which is about the forgiveness of sins (Lk. 1.77; 3.3; 5.17-26, 32; 7.36-50; 11.4; 24.47) and with Jesus who is declared δίκαιος at his death (23.47).[162] Therefore, there is a considerable likelihood that this servant figure may lie behind some ideas in Luke's passion narrative.

At the heart of my proposal is the realization that ἄνομος in Luke 22.37, which is usually translated 'transgressor', is used in parallelism with ἁμαρτωλός, which is translated 'sinner' in the OT (Ps. 31.5; Isa. 6.7). If we read that Jesus is counted among the ἄνομον (sinful) yet dies as δίκαιον (righteous), does this present an atoning picture? Further in 22.7 when it was necessary for the passover lamb to be slain, is there more at stake than simply the actions of a faithful Jew who carried out the festival requirements? In some way does Luke perceive a role for Jesus as the passover lamb, and is his death necessary in some way for the gospel of forgiveness? Is the Lukan Jesus God's pastoral offering who is counted among the sinful and carries the sin of many (Isa. 52.12)?

If so, this complements our motif and strengthens the reason why he chose not to use the quote from Zechariah from Mark.

4.6 Summary

In this chapter we have seen four repetitions of the Davidic shepherd king motif. First, we saw how Jesus sent the seventy disciples out like lambs in the midst of wolves as a shepherd in the household mission. We noted how prominent this passage was due to its placement near the beginning of the travel narrative and its mission which prefigures the Acts household conversion narratives into Gentile territory. While God sends Jesus (10.16), Jesus also sends the disciples (10.3), and as both are shepherds this prefigures a future role for them as shepherds of the flock. This is a motif Luke uses in the Miletus speech. We also noted that Isaiah 40.11 and Ezekiel 34 were behind the motif, and the shepherd from Ezekiel especially had a focus on eating.

161. Mallen, *Reading*. Also Sanders, 'Isaiah in Luke', p. 20; Koet, 'Isaiah in Luke-Acts', p. 80.

162. In the passion narrative Jesus is also repeatedly found not guilty of his charges (23.4, 14-15, 22).

Secondly, in Luke 12.32 we have a unique shepherd saying attached to a Q passage. Thus, we find the motif being used in Jesus' ministry years when he is teaching his disciples that it is God's nature to care and provide for his people. Jesus also describes his disciples as a *little flock* which situates him as the shepherd in the text. The passage is drawing on an echo to Ezekiel 34 where there is also a focus on the flock being fed, and where the Lord's Davidic shepherd is given the role of leading the flock.

Thirdly, we saw how the parable of the lost sheep focuses on the role of the faithful shepherd who seeks out the lost sheep, and so we renamed it 'the parable of the faithful shepherd'. We found it is most likely to be from Luke's own source due to its internal features and particularly its unity with the following two parables. The parable's setting helps the reader understand that the parable critiques the religious leaders who are grumbling at Jesus' table fellowship with toll collectors and sinners. The response of Pharisees and scribes causes Jesus to tell them the parable of the faithful shepherd, which is particularly appropriate to religious leaders whom scripture identifies as shepherds. This setting and parable together again suggest an echo of Ezekiel 34, where there is a strong critique of the shepherds of Israel who have looked after themselves and not the Lord's flock.

In the parable there is a vivid description of a faithful shepherd which Jesus enacts both in this particular encounter and on his journey to Jerusalem. The parable has a theological emphasis where we learn of God's care for his flock, and a christological emphasis where Jesus is the Lord's Davidic Shepherd. The placement of this parable at the midpoint of the Gospel and that it expresses the heart of the Third Gospel, certainly satisfies Freedman's criterion for a high efficacy for the motif. It also does seem to suggest that Luke has carefully wrapped text around this central point which makes the parable/s stand out as a call for the shepherds of Israel to seek out the lost sheep.

Finally, we saw the motif used in the Miletus speech in Acts 20 when Paul addresses the Ephesian church leaders. We noted that this speech is the only one recorded to Christians and it is likely that it was recorded by Luke for the benefit of all church leaders. The motif extended to the church of God as the 'flock' and the leaders as 'shepherds'. They are warned and encouraged to be faithful as Paul was faithful, and to be on their guard against false teachers who are described as wolves who will come among them to harm the flock. The motif is emphasized by the exposition of the Godhead and recalls Ezekiel 34. The Gospel shows Jesus who faithfully lives out Ezekiel's Davidic shepherd while in Acts, Paul mirrors such faithful actions and he calls other leaders to imitate him.

We have found four passages or sayings which are all unique to Luke and use the shepherd motif; Jesus is the faithful Davidic shepherd of Ezekiel 34, and the call is for leaders to act likewise – the motif holds currency for all. Even though Luke omitted Mark 6.34 and 14.27, these four shepherd passages still stand within Luke's narrative. They do not suggest this is Luke's predominant motif, but they are significant and show a previously unrecognized feature of the Lukan Jesus' earthly ministry.

5

JESUS, THE SEEKING AND SAVING DAVIDIC SHEPHERD

We have seen that the motif of the shepherd has continued in the Lukan narrative beyond the infancy narrative. Now we turn to the supreme example – the story of Zacchaeus, where Jesus is the Son of Man who has come to seek out and save that which is lost (19.10). We began this book by noting that Marshall believes this saying sums up the central message of the Gospel and Miura, that *Davidic Shepherd* imagery sums up the earthly ministry of Jesus in Luke 19.[1] Marshall's statement in particular implies that 19.10 expresses the *telos* or *fulfilment* of Jesus' ministry years and holds a semantic key for the Gospel. It is now time to test this statement out.

We will first discuss the summative nature of 19.10 and show how this pericope, to which the saying is attached, is so resonant with the wider Lukan narrative. We will note the placement of the narrative and its content and demonstrate that it is the *telos* of Jesus' *Reisebericht*.

Secondly, we will review what has been called the 'vindication' argument which suggests that Zacchaeus customarily gives away half his income and restores fourfold anyone from whom he has extorted money. This is an important debate as it casts a very different picture of Jesus as the Davidic shepherd king. If Jesus is showing that Zacchaeus is already a member of the kingdom community, then he does not need a saviour and Jesus' role as reaching to the margins for the sheep is significantly changed.

Thirdly, we will give a detailed exegesis of 19.1-10 showing how this pericope is a salvation story, where Jesus as a Davidic shepherd king seeks out and saves Zacchaeus. We will note that salvation begins in Zacchaeus' house, is multi-layered and affects many areas of his life. We will also see how salvation is shown to be fully universal in this pericope; it is open to both genders, and to all races and social classes.

Fourthly, we will consider what this adds to our knowledge of the Davidic shepherd king motif; and finally, we will consider what the summative nature of 19.10 means with regard to 4.18-19, the programmatic saying of the Gospel. We will suggest that Luke has two programmatic sayings: one at the beginning of his ministry years (4.18-19) and one at the end (19.10).

---

1. Marshall, *Historian and Theologian*, p. 116; Miura, *David*, p. 240.

5.1 The summative nature of 19.10

This study accepts that 19.10 has a summative role for the Gospel. Any narrative is cumulative and works toward a *telos* or goal in a storyline. While we acknowledge that stories have more than one climax and certainly Jesus' death, resurrection and ascension is paramount, other key places in the text are also important in reading the text. The story of Zacchaeus is Jesus' last encounter in his ministry years we suggest is one of those places.[2] Mark's final pericope is the healing of the blind beggar (Mk 10.46), but as Luke inserts the story of Zacchaeus after this healing story, his ending and narrative emphasis are quite unique. Luke's emphasis is now on the Davidic shepherd king who seeks out and saves the lost sheep.

Jesus' ministry begins formally when he is in the synagogue in Nazareth and this is where the accepted programmatic saying of the Gospel is located (4.18-19). The saying encapsulates the ministry of Jesus; that is, it tells the reader what the Lukan Jesus' ministry is; it is a mission to the poor, the captive, the blind, and the oppressed; it is a message in which the year of Jubilee is declared to bring hope to the poor. As the ministry of Lukan Jesus proceeds, there is encounter after encounter where Jesus enacts this mission statement (4.18-19). For example, we find many pericopae which deal with the poor and related topics such as wealth, women, and widows (4.25; 6.20-25; 7.11-16; 7.36-50; 12.13-34; 18.18-30). We see captives to sickness being released (5.12-16, 17-26; 8.26-39; 13.10-17), the blind seeing again (7.21-22; 18.35-43), and the oppressed going free (7.36-50). All of these categories overlap and express Luke's central theme of universal salvation. Salvation is available to all people regardless of gender, ethnicity, or social status. Ultimately we find these three key paradigms of universal salvation are all outworked in the story of Zacchaeus.

Luke has placed the Zacchaeus story in its immediate context carefully to parallel and contrast especially with the rich ruler (18.18-30), the healing of the blind man (18.35-43), and the parable of the Pharisee and the toll collector (18.9-14). It also has strong links with the earlier 'lost' parables, the healing of the crippled woman (13.10-17), the sending of the seventy, the sinful woman (7.36-50), the calling of Levi (5.27-32), and the birth narrative. While many Lukan stories could be said to have some parallels, the Zacchaeus story has so many linguistic and thematic resonances with other stories that this suggests the Zacchaeus story has a summative role for the Lukan narrative. Further, Luke seems to use these parallel stories to build a cumulative intratextual platform which helps the reader to be able to interpret the Zacchaeus pericope. I will demonstrate this now.

5.1.1 The rich ruler (18.18-30) and Zacchaeus

There are many parallel features between the Zacchaeus pericope and the story of the rich ruler. Both men are wealthy (18.23; 19.2), exercise rulership (18.18; 19.2),

---

2. The end of the travel narrative is generally accepted to be at 19.28 after the parable spoken in Zacchaeus' house (19.11).

and seek Jesus out (18.18; 19.3). The rich ruler asks Jesus a question (18.18) and Zacchaeus is seeking to see Jesus (19.3). Both are shown to have good intentions in approaching Jesus. The text notes that the rich ruler becomes περίλυπος when Jesus replies that as well as keeping the commandments he should sell his possessions and give the money to the poor (18.23), showing that his desire had been to follow Jesus' advice. Zacchaeus goes to great lengths to see Jesus by running ahead and climbing a tree, even though he may face further ridicule from the community in this act. Thus, he is able to overcome the obstacles of the crowd and his height[3] to gain a glimpse of Jesus as he passes by, and shows his good intentions in approaching Jesus. The stories therefore, bear much in common that link them together and this suggests they are related.

The rich ruler story is primarily about entering the kingdom (18.24) and the reader with the crowd wonders whether the rich can enter the kingdom of God when they hear Jesus' riddle (18.25) when the question is asked, 'Who then can be saved?' (18.26). No reply is given, only Jesus' words, 'What is impossible for mortals is possible for God' (18.27). The question is yet to be fully answered. Can a rich person enter the kingdom? The rich ruler seems unable to relinquish his possessions in keeping with the general tenor of Luke's presentation of the tyranny of wealth (6.24; 12.16-21, 34; 14.7-11, 15-24; 15.25-32; 16.19-31).

Maxwell notes that in 18.18-30, Luke has created a narrative gap for the reader to fill.[4] This gap creates a space where the audience must consider the plight of the rich and whether they can indeed be saved (18.26). This question is left hanging until Zacchaeus, a man who is rich, relinquishes his wealth (19.8); this is a literary twist, an unexpected event and gives the wider narrative a sense of closure. Aside from the women who support Jesus (8.1-3) who are given little narrative space, no rich person has managed to enter the kingdom. When Zacchaeus welcomes Jesus with joy this implies he has entered the kingdom, echoing in the reverse sense the story of the rich man.

As the two stories are tied together narratively, the first laying a platform for the second, we have evidence from the wider narrative that the Zacchaeus pericope is a salvation story. It is about Zacchaeus entering the kingdom.

5.1.2 *The blind man (18.35-43) and Zacchaeus*

The healing of the blind man also bears many parallels with the Zacchaeus pericope, and we note the first immediately precedes the second. The narrative links are the location in Jericho (18.35; 19.1), Jesus is passing by (18.37; 19.1), and the crowd forming a barrier to each individual (18.39; 19.3). Both men have

---

3. The text describes Zacchaeus as τῇ ἡλικίᾳ μικρός (19.3). ἡλικία can relate to age (Jn 9.21), maturity (Lk. 2.52) or bodily stature (Lk. 19.3). BDAG, pp. 435–6. In 19.3 it refers to height as it is a physical description unlike 2.52. Bock, *Luke,* p. 1517, n. 5; Fitzmyer, *Luke,* p. 1223.

4. Maxwell, *Hearing,* p. 145.

a salvific encounter (18.41-2;[5] 19.9), both show determination in reaching Jesus (18.39; 19.4) and demonstrate a good response to him (18.43; 19.6, 8). There are linguistic parallels in the use of ἵστημι (18.40; 19.8) and κύριος (18.41; 19.8). Both pericopae echo the Nazareth Manifesto; Jesus is named as Jesus of 'Nazareth' (18.37), and in 19.10 the content of the manifesto is recalled (see section 5.5). There is a Davidic connection with the blind man calling out υἱὲ Δαυίδ twice (18.38, 39) while in 19.10 there is a clear echo of Ezekiel's Davidic shepherd king who seeks out and saves the lost. There are also narrative contrasts which further suggest the two stories are linked. The central character in one is a beggar, while the other is rich (18.35; 19.2), and there is a spatial contrast where one is sitting down while one has climbed a tree and has an elevated position (18.35; 19.4). The result of each man's salvific encounter also illustrates different aspects of salvation: the blind man receives his sight[6] and Zacchaeus finds acceptance and salvation and responds with economic reform.[7]

The story of the blind man marks a return to the Davidic theme from the infancy narratives.[8] The blind man calls 'Son of David' twice, signalling a return to the infancy narrative's Davidic theme. The *primacy effect* has made readers sensitive to the Davidic motif. The Davidic shepherd king motif is recalled again in the story of Zacchaeus (19.10). This causal chain shows a clear ordering of the Lukan narrative and the Davidic motif as a *Leitwort*. This chain begins with the healing of the blind man and this sets the stage for Zacchaeus, the lost sheep (19.10), who will meet with the Davidic shepherd king.

5.1.3 The parable (18.9-14) and Zacchaeus

The Zacchaeus pericope is set in parallel to the parable of the Pharisee and the toll collector (18.9-14). Both pericopae have central characters who are τελῶναι (18.10; 19.2) and discuss money and possessions. In 18.12 the Pharisee states he gives a tithe of his income which is an assertion of his religious superiority,[9] and Zacchaeus is πλούσιος (19.2) and speaks of his ὑπαρχόντων (19.8). Both toll collectors demonstrate a Lukan ideal of true humility (18.13-14; 19.4, 6, 8). We see this in the parable when the toll collector distances himself in the temple and does not draw attention to himself but speaks to God. It is further evident in his

---

5. The blind man asks to receive his sight (18.41) and this fulfils 4.18. This is the only pericope where someone's sight is restored, although it has been implied in 7.21-22 and the blind are called to a feast in 14.13, 21 showing Jesus' care and concern for the blind. The blind man asks to receive his sight (18.41) and this fulfils 4.18.

6. Luke uses σῴζω here (18.42)

7. 19.9 uses σωτηρία. This is the only instance of the noun for salvation outside of the infancy narrative and in the John the Baptist pericope (3.6). With the theme of salvation being so prominent, this makes this a significant echo of the narrative beginnings where Jesus is the Saviour (2.11).

8. Nolland, *Luke*, p. 897.

9. Bock, *Luke*, p. 1464.

actions when he does not look up to heaven, but beats his breast and declares he is 'the sinner' (τῷ ἁμαρτωλῷ). Humility is seen in Zacchaeus when he risks ridicule in running to secure a place to see Jesus when he passes by, and also when Jesus speaks to him he responds with obedience, joy, and haste. Further, Zacchaeus shows humility when he does not respond to the crowds' charge in 19.7 but instead calls Jesus κύριος and gives half of his possessions away to the poor. Both characters are presented as people who are model respondents.[10]

The parable makes clear that a right relationship with God is not centred only in what we do with our money, but in our humility to God. In the parable we have a positive and negative example. The Pharisee practices tithing and fasting which are good religious practices, but are seen to be inadequate in themselves as right responses to God. The toll collector, conversely, is a model respondent as he humbles himself before God, acknowledging that he is a sinner and in need of God's mercy (18.13). This clear picture of a repentant sinner will help the reader interpret Zacchaeus' response as one of humility and repentance before Jesus to whom he responds (19.6) and acknowledges as κύριος (19.8).

The parable articulates how toll collectors are viewed by society; that is, they are viewed in the same way as thieves, the unrighteous, and adulterers. This setting will help the reader interpret why the crowd forms a barrier against Zacchaeus (19.3) and why they call him a sinner (19.7). The Pharisee will pejoratively judge the toll collector (18.11) and in the same way the crowd will judge Zacchaeus (19.7). The linguistic use of ἁμαρτωλός further ties the passages together (18.13; 19.7).

This parable makes clear a Lukan perspective relating to δίκαιος and ἁμαρτωλός which is crucial for the Lukan narrative as a whole and the Zacchaeus pericope in particular. The parable is told to those who think they are δίκαιοι (18.9), and the Pharisee will call the toll collector ἄδικος (18.11). The toll collector, however, will call himself ἁμαρτωλός using the definite article (18.13), and is declared δίκαιος (18.14).[11] The implication in the parable is that the one who thinks he is δίκαιος may be ἄδικος, but the one who acknowledges he is ἁμαρτωλός is justified and put right with God. This is the only Lukan pericope where someone calls themselves ἁμαρτωλός using the definite article and this is significant.[12] Thus, we have a toll collector acknowledging the full weight of his sin by calling himself 'the sinner'

---

10. Other examples of model respondents are Mary (2.38), the shepherds (2.15), the sinful women (7.38), and the leper who falls at Jesus' feet (17.15-16).

11. Wallace suggests that Luke's context points to the article functioning as *par excellence* rather than simple identification and the man 'is declaring that he is the worst of all sinners … This seems to fit well with the spirit of his prayer, for only the Pharisee explicitly makes a comparison with the other person present.' If it was simple identification then the tax collector is recognizing the presence of the Pharisee and making a distinction between the two of them. Daniel B. Wallace, *Greek Grammar Beyond the Basics: An Exegetical Syntax of the New Testament* (Grand Rapids: Zondervan, 1996), p. 223.

12. Simon Peter will call himself ἁμαρτωλός (5.8) without the definite article.

and as a result the reader finds him justified.[13] This supports Jesus' explanation of his mission at 5.32 that he has not come to call the righteous but sinners to repentance. The Pharisee sees himself as righteous, while the toll collector sees himself as the sinner, and thus, in his repentant plea to God, finds justification and the forgiveness of sins. This information will help the reader understand that Zacchaeus, the chief toll collector, also finds justification and the forgiveness of sins.

5.1.4 The crippled woman (13.10-17) and Zacchaeus

The story of the healing of the crippled woman also parallels the Zacchaeus story primarily because both stories contain specific classifications as a daughter or son of Abraham.[14] Aside from the genealogy which recalls Jesus' lineage and where we hear who is the son of whom (3.23-38), Luke only uses the phrase to describe Zacchaeus (υἱὸς Ἀβραάμ, 19.9). What Luke does do, however, is refer to the crippled woman in 13.16 as θυγατέρα Ἀβραάμ, an uncommon expression (4 Macc. 14.20; 15.28; 17.6; 18.20).[15] There are other interesting parallels, while also many differences.

Both stories are unique to Luke, centre on one person, use the Greek ἔδει/δεῖ (13.16; 19.5) and κύριος (13.15; 19.8), which convey a soteriological centre to each story. Both stories have a physiognomic aspect that plays a strategic role in the plot. The woman is bent and, according to physiognomic tradition, her condition would have been understood as moral.[16] Similarly, Zacchaeus' height could have been interpreted as reflecting a 'small spirit' or divine judgement.[17] Both stories involve plots where Jesus seeks out the person. In 13.12 Jesus approaches the woman, and Luke's use of ἀπολύω in the perfect, passive, indicative (ἀπολέλυσαι) indicates the divine agent of her healing; in 19.10 it is Jesus who seeks out Zacchaeus. Both stories also include a negative response to Jesus' encounter: in 13.14 the leader of the synagogue reacts to Jesus, and in 19.7 the crowd react to

13. This parable illustrates 16.14-15 where Jesus says to the Pharisees that they are those who justify (δικαιόω) themselves in the sight of others, but that God knows their hearts. As lovers of money they are indirectly revealed as an abomination in the sight of God.

14. Acts 13.26 talks about being a descendant of Abraham.

15. Mikeal C. Parsons, *Body and Character in Luke and Acts: the Subversion of Physiognomy in Early Christianity* (Grand Rapids: Baker Academic, 2006), p. 87.

16. Ibid., p. 86. Polemon the Platonic philosopher writes that 'if you see that the back is broad, it is an indication of mighty and strong men, and it indicates great anger. If it is the opposite of that, it indicates weakness and the contrary of what the broad and strong back indicated.' Richard Foerster (ed.), *Scriptores Physiognomonici Graeci et Latini* (Leipzig: Teubner, 1983), 2, p. 208.

17. Parsons, *Body and Character*, pp. 99, 101. Pseudo-Aristotle said: 'These are the marks of a small-minded person. He is small limbed, small and round, dry, with small eyes and a small face, like a Corinthian or Leucadian' (808a30).

Jesus. Finally, both stories contain an allusion to the LXX: 13.17 is a clear parallel to Isaiah 45.16[18] and 19.10 to Ezekiel 34.

These stories follow the Lukan pattern where there are parallel stories of a man and a woman, and the two stories demonstrate that salvation is universal for both genders. Both characters are on the edges of society and respond well to Jesus. Jesus is shown to be the one who releases the captive woman from the power of Satan echoing Isaiah 61.1-2 and Luke 4.18. Zacchaeus' salvation releases him from his estrangement from the community, while the use of σωτηρία (19.9) and σῴζω (19.10) also suggests a salvation that is transcendent.

5.1.5 The sinful woman (7.36-50) and Zacchaeus

The story of Zacchaeus and the sinful woman have clear parallels. They are both set in the context of hospitality (7.36; 19.5). Simon accuses the woman of being ἁμαρτωλός (7.39) and the crowd do likewise to Zacchaeus (19.7). The implication is that the woman and Zacchaeus are sinners because of their occupations (7.37; 19.2, 8). Jesus reveals Simon's attitude to the woman is wrong (7.40-47) and similarly, Jesus does this for the crowd who have ostracized Zacchaeus. Further, Simon's murmuring (7.39) and the crowd's murmuring about *Jesus* (19.7) are wrong. The woman anoints Jesus' feet with her tears and μυρόν, a very costly perfume (7.37-38) from an alabaster jar, and Zacchaeus makes a very costly resolve with his money (19.8). When the woman enters the Pharisees' house and responds to Jesus with tears and anoints his feet, she faces public ridicule. Similarly, when Zacchaeus climbs the tree and responds to Jesus publicly, he lays himself open to public humiliation. There are also linguistic parallels in the salvific language of σῴζω/ σωτηρία (7.50; 19.9, 10). We again have a story of a man and a woman, although this is not the focus of the parallel.

Both narratives reveal that the characters have been forgiven a great debt. The parable of the two debtors describes the scale of the woman's debt (7.41-42), and the use of the ὅτι (7.47) shows the link between her debt and her love. As Jesus says to Simon, 'Therefore, I tell you, her sins, which were many, have been forgiven; for (ὅτι) she has shown great love' (7.47). Zacchaeus' debt is shown in his costly resolve (19.8). The parable in the sinful woman story lays the platform to interpret Zacchaeus' resolve with his money as one who has been forgiven a great debt and so generously gives half of his money away. In both stories, therefore, we see Jesus in the role of saviour of sinners. Zacchaeus' level of generosity causes the reader to hear the echo of this story and Jesus' words that 'her sins are forgiven' (7.48).

5.1.6 Levi (5.27-32) and Zacchaeus

The calling of Levi and the following banquet also parallels the Zacchaeus story. Both characters in the narratives, Levi and Zacchaeus, are toll collectors. Jesus

---

18. Bock, *Luke*, p. 1219; Fitzmyer, *Luke*, p. 1014; Marshall, *Gospel*, p. 559; Nolland, *Luke*, p. 725.

calls Levi to follow him and he does so immediately (5.27-28) and so does Zacchaeus (19.5-6). The narratives involve table-fellowship and both have crowds listening to the proceedings (5.29; 19.3, 7). The Pharisees and scribes grumble (5.30) and so do the crowds (19.7). The setting for Levi's banquet implies rejoicing (5.29) and Zacchaeus rejoices (19.6). Repentance (μετάνοια) in the Levi story suggests a reorienting of his life around God's purposes,[19] while 5.28 implies that he does not give up all his possessions.[20] In the same way Zacchaeus' welcome of Jesus does not mean he gives up all of his possessions, though he does give up a sizeable portion that suggests he reorients his life to reflect God's care for the poor (19.8). Most importantly, each pericope ends with significant mission statements from Jesus' lips and 19.10 recalls the earlier 5.32.[21]

There is a narrative contrast as Levi leaves his job as toll collector while Zacchaeus does not. Further, Luke uses the language of μετάνοια in the story of Levi, but only implies it through the gaps in the Zacchaeus story. This gap is 'logically constrained to the text'[22] and cohesive within the narrative, which are criteria that support the parallels and contrasts in 5.27-32 and 19.1-10. These links coupled with the language of μετάνοια in 5.32 helps the reader interpret Zacchaeus' response to Jesus as one of repentance.

5.1.7 Summary

Luke 19.1-10 works in parallel with many other Lukan Gospel stories. Its language, style and content resonate with many other pericopae, making it a pivotal story in the wider narrative. It completes the sense of universal salvation through the story of the rich ruler (the rich can be saved), the story of the crippled women (both genders can be saved), and the story of the sending of the seventy (all ethnicities can be saved). The stories lay an interpretative base with which we can fully understand the story of Zacchaeus. Jesus is the one who has come to call sinners to repentance (5.29-32), he forgives the repentant sinner (7.36-50), he brings transcendent salvation to households (10.1-24), and salvation is universal and comes to both men and women (13.10-17). Further, Jesus exalts the sinner who humbles himself (18.9-14), he shows us that salvation is not just about what we do with our wealth but about our relationship with God (18.18-25), and as the Son of David he brings salvific sight (18.35-43). Jesus is the Davidic shepherd king (18.38, 39; 19.10) and a faithful shepherd who seeks out the lost sheep. To understand the message of Zacchaeus, it must be read within the context of the character and mission of Jesus throughout his ministry. Luke has painted a

19. Green, *Gospel,* p. 246.

20. Luke 5.28 states Levi left everything, but then in 5.29 he gives a banquet for Jesus. This tension in the text is resolved by understanding that it does not simply mean giving away all his possessions, but a fundamental reorienting of purpose around Jesus and his mission as physician to the sinner.

21. Adams, *Sinner,* p. 171.

22. Eagleton, *Literary Theory,* p. 73.

cohesive picture where one story illuminates another, and culminates in 19.1-10. It is an ordered narrative where beginnings and progression build to a significant climax; a story with gaps and blanks to engage the reader and a story which ends with an important mission statement (19.10): the Son of Man has come to seek and save the lost.

The placement of the Zacchaeus pericope at the end of the travel narrative suggests its narrative's importance, and further, by inserting this pericope into the Markan outline, Luke gives the reader a unique end to Jesus' journey to Jerusalem. Jesus enters Jerusalem as the Davidic shepherd king who brings salvation to all, and especially to those on the margins of society.

5.2 Zacchaeus – the saint (a vindication reading)

The nature of the Zacchaeus pericope has given rise to various form critical classifications,[23] and here we will examine the debate which surrounds the classification of 19.1-10 as a vindication story.

The centre of the controversy stems from v. 8 where the question is asked how to best interpret δίδωμι and ἀποδίδωμι. These verbs are written in the present active indicative and have traditionally been read as futuristic presents; however the verbs can equally be read as simple present iterative verbs showing Zacchaeus' customary action. This debate is important because it affects a Lukan theology of salvation which, in turn, affects a reading of the Davidic shepherd king in the narrative. A vindication reading pushes towards a works-based theology with an emphasis on what we do to achieve salvation and where the human sinful condition is underplayed. In so doing, it does not recognize the need of a cosmic Saviour and we find Jesus in the role of a life coach. A salvation reading, on the

---

23. Bultmann classifies the story as a 'biographical apophthegm' because of the many details given about Zacchaeus; Conzelmann, Hamm and Kariamadam, a 'conversion story'; Fitzmyer and Nolland, probably a 'pronouncement story' with a climax in 19.9 when Jesus announces, 'Salvation has come to this house today, because he too is a son of Abraham'; Talbert a 'quest type of pronouncement story'; Marshall and Dibelius that it is a 'personal legend' with an historical core; O'Toole and Tannehill a 'quest story'; Mitchell a 'vindication story'; and Ravens classifies it as a salvation by vindication story. See Bultmann, *Synoptic Tradition*, pp. 55–7; Conzelmann, *Theology of St. Luke*, p. 229; Dennis Hamm, 'Luke 19:8 Once Again: Does Zacchaeus Defend or Resolve', *JBL* 107 (1988): 436–7; P. Kariamadam, *The Zacchaeus Story Luke 19:1-10: A Redaction-Critical Investigation* (Kerala, India: Pontifical Institute of Theology and Philosophy, 1985), pp. 56–8; Fitzmyer, *Luke*, p. 1219; Nolland, *Luke*, p. 904; Talbert, *Reading Luke*, p. 205; M. Dibelius, *From Tradition to Gospel* (trans. B. L. Woolf; London: Ivor Nicholson and Watson, 1934), pp. 118, 293; Marshall, *Gospel*, p. 695; Robert F. O'Toole, 'Literary Form of Luke 19:1-10', *JBL* 110 (1991), pp. 107–16; Tannehill, *Narrative Unity*, 1, pp. 111–12; Alan C. Mitchell, 'Zacchaeus Revisited: Luke 19:8 as a Defense', *Biblica* 71 (1990): 153–76 ; D. A. S. Ravens, 'Zacchaeus: The Final Part of the Triptych?' *JSNT* 41 (1991): 19–32.

other hand, places an emphasis on the actions of God to initiate salvation and on human actions as a result of salvation. In this reading the Davidic shepherd really does have a seeking and saving role for the people of God.

Godet challenged the traditional view in the latter part of the nineteenth century when he saw the interpretative problem of translating ἀποδίδωμι as a futuristic present. While he could understand δίδωμι to mean 'as of now I give away', he queried what sense it would make to understand ἀποδίδωμι in the same way. If this was a salvation story then how do we understand a repentant sinner already making plans for what he would do to restore those he would defraud or extort money from?[24] The tension he sees is real, as there is an interpretative problem. In support of this view, Godet also suggests that Luke's use of σταθείς (19.8) denotes a firm and dignified attitude, which he proposes 'suits a man whose honour has been attacked'.[25] Furthermore, the use of ἰδού (19.8) heralds the unexpected revelation for the crowd rather than an expression of resolve. Godet's concerns have been reiterated and expanded as the following analysis demonstrates.

Fitzmyer, for example, also queried the traditional view.[26] First, Zacchaeus does not beg for mercy (17.13; 18.38) or express sorrow (15.21; 18.13) as one might expect in a salvation story. Secondly, Jesus makes no reference to Zacchaeus' faith (7.50; 8.48), repentance or conversion (15.7, 10), or discipleship. Fitzmyer, therefore, reads Jesus' pronouncement of salvation as unrelated to the forgiveness of sins, but argues Jesus' pronouncement is given to make sure the crowd understands that as a Jew, a son of Abraham, he has as much claim to salvation as any other Israelite. He refutes that Zacchaeus *has become*[27] a child of Abraham in a Pauline sense (Gal. 3.7, 29; Rom. 4.16-17) and yet reads v. 10 as summing up this episode as the 'soteriological message of the entire travel account and the Lucan Gospel'.[28] In the light of these features, and coupled with the present tense verbs of v. 8, he takes the thrust of this pericope to be Jesus' vindication for Zacchaeus' customary actions.

White also believes this pericope does not contain the necessary elements to make it a salvation story and that Luke is interested in vindicating Zacchaeus from a false stereotype that toll collectors are all corrupt.[29] He notes that first, there is no clear indication that Zacchaeus is a sinner and there is no mention of sin. Secondly, Zacchaeus' speech and behaviour are not contrite and self-effacing, such as in 8.40 where Jairus falls at Jesus' feet;[30] 15.21 where the prodigal son says he is no longer worthy to be called a son; or 18.13 where the toll collector

---

24. Godet, *St. Luke*, 2, pp. 217–18.

25. Ibid., 2, p. 217.

26. Fitzmyer, *Luke*, pp. 1220–1.

27. Fitzmyer says: 'This does not mean that Zacchaeus *has become* a child of Abraham in some spiritual sense (as in Pauline usage. Gal 3:7, 29; Rom 4:16-17)'. Ibid., p. 1221.

28. Ibid., p. 1221.

29. Richard C. White, 'Vindication for Zacchaeus?' *ExpTim* 91 (1979-80), p. 21.

30. I assume White means 8.41 where Jairus falls at Jesus' feet.

beats his breast and acknowledges himself a sinner. Thirdly, the story does not show deference to the power of Jesus nor a petition for his mercy (9.37; 17.13). Fourthly, the story does not contain a forgiveness pronouncement of Jesus that notes his faith (5.20; 7.47). Finally, White notes the observers do not react, either positively (5.26) or negatively (7.49), to the power of Jesus to effect change, which is a typically Lukan response.[31]

Mitchell believes Luke is trying to explode a false stereotype[32] and to show 'how salvation came to a loyal Jew … without necessarily implying that Jesus saw him as a sinner'.[33] At the heart of Mitchell's critique of a 'salvation reading' is a belief that salvation (σωτηρία) is not only about the forgiveness of sins, but also that salvation refers to the Davidic Messiah who rescues us from our enemies (1.69, 71), which he claims has nothing to do with sin and repentance.[34] He goes on to note that the Zacchaeus story lacks any reference to sin and repentance, and the programmatic verses (4.18-19) lack any reference to the forgiveness of sins.[35] Furthermore, he suggests that Luke records the pericope to answer the question of how we can have material possessions and still be saved and also as an apologetic to explain how the Jews are included in universal salvation.[36] That is, it shows us how the promises of the OT are still valid for Jews.

Mitchell's argument makes much of the reference to Zacchaeus as son of Abraham (19.9), claiming that this provides the necessary interpretative link to the Genesis account where Abraham is justified by works through his hospitality.[37] He suggests Luke ties salvation to good works in 3.1-20 by linking the quote from Isaiah (3.4-6) which ends with all flesh seeing the salvation of God (v. 6), through the word οὖν at the beginning of v. 7 and again in v. 10. According to Mitchell, the word οὖν functions as a link word which shows how this salvation is fulfilled. That is, it is fulfilled by our actions which are fruits worthy of repentance. He proposes that Luke drew on traditions not only of Abraham, but also of Rahab[38] as models of hospitality,[39] to show justification by works, and showing how the promises of the old covenant are still in effect and coming to

---

31. White, 'Vindication', p. 21.

32. For example, he argues that there are false stereotypes uncovered in the stories of the call of Levi (toll collectors can leave everything and follow Jesus), dinner at Simon's house (the sinful woman is the one who understands forgiveness more fully than the Pharisee), and the Good Samaritan (the Samaritan and not the religious leaders is the one who helps the injured man). Mitchell, 'Zacchaeus Revisited', pp. 153–76 (p. 153).

33. Mitchell, 'Zacchaeus Revisited', p. 153; Mitchell, 'The Use of συκοφαντεῖν in Luke 19:8: Further Evidence for Zacchaeus's Defense', *Bib* 72 (1991): 546–7.

34. Ibid., pp. 159–60.

35. Ibid., p. 159, n. 14.

36. Ibid., p. 163.

37. Ibid., pp. 169–72.

38. John Drury, *Tradition and Design in Luke's Gospel: A Study in Early Christian Historiography* (London: Darton. Longmann and Todd, 1976), pp. 73–4.

39. Here he uses Jas. 2.18-25 as evidence of the tradition.

fruition for Jews in Christianity.[40] Mitchell quotes James 2.21 where Abraham is justified by good works and believes that this is a tradition Luke is likely to have drawn on.

For Ravens, a combination of factors leads him to argue strongly against a future sense for the two verbs.[41] He notes this story is at a climax in the narrative because this is the last story before Jesus enters Jerusalem and because Zacchaeus is the ἀρχιτελώνης (19.2). He correctly notes that Luke always portrays τελῶναι responding well to Jesus,[42] but takes this to imply a customary action from v. 8, rather than a future response or a response relating to Zacchaeus' actions in v. 6. He also notes the absence of the language of repentance suggesting its absence means he has no sins to repent from.

Ravens examines the Zacchaeus pericope in light of the anointing story (7.36-50) and the story of the rich man and Lazarus (16.19-31), which he suggests together function as a triptych. This he admits is 'involved and circumstantial'[43] and centres on the meaning of the names of principal characters in each passage. In 7.36-50 Simon's name in the Hebrew form means 'hearing', echoing Simon's need to hear what Jesus has to say (7.40), and in 16.19-31 Lazarus finds help ultimately from God echoing his name's Hebrew root, 'El'azar' (God has helped). Therefore, he suggests, Zacchaeus' name, which means innocent, gives Luke's view of his character in the text making it a vindication story.

Ravens also looks to evidence external to the pericope, noting that Luke has interrupted the Markan narrative's order so that 19.1-10 follows the healing of the blind man, which follows mention of the disciples' lack of understanding (18.31-34). This he suggests functions as a prelude to the Zacchaeus story where Jesus opens the eyes of the crowd to Zacchaeus' true status.

To justify his position, Ravens further notes that Luke uses πάντες διεγόγγυζον (19.7) pejoratively of the crowds' response,[44] and that being a toll collector does not mean being a sinner in Luke.[45] To support this, he interprets σταθείς to mean standing firm in belief, and Zacchaeus calling Jesus 'Lord' as Luke paints Zacchaeus in a favourable light. The crowd seem to assume that all τελῶναι are ἁμαρτωλοί and therefore outside the covenant, but Luke subverts that.[46]

Green positions Zacchaeus as a model of one on the margins who has already understood the values of Jesus' mission and for whom salvation means restoration

---

40. Mitchell, 'Zacchaeus Revisited', p. 167.

41. Ravens, 'Zacchaeus', pp. 19–32 (28).

42. Ravens correctly notes the τελῶναι are one of three groups the Baptist addresses when they come to him to be baptized (3.10-14), are at Levi's banquet (5.29), and at 7.29, in a narrative comment, the reader finds out that the τελῶναι went home justified. He fails to note another positive example in the parable of the toll collector and the Pharisee (19.9-14) where it is the toll collector who is a model respondent. Ibid., p. 22.

43. Ibid., p. 28.

44. Ibid., p. 24.

45. Ibid., p. 25.

46. Ibid., pp. 22–3.

to the community of God.[47] He suggests that Zacchaeus has understood the message of John (3.10-14) and also of Jesus' economic justice and almsgiving.[48] He also notes the lack of conversion language,[49] and interprets his response of joy and immediate and exact obedience (19.5) as showing that 'he is one who embraces the values and claims of the kingdom of God'.[50]

Lieu agrees with the vindication position and further notes that repentance is not discussed and that Jesus brings salvation often to those whom society traditionally despises by restoring them and giving them recognition.[51]

In summary: 19.1-10 as a vindication story
Δίδωμι and ἀποδίδωμι are present tense verbs that could present Zacchaeus as customarily giving half his possessions to the poor and if he finds he has defrauded anyone of anything, restoring them fourfold. On this reading, the crowd claim he is a sinner but Jesus shows this to be false by declaring him to be a son of Abraham as evidenced by his good deeds. Jesus is interested in unearthing false stereotypes particularly concerning people on the margins.

In support of this, the claim is made that this pericope does not contain all the language or components of a salvation story revealing that it is indeed a vindication story of a righteous man. The specific critiques centre on: (1) the omission of the language of sin and repentance; (2) Jesus does not declare Zacchaeus' sins forgiven, implying there are none to forgive; (3) Zacchaeus' speech and behaviour are not contrite or self-effacing as one would expect in a salvation story; (4) Zacchaeus does not declare his faith; and (5) there is no crowd response to his actions or Jesus' statement.

However, there is considerable evidence that this position is not the best reading of the pericope and that the Zacchaeus story is indeed a salvation story with δίδωμι and ἀποδίδωμι showing a new sense of resolve.[52] We will now turn to the evidence from the text to support this claim.

---

47. Green, *Gospel,* pp. 672–3.

48. Ibid., p. 671.

49. Green notes that Luke does not mention Zacchaeus' need for repentance, an act of repentance or faith, or Jesus calling him to repentance and therefore that this is not a story of conversion. He does state that if v. 8 had a futuristic sense then 'verse 8 would refer to his repentance, while vv. 9-10 would refer to his being saved'. Ibid., pp. 671–2.

50. Ibid., p. 670.

51. Judith Lieu, *The Gospel of Luke* (Epworth Commentaries; Peterborough: Epworth Press, 1997), p. 148.

52. This view that Zacchaeus is showing a new resolve is held by many scholars. Adams, *Sinner,* p. 175; Bock, *Luke,* pp. 1519–20; Hamm, 'Luke 19:8', pp. 431–7; Dennis Hamm, 'Zacchaeus Revisited Once More: A Story of Vindication or Conversion?' *Bib* 72 (1991): 248–52; Hendriksen, *Gospel of Luke,* p. 856; Kariamadam, *Zacchaeus Story,* p. 39; R. C. H. Lenski, *The Interpretation of Saint Luke's Gospel* (Minneapolis: Augsburg Publishing, 1946), p. 943; William P. Loewe, 'Toward an Interpretation of Lk. 19:1-10', *CBQ* 36 (1974): 326; Marshall, *Gospel,* pp. 697–8; Méndez-Moratalla, *Paradigm of*

5.3 Zacchaeus – the sinner (a salvation reading)

The Zacchaeus pericope comes at the end of the travel narrative and contains many of the Lukan themes of salvation, the lost, and Jesus' mission. It does not contain all the language of salvation, but it uses many of the ideas and concepts of sin, repentance, and salvation which clearly place it within the domain of a salvation story. The Zacchaeus story resonates with many other pericopae which lay an interpretative base for the interpret gaps and blanks we encounter. As narrative works as a unity to create meaning, repetition, arrangement and echoes are significant in Luke's narrative. Luke himself states his writing is ἄνωθεν (from the beginning of something),[53] καθεξῆς (in orderly sequence),[54] and ἀκριβῶς (carefully or accurately);[55] no story in a narrative stands alone, as narrative is cumulative and cohesive and ordered. The beginning of the narrative set the trajectory for Jesus' role as the Davidic shepherd king and now we will now look at details in the text which support a salvation reading where Zacchaeus is the sinner sought out and saved by this king.

In 19.1, we find Jesus is on his journey to Jerusalem (9.51-52) and is passing through Jericho (19.1). Jericho is about 20 kilometres from Jerusalem, at the border between Perea, under Herod Antipas' control, and the province of Judea.[56] The city was known as an agricultural centre, a winter playground for Jerusalem aristocracy, and, as a relatively wealthy crossroad city near to Jerusalem, it was a likely place for a toll collection point.[57] There is generally considered to be no intrinsic link with Jericho in the Zacchaeus story other than recording the actual historical location,[58] but rather it brings Jesus nearer his narrative travel destination, Jerusalem.

Conversion, p. 174; James A. Metzger, *Consumption and Wealth in Luke's Travel Narrative* (BIS, 88; Leiden: Brill, 2007), pp. 173–4; George W. E. Nickelsburg, 'Riches, the Rich, and God's judgment in 1 Enoch 92-105 and the Gospel of Luke', *NTS* 25 (1978-79): 340; Nolland, *Luke,* pp. 905–6; O'Hanlon, 'Zacchaeus', p. 16; O'Toole, 'Literary Form of Luke 19:1-10', pp. 114–15; Sharon H. Ringe, *Luke* (WBCom; Louisville: Westminster John Knox Press, 1995), p. 232; Eduard Schweizer, *The Good News According to Luke* (trans. David E. Green, 1984; Atlanta: John Knox, 1913), p. 292; Talbert, *Reading Luke,* pp. 205–6; Robert C. Tannehill, 'The Story of Zacchaeus as Rhetoric', in *The Shape of Luke's Story: Essays on Luke-Acts* (Eugene: Cascade, 2005), pp. 75–6; Mikeal C. Parsons, '"Short in Stature": Luke's Physical Description of Zacchaeus', *NTS* 47 (2001): 57; Nigel M. Watson, 'Was Zacchaeus Really Reforming?' *ExpTim* 77 (1965–66), p. 282; Yamasaki, *Watching Biblical Narrative,* p. 201; John O. York, *The Last Shall Be First: The Rhetoric of Reversal in Luke* (SSNTSS, 46; Sheffield: JSOT, 1991), p. 159; Arthur A. Just Jr., *The Ongoing Feast: Table Fellowship and Eschatology at Emmaus* (Collegeville: Liturgical Press, 1993), pp. 188–93.

53. 'ἄνωθεν', BDAG, p. 92.
54. 'καθεξῆς', BDAG, p. 490.
55. 'ἀκριβῶς', BDAG, p. 39.
56. Safrai and Stern, *Jewish People,* 1, p. 333.
57. Ehud Netzer, 'Jericho', *ABD* 3, p. 739.
58. Nolland, *Luke,* p. 904.

The introductory remarks about Zacchaeus in v. 2 set him up to be of high interest in the Lukan narrative. Zacchaeus is a ἀρχιτελώνης and he is πλούσιος. Zacchaeus is not simply any τελώνης, but a ruler of others. Those in places of power and status walk a precarious road in Luke's perspective regarding the kingdom of God, and this is not any man of status, he is a Jewish man working as a ruler of the toll collectors for the Romans. Furthermore, as one who is rich and as the *chief toll collector,* he is clearly a successful toll collector as he collects the indirect taxes on agricultural produce and other goods coming from Judea to Perea.[59] The use of πλούσιος recalls 18.23 and the rich ruler who is seeking salvation (18.18, 26).

'Zacchaeus' is the Greek form of the Jewish name Zakkai or Zacchi (Neh. 7.14; Ezra 2.9; 2 Macc. 10.19; Josephus, *Life* 1.239) and may be an abbreviated form of Zechariah.[60] Zacchaeus' name in Hebrew means 'clean, innocent' [61] and is often used in Hebrew parallelism with צדיק, 'righteous, upright'. Although Zacchaeus' name means clean or innocent it is not generally considered significant to the pericope.[62] There are many interesting possibilities in Luke's inclusion of his name.

First, Bauckham argues that as a named account, it is possible that Zacchaeus was either known to the author or was the source for the story.[63] This is quite possible; it is not often that Luke provides the reader with an individual's name.

Secondly, we know that Zacchaeus is a Jew and this makes sense of Jesus declaring that he is a son of Abraham (19.9).[64] It is significant however, that in the parallel statement in 13.16 where Luke describes the crippled woman as a daughter of Abraham, Luke does not name her, suggesting that the inclusion of his name is not only to confirm ethnicity.

Thirdly, his name is also coupled with the knowledge that he is ἀρχιτελώνης, and this sets the reader up with the inevitable conflict that would arise from a Jewish man working for the Romans. As we have noted, Zacchaeus is not simply any τελώνης, but a ruler of others, and his status as πλούσιος, demonstrates to the reader that he is a man of some status in the community. The combination of information (ἀρχιτελώνης and πλούσιος) implies this community status is infamous.

Fourthly, as a thoroughly Jewish name, there is an element of irony or conflict with his occupation for the Roman oppressors.[65] This helps the reader to make sense of 19.3 where the crowd have formed a barrier and so he cannot see Jesus.

---

59. Otto Michel, 'τελώνης,' *TDNT* 8: 97; Marshall, *Gospel,* p. 696; Safrai and Stern, *Jewish People,* 1, p. 333.

60. Marshall, *Gospel,* p. 696; *Contra,* Bock, *Luke,* p. 1516; Fitzmyer, *Luke,* p. 1223.

61. *TWOT,* p. 240; Fitzmyer, *Luke,* p. 1223.

62. Bock, *Luke,* p. 1516; Nolland, *Luke,* p. 904.

63. Richard Bauckham, *Jesus and the Eyewitnesses: The Gospels as Eyewitness Testimony* (Grand Rapids: Eerdmans, 2006), pp. 39–55.

64. Fitzmyer, *Luke,* p. 1223; Bock, *Luke,* p. 1517.

65. O'Hanlon suggests this is ironical because of his role with the Romans and Lieu

Finally, the inclusion of his name also adds interest when in 19.5 Jesus mysteriously knows his name. Zacchaeus' name is also introduced by a Septuagintal expression ὀνόματι καλούμενος.[66] Luke uses ὀνόματι and καλούμενος frequently, but it is less common that he combines the two words.[67] This 'pleonastic' expression'[68] (ὀνόματι καλούμενος) while being stylistically Septuagintal, also provides a deliberate pause in the narrative. This sharpens the reader's focus for 19.5 when Jesus will miraculously call Zacchaeus by his name. Jesus' miraculous knowledge of Zacchaeus' name is consistent with his ministry in the power of the Holy Spirit (4.1, 14, 18; 5.17) where he finds divine empowerment. This empowerment relates not only to miraculous deeds (19.37), but to divine knowledge. For example, the Lukan Jesus demonstrates miraculous foreknowledge of Simon's catch of fish (5.4), and further, in the story of the rich ruler Jesus shows remarkable insight into the man's struggle to understand the law (18.19-22). Luke also describes Jesus praying all night before choosing the disciples (6.12) which suggests Jesus is seeking divine knowledge, and he also encourages the disciples to allow the Holy Spirit to give them divine knowledge if they are in court (12.12). In 19.5 therefore, when Jesus knows Zacchaeus' name, it is consistent with the Lukan Jesus who is exercising divine knowledge.[69]

Roman taxes were collected in two forms in Palestine at this time; direct taxes (land and head taxes) collected by the Jewish councils and indirect taxes (tolls, customs, and duties) collected by private contractors.[70] Zacchaeus is a private contractor, and as such would have added his own charge onto the state toll charge, to which an individual had no recourse to disagree. This lay the system open to abuses and Luke's description that he was πλούσιος implies his wealth was made through fraudulent means, adding intensity to his characterization. O'Hanlon therefore rightly notes that, 'the function of ἀρχιτελώνης in the narrative is to emphasise the richness of the tax collector and the *magnitude of his sinfulness*'.[71] Jesus' mission to call sinners to repentance is clear in 5.32 and this parallel story creates an echo here.

Luke's emphasis on Zacchaeus' Jewish name, his social status as ἀρχιτελώνης, and his wealth sets Zacchaeus up in the narrative to be an arch-sinner. This point

because his name means 'righteous'. John O'Hanlon, 'Zacchaeus', p. 12; Lieu, *Gospel of Luke*, p. 147.

66. ὀνόμα and καλέω are sometimes contained in close proximity in the LXX, so this suggests an example of Luke's use of Septuagintal language (Exod. 3319; 34.5; Judg. 18.29).

67. Luke uses a combination of these two words also in 1.31, 61; 2.21.

68. Nolland describes this combination of words as 'pleonastic'. Nolland, *Luke*, p. 904.

69. John also knows of this tradition (Jn 1.48).

70. Michel, 'τελώνης', *TDNT* 8: 97. When Archelaus' reign as ethnarch ceased and he was exiled in 6 CE, the Roman tax system was revised and a census called. Safrai and Stern, *Jewish People*, 1, pp. 330-4.

71. O'Hanlon, 'Zacchaeus', p. 12. Emphasis is mine.

is overlooked or underplayed by White, Mitchell, Ravens, Green and Lieu.[72] Thus, we find that the information that Zacchaeus is πλούσιος and ἀρχιτελώνης is significant for interpreting Zacchaeus' characterization as a sinner. This makes Zacchaeus an ideal candidate for the seeking and saving Davidic shepherd king who seeks the lost and scattered sheep (Ezek. 34.12).

In v. 3 we find Zacchaeus is seeking (ζητέω) to see (εἶδον) Jesus, but he is unable to do so because there are two barriers – the crowd that has gathered to see Jesus are blocking his vision and Zacchaeus is short in stature and so cannot look over the crowd.[73] This quest however, is positive and suggests 'a christological backbone' to the pericope.[74] Earlier in the narrative Herod had been 'seeking' to see who Jesus was (9.9) but 23.8 shows us that he was hoping to see him perform a sign. Luke shows this motivation as negative. In 11.16 people are also 'demanding' a sign from heaven to test Jesus, and in 11.29 Jesus calls the generation *evil* as it is 'asking' for a sign. In contrast, Zacchaeus' motivation to see Jesus is not sparked by a negative motivation such as Herod's in 9.9, 23.8 or the people in 11.16, 19, and his place in the tree makes him unobtrusive. This positive characterization coupled with his marginalization from the crowd further strengthens his candidature for a saving encounter with the Davidic shepherd king.

The notion of 'sight' is significant in the Gospel and 'seeing' as a metaphor for spiritual sight was common in religious literature of the ancient world.[75] In 4.18-19 in Luke's programmatic saying, Jesus announces that through him as God's anointed, the blind will see again and, under Hamm's chiastic analysis of 4.16-20, τυφλοῖς ἀνάβλεψιν forms the centre of the chiasm.[76] This is demonstrated below:

A and *he stood up* to read
B and there *was given* to him the book of the prophet Isaiah
  C he *opened the book* and found the place where it is written
    D 'The Spirit of *the Lord* is upon me, because he has anointed me
      E *to proclaim good news* to the poor
        F he *has sent* me to proclaim release to *captives*
          G **and *recovering of sight to the blind***
        F¹ to *set at liberty* those who are oppressed
      E¹ *to proclaim*

72. White, 'Vindication', p. 21; Mitchell, 'Zacchaeus Revisited', p. 153; Ravens, 'Zacchaeus', p. 25; Green, *Gospel*, pp. 672–3; Lieu, *Gospel of Luke*, pp. 147–8.

73. Another possible avenue explored is the ancient world of physiognomy where Parsons has suggested Zacchaeus' short stature may be perceived by the ancient world as indicating that he was a 'sinner'. See Parsons, 'Short in Stature', pp. 50–7 (p. 55); Parsons, *Body and Character*, pp. 97–108.

74. O'Hanlon, 'Zacchaeus', p. 13.

75. Dennis Hamm, 'Sight to the Blind: Vision as Metaphor in Luke', *Bib* 76 (1986): 457.

76. Hamm acknowledges the earlier work of Meynet (1982) and Lund (1942). Ibid., pp. 458–9.

D¹ the acceptable year of *the Lord.'*
C¹ And he *closed the book*
B¹ and *gave it back* to the attendant
A¹ and *sat down.*[77]

Furthermore, in 7.21 Luke records an important summary healing statement which specifies the blind receiving their sight, and then in 7.22 various healings are named using LXX allusions to Isaiah 29.18; 35.5;[78] 61.1. The blind receiving their sight is the only healing that is common to both verses, and its double linguistic use is intriguing as Luke writes of the blind receiving their sight last in v. 21 and first in v. 22, suggesting a Lukan emphasis where Jesus' soteriological mission and sight are connected.[79] This is demonstrated below:

ἐν ἐκείνῃ τῇ ὥρᾳ ἐθεράπευσεν πολλοὺς ἀπὸ νόσων καὶ μαστίγων καὶ πνευμάτων πονηρῶν καὶ **τυφλοῖς πολλοῖς ἐχαρίσατο βλέπειν.**
(καὶ ἀποκριθεὶς εἶπεν αὐτοῖς· πορευθέντες ἀπαγγείλατε Ἰωάννῃ ἃ εἴδετε καὶ ἠκούσατε·)
τυφλοὶ ἀναβλέπουσιν, χωλοὶ περιπατοῦσιν,
λεπροὶ καθαρίζονται καὶ κωφοὶ ἀκούουσιν,
νεκροὶ ἐγείρονται, πτωχοὶ εὐαγγελίζονται·. (7.21-22)

This statement is important because it confirms Jesus as the Messiah[80] and its likely echo of Isaiah 61, the source for the programmatic saying, lends weight to its significant content. That salvific sight is central to both passages makes a double statement of its importance for the narrative.

In the pericope immediately prior to Zacchaeus, the blind man asks to receive his sight (ἀναβλέπω; 18.41) and has an uncanny ability to perceive Jesus as the 'Son of David'. The blind man seems able to 'see' something of Jesus' nature, a revelation that his disciples do not appear to have received (18.34). When the blind man receives his sight the Nazareth manifesto is fulfilled (4.18-19), at least in part, and while 7.21-22 has claimed Jesus has already done so, Luke has not

---

77. Italics original. Green's analysis notes the quote from Isaiah is at the centre, and at the centre of that are two sayings of release (to proclaim for the captives' release; and to send forth the oppressed in release). However, I note that even under his analysis the blind receiving their sight is between these two sayings and lies at the centre of the verse. Green, *Gospel,* p. 210. Bock follows Tiede's analysis, which shows the centre as the same as Hamm's. Bock, *Luke,* p. 399.

78. Isaiah 35.5 is within the context of σῴζω (Isa. 35.4).

79. In 2.30 Simeon says his 'eyes have seen your salvation' and 2.32 talks of Jesus being a 'light' to the Gentiles. Both examples link seeing and salvation language.

80. Fitzmyer regards Jesus' reply as nonmessianic, although his words are so closely reflective of the works expected of the Messiah that there seems to be a messianic claim being made either directly or as an allusion. Bock, *Luke,* p. 668; Marshall, *Gospel,* p. 292; Nolland, *Luke,* p. 330; Fitzmyer, *Luke,* p. 667.

opened this window clearly for the reader until the end of Jesus' ministry. That is, it is not until 18.35-43 that the reader 'sees' Jesus heal the blind. This accelerates the ending of the travel narrative as Jesus' ministry is shown to be nearly complete. While blind Bartimaeus ends the Markan journey (Mk 10.46-52), for Luke, Jesus' ministry still has one more important dimension which will be added with Zacchaeus who is seeking to *see* Jesus.

In light of Luke's use of salvific sight as a metaphor, and the positive characterization of Zacchaeus when he is seeking 'to see who Jesus is', this action can be seen as 'the first step in Zacchaeus' own repenting'.[81]

The parable of the toll collector and sinner (18.9-14) also bears many parallels to the Zacchaeus pericope as we have seen, and its close proximity has already created an ideologically sympathetic attribute to a toll collector who shows humility and repentance. This parable, I suggest, provides the reader with a Lukan lens with which to read the character of Zacchaeus who is on a quest to encounter Jesus, albeit at a distance at this stage.

In v. 4, Luke also shows Zacchaeus is eager to see Jesus with the pleonastic expression which highlights Zacchaeus' actions of 'running on ahead' (προτρέχω), followed by 'in the front' (εἰς τὸ ἔμπροσθεν). This further confirms Zacchaeus' honest desire to see Jesus which will also be shown when he climbs a sycamore tree which could have led to the possibility of public ridicule.[82] The ancient world found the movements of dwarfs comical and they were sought after as party entertainment; thus, the image of height-challenged Zacchaeus running ahead, Parsons suggests a 'cruel and ribald mockery'.[83] Although he is a man of considerable social status and wealth through his infamous role as ἀρχιτελώνης, it is a positive attribute that Zacchaeus is willing to face public humiliation to gain access to Jesus. The sinful woman parallel has also shown a woman who risked public ridicule in approaching Jesus. This story's many close links further place the Zacchaeus story within a salvific domain. Certainly, Zacchaeus' actions negate White's belief that Zacchaeus' behaviour is not contrite or self-effacing, and confirms Zacchaeus' intention as more than a sight-seeing tourist. His desire is shown as honourable by Luke.

The language and Lukan theme of salvation is firmly established in vv. 5-6. As Klein rightly says, 'with the coming of Jesus the matter is turned around. It is not Zacchaeus who sees Jesus, but Jesus looks up and catches sight of him'.[84] The significance of Jesus seeking Zacchaeus out and the salvific language is underplayed in a vindication reading, a key weakness in this theory. It is here in Zacchaeus' house that I suggest the salvific event occurs. That is, salvation occurs in Zacchaeus' house, which I will now demonstrate.

In v. 5 Jesus speaks to Zacchaeus with an imperative, σπεύσας κατάβηθι. Luke uses σπεύδω in the context of divine command in Acts 20.16; 22.18, 21. In Acts 20.16 Paul is hastening to arrive in Jerusalem for Pentecost in line with the

---

81. Yamasaki, *Watching Biblical Narrative*, p. 193.

82. O'Hanlon, 'Zacchaeus', p. 13; Green, *Gospel*, p. 669.

83. Parsons, *Body and Character*, p. 103.

84. Klein, *Das Lukasevangelium*, p. 601. Author's translation.

divine plan for his mission (Acts 20.22-24), while in Luke 2.16 σπεύδω recalls the shepherds as model respondents, hurrying to Mary and Joseph and the baby lying in the manger. In Luke 19.5 there is this sense of divine command, especially with the salvific language that follows. Indeed, 'Jesus knew Zacchaeus' name by virtue of his superhuman omniscience',[85] leading the reader to expect a salvific encounter on a divine timetable.

The use of καταβαίνω is interesting as it may suggest functional repentance. It is a sign of Zacchaeus' acknowledgement of this divine command that he responds quickly and comes down from the tree. In v. 8 he will go on to address Jesus as κύριε, which may be another sign of repentance. Luke favours showing people responding to Jesus by a physical action of falling down before him. For example, Simon falls down and acknowledges his sin before Jesus (5.8),[86] the Gerasene demoniac falls down before him (8.28)[87] and the leper who is healed prostrates himself in front of Jesus (17.16).[88] Luke also has the sinful woman anointing Jesus' feet (7.38) rather than his head in the Markan anointing story (Mk 14.3).[89] When Zacchaeus therefore comes down from the tree, Luke paints him as responding appropriately to Jesus.[90]

Luke's use of σήμερον could be viewed as temporal and non-theological, but its context makes this option unlikely as σήμερον will be repeated and linked with σωτηρία in 19.9.[91] As Wolter further notes: 'For the first time since 4.21 and his own first words in public, Jesus speaks again of σήμερον … That the word has salvific significance here as well, is beyond question.'[92] Luke uses σήμερον extensively in a theological sense,[93] and in 19.5 Jesus calls for a response from Zacchaeus. Further, 19.5 and 19.9 are parallel statements with σήμερον at the beginning of each verse and with σωτηρία coming between σήμερον and οἶκος. This points to this encounter in Zacchaeus' house as salvific. The parallels are demonstrated overleaf:

85. Bovon, *Lukas 3*, p. 274. Author's translation.

86. This pericope is primarily Lukan; the response, unique.

87. This physical response of falling down before Jesus (προσπίπτω) is Lukan. Mark uses προσκυνέω, to worship.

88. This pericope is Lukan. He uses the physical picture of the man ἔπεσεν ἐπὶ πρόσωπον παρὰ τοὺς πόδας αὐτοῦ.

89. These are not directly parallel stories but bear strikingly similar features. They are both in the house of a man named Simon when a woman comes to anoint Jesus, people react at the costly act which could have instead helped the poor, but Jesus defends her actions.

90. This may suggest a christological framework.

91. Fitzmyer, *Luke*, p. 1224; O'Hanlon, 'Zacchaeus', p. 15; Marshall with some reserve, *Gospel*, p. 697. Green says the term is highly suggestive as in other places it has been linked to salvation. Green, *Gospel*, p. 670.

92. Wolter, *Das Lukasevangelium*, p. 612. Author's translation.

93. Refer 2.11; 4.21; 5.26; 13.31, 33; 23.43.

(19.5) σήμερον γὰρ ἐν τῷ οἴκῳ σου δεῖ με μεῖναι

(19.9) σήμερον σωτηρία τῷ οἴκῳ τούτῳ ἐγένετο

Furthermore, the concept of salvation is clearly evident in Luke's use of δεῖ when Jesus says he *must* stay in Zacchaeus' house.[94] This word, which expresses divine necessity, is critical to the narrative and it is loaded with cultural overtones. It has a Hellenistic background where the thought is of a neutral deity who is in control of the course of the world.[95] Luke has taken this term and given the deity a name and embedded the understanding of God who is not neutral, but is actively pursuing his plan of salvation for the world in his son Jesus who is Saviour (2.11).

When Luke uses δεῖ, the soteriological interpretative framework has been set. The additional use of σήμερον confirms this. This verse shows the reader that Jesus is in control of this encounter with Zacchaeus. While Zacchaeus was seeking to see Jesus, Jesus is displaying his greater desire to meet with him. Méndez-Moratalla suggests the use of δεῖ points to repentance. He says:

> Luke's emphasis on divine initiative displayed in the ministry of Jesus and expressed in terms of 'necessity' ... aims at repentance. That is the expected response to the divine salvific initiative articulated as 'the call of sinners to repentance' (5:32), 'the seeking of the lost' (19:10), which is toward those despised by members of the socio-religious strata, namely, to the sinners, the toll collector, the lost.[96]

Furthermore, Jesus' words ἐν τῷ οἴκῳ σου δεῖ με μεῖναι cannot be underestimated. This is a clear reference to Middle Eastern hospitality, that is, table fellowship,[97] and the salvific nature of Jesus' request is paramount. Luke's narrative has consistently foregrounded Jesus' table fellowship and the role eating and drinking has in the purposes of God. The Zacchaeus pericope is another example of Jesus eating with a sinner and showing his acceptance of them as a result. Luke favours the use of μένω (and ἐπιμένω). Unlike Matthew and Mark, who only use it once each respectively for hospitality in a house (Mt. 10.11; Mk 6.10), Luke uses it seven times in the Gospel (1.56; 8.27; 9.4; 10.7; 19.5; 24.29 [twice]) and thirteen times in Acts (Acts 5.4 [twice]; 9.43; 16.15; 18.3, 20; 20.5, 23; 21.7-8; 27.31; 28.12, 14).[98]

---

94. Bock, *Luke*, p. 1518; Fitzmyer, *Luke*, pp. 179–80; Walter Grundmann, 'δεῖ, δέον ἐστί', *TDNT* 2: 22–3; Marshall, *Gospel*, p. 696; Nolland, *Luke*, p. 905; O'Hanlon, 'Zacchaeus', p. 15.

95. Grundmann, 'δεῖ, δέον ἐστί', *TDNT* 2, p. 21.

96. Méndez-Moratalla, *Paradigm of Conversion*, p. 165.

97. Matson, *Household*, p. 72; D. E. Smith, 'Table Fellowship as a Literary Motif in the Gospel of Luke', *JBL* 106 (1987), p. 636; Just, *Ongoing Feast*, p. 188.

98. He also uses ἐπιμένω in Acts 10.48; 15.34; 21.4, 10; 28.12, 14.

Adams, following Marshall, describes Jesus' offer of fellowship to Zacchaeus as extending an offer of forgiveness.[99] For there to be forgiveness, the implication is that there is sin to be forgiven. While in the Western world this may not seem explicitly related to the forgiveness of sins, the Middle Eastern world knew all that it implied.

In Moessner's description of the Lukan journey he explores the motifs of 'food' and 'meal' as metaphors for proper relationship with Jesus. Meal imagery, he suggests, is

> paradigmatic of the disciples' relationship of submission and total dependence upon their Lord. For not only were the disciples dependent upon their identification with Jesus to receive hospitality from their hosts but also the home meal became the fullest expression of the relationship of blessing and salvation to the presence of the Lord in their midst.[100]

N. T. Wright goes so far as to suggest that in the encounter in Zacchaeus' house, Jesus is implicitly claiming to be and do what the temple was and did[101] – that is, in this act of hospitality, Jesus was offering forgiveness of sins and restoration, roles of the Jerusalem temple, thereby offering Zacchaeus a 'bypass'.

> If one was with Jesus, one did not need the restoration into the covenant membership which was normally attained by going to Jerusalem and offering sacrifices in the temple: 'Today salvation has come to this house; this man too is a son of Abraham!' (Luke 19:9).[102]

This is consistent with the household mission in Luke 10.1-24, which we found to have a foundational role in the household Gentile mission in Acts and where entering the house and offering peace was tantamount to salvation. In 19.5-6, Luke again presents the reader with a picture of Jesus entering a house and bringing salvation. In a very real way, Jesus being present was enough for salvation, and supports Wright's suggestion that the Lukan Jesus does supersede the role of the temple by being a new 'sacred space'. Forgiveness for Zacchaeus was enabled by Jesus' invitation and was entered into by his response and not by a visit to the temple.[103] In this act of invitation therefore, and surrounded by language

---

99. Adams, *Sinner*, p. 172. Marshall also says that Jesus' decision to stay with Zacchaeus is, 'a sign of fellowship and ultimately of forgiveness'. Marshall, *Gospel*, p. 697.

100. Moessner, *Lord of the Banquet*, p. 151.

101. N. T. Wright, 'Jerusalem in the New Testament', in *Jerusalem Past and Present in the Purposes of God* (ed. P. W. L. Walker; Cambridge: Tyndale House, 1992), p. 58.

102. Wright, 'Jerusalem', p. 58.

103. Luke's Gospel begins and ends in the temple (1.8; 24.53), giving the temple a special narrative place in the Gospel. He also shows a unique interest in what happens in the temple when Jesus dies, as he brings the tearing of the temple curtain forward to *before* Jesus dies (23.45). Mark and Matthew both place it after the death (Mk 15.38; Mt. 27.51).

of necessity (δεῖ), σήμερον, and μένω in v. 5, and with the backdrop of Zacchaeus seeking to see Jesus (ζητέω, εῖδον), Luke has drawn heavily on salvation language. The absence of some salvation language is given as primary evidence for a vindication reading of the pericope, and yet Luke's language is clearly salvific, while not containing every possible Lukan salvific word.

It is of note that after this unit (19.1-27), Jesus will enter Jerusalem and go straight to the temple and cleanse it (19.45-46). Perhaps another reason Luke has inserted the Zacchaeus pericope into the Markan journey, is that Wright is correct that the Lukan Jesus was redefining the role of Jerusalem and the temple. Luke 13.35 has suggested that, for the Lukan Jesus, the temple has become a place where God no longer dwelt when he says ἰδοὺ ἀφίεται ὑμῖν ὁ οἶκος ὑμῶν, and this will be affirmed in Stephen's words (Acts 7.48-49). While Luke continues to refer to the temple in his Gospel narrative and in Acts,[104] it is possible that Luke views the temple and the forgiveness of sins in a new way and the house is a new salvific space. Certainly Jerusalem, which is inextricably tied to the temple, becomes a narrative marker for the progression of the gospel rather than the preeminent place where the temple was located. Locations in the travel narrative help to show Jesus' journey to Jerusalem, and thereafter they become linked to the spread of the gospel (24.47; Acts 1.8).

When Jesus enters Zacchaeus' house, the belief of the crowd in 19.7 is that he enters a ritually unclean house. *M.Tohorot* 7.6, which discusses purity, says: 'The tax collector who entered the house – the house is unclean.' Jewish tradition likened toll collectors to Gentiles who were ritually unclean. *M.Ohol.* 18.7 notes the 'dwelling places of gentiles [in the land of Israel] are unclean' and *Jub.* 22.16 says:

Separate thyself from the nations, and eat not with them:
And do not according to their works,
And become not their associate;
For their works are unclean,
And all their ways are a pollution and an abomination and uncleanness.

For the Jewish person, remaining separate was essential, as God could not mix the holy with the profane.[105] This is evident in the Prayer of Benediction, *Havdalah*, which says:

Blessed are you, Lord our God, king of the world, who divides holy and profane, between light and darkness, between Israel and the peoples, between the seventh day and the sixth day of work. Blessed are you Lord, who divides between sacred and profane.

While scholars are uncertain what this means, it shows that Luke does see the temple and Jesus as being connected.

104. The Gospel begins and ends in the temple (1.9; 24.53) and this continues in Acts (3.1; 5.25).

105. John H. Elliott, 'Purity', in *The Social World of the New Testament: Insights and Models,* (eds Jerome H. Neyrey and Eric C. Stewart; Peabody: Hendrickson, 2008), p. 103.

The mission to households has established a radically inclusive attitude to mission where there is a breaking down of concern over table fellowship,[106] and the Zacchaeus pericope is a further example of this mission strategy in action. In fact, because it is the final pericope in the travel narrative and so culminates themes of the Gospel, this may be not only another recollection of the household mission, it may highlight this theme as of special interest to the Lukan Jesus. As Matson says, 'Jesus' declaration to Zacchaeus (in v. 9) highlights the sphere of the house as the place for the restoration and cleansing of "sinners".[107]

Zacchaeus responds with joy and haste to Jesus' command in v. 6 and Luke reiterates σπεύσας κατέβη. Zacchaeus also welcomes (ὑποδέχομαι) Jesus, another clear reference to hospitality.[108] The notion of δέχομαι and its cognates often means to welcome or receive a guest (2.28; 9.5, 11, 53; 10.8, 10, 38; 19.6; Acts 7.59) and yet, clearly these references are set within mission mandates where the focus is on receiving not only the guest, but the message of the kingdom. The word-group is also used explicitly with regard to receiving the kingdom message (8.13; 16.9; 18.17; Acts 8.14; 11.1; 17.11). In 19.1-10, Fitzmyer notes that there is no mention of faith, as evidence for a vindication reading.[109] Yet, the context for Zacchaeus welcoming Jesus suggests he is welcoming the kingdom and points to this encounter as salvific.

Zacchaeus' response to Jesus is not only to welcome him with haste, but with joy (χαίρω). His response with χαίρω, especially within the salvific context of v. 5, points the reader to his conversion.[110] We have noted the role of joy in the parable of the faithful shepherd and here we have another example where salvation and joy are linked.

Verse 7 forms a pivot in the narrative as the opinions of the crowd are revealed and they are πάντες (all) found grumbling (διαγογγύζω). As we have seen, Luke uses this word pejoratively (5.29; 15.2) and there is likely to be an exodus echo behind the word. The crowd seem unable and unwilling to embrace Jesus' compassionate welcome of Zacchaeus and the crowd charge Zacchaeus as ἁμαρτωλός. Bovon highlights that 'Luke has accustomed his readers to jealous recriminations situated near scenes of pardon, reconciliation, healing and deliverance'.[111]

Luke points to the crowd's charge as deficient through his use of διαγογγύζω, and scholars holding the vindication position have made the assumption that

---

106. Matson, *Household*, p. 43; Jerome H. Neyrey, 'Ceremonies in Luke-Acts: The Case of Meals and Table Fellowship', in *The Social World of Luke-Acts: Models for Interpretation* (ed. Jerome H. Neyrey; Peabody: Hendrickson, 1991), p. 381.

107. Matson, *Household*, p. 74.

108. Green, *Gospel*, p. 670. Green says both 'stay at your house' (v. 5) and ὑποδέχομαι (v. 6) represent hospitality.

109. Fitzmyer, *Luke*, p. 1224.

110. Méndez-Moratalla, *Paradigm of Conversion*, pp. 166-7. O'Hanlon notes the verb is used frequently by Luke to show eschatological joy which springs from the reception of salvation. O'Hanlon, 'Zacchaeus', p. 15.

111. Bovon, *Lukas 3*, p. 275. Author's translation.

Zacchaeus must therefore be righteous. However, this does not necessarily have to follow. From a narrative perspective, the grumbling may imply that the crowd, and here Luke uses πάντες, do not understand who Jesus is and what his mission entails. It does not have to imply that Zacchaeus is δίκαιος. The crowd's reaction is undoubtedly a result of their misunderstanding of the salvific nature of Jesus' encounter and invitation in vv. 5–6. They do not yet appear to understand that Jesus offers forgiveness of sins. Furthermore, the crowd's reaction may be a deliberate parallel to the disciples' lack of understanding at 18.34. The result is that at the end of Jesus' ministry outside Jerusalem, Luke makes it clear that neither the disciples nor the crowd understand his mission.

The negative reaction of the crowd parallels the reaction of the elder brother in the prodigal parable (15.25-32), and so looking to the wider Lukan narrative is again helpful. The older brother cannot accept his father's welcome of the younger son whose sin was so blatantly visible to the community. He cannot understand how their father has put the younger son's immense sin fully behind him when he simply returns home. This parallel story may be Luke's key to help the reader perceive that it is not that Zacchaeus has not sinned, but that forgiveness is complete through a turning to God.

There are other echoes between the two units that encourage the reader to view the pericope as a salvation story. The lost parables talk of being found within the context of repentance and joy. These explicit references in the parables find further expression in Zacchaeus who is one of the lost sheep of Israel that Jesus finds (19.9-10), the one who shows repentance through his action in responding to Jesus (19.5-8) and then joyfully responds to Jesus (19.6). There are also the linguistic parallels with the use of ζητέω (15.8; 19.3, 10), δεῖ (15.32; 19.5), χαίρω/χαρά (15.5, 7, 10, 32; 19.6), ἁμαρτωλός (15.2; 19.7) and ἀπόλλυμι (15.4, 6, 8, 9, 17, 24, 32; 19.10). Thus, the Zacchaeus pericope resonates with the parable and it is likely that interpreting the latter narratively speaking (19.1-10), with respect to the former (18.9-14), is a natural response to a cohesive text. The parallels with the story of Levi further suggest that Zacchaeus is a sinner in need of repentance and this is a story of a sinner who finds salvation.

More latterly, Rowe has noticed that 'Luke uses ἁμαρτ-cognates thirty-seven times in Luke-Acts, and *in every case* "sin" and "sinner" is a moral-theological category related to the need of repentance, forgiveness and salvation'.[112] While the crowd has an incorrect understanding of the Lukan Jesus' view of ἁμαρτωλός (and δίκαιος), Rowe is correct that the term is used by Luke to confirm this as a salvation story. Luke's biographical detail in 19.2 has already provided the reader with the parameters to establish that Zacchaeus is a sinner, and in view of the pejorative way Luke portrays the crowd, it may in fact point also to their sin in excluding Zacchaeus and grumbling at Jesus' action.

In v. 8 Zacchaeus issues a statement of resolve that he will give half of his money to the poor and give back in fourfold restitution to anyone he has defrauded. At the first level, this resolve is a *result* of the saving action in vv. 5-6

---

112. Rowe, *Early Narrative Christology*, p. 87. Author's italics.

rather than it being the moment that initiates his salvation. For Luke, knowing God is inextricably tied to ethical action as Zacchaeus demonstrates, and this ethical action is an important dimension in a multi-layered salvation. The earlier interchange between Jesus and the lawyer (10.27), which draw on the *Shema* and Lev. 19.18, demonstrate that loving God and loving people are tied together; the same dynamic is evident in 18.18-35. The two actions are not separated for they reflect God's character and nature which cares for the poor (Exod. 22.21-24; Deut. 10.17-19). This resonates with Ezekiel 34's emphasis on the practical needs of the sheep being met; God wants his sheep found, fed, healed, and restored. Salvation is about being found by the shepherd and then fed. Zacchaeus' resolve to give away money to the poor reflects the faithful shepherd he has encountered. In this he takes on an aspect of God's mission for himself. This is the same cycle we saw in the household mission when Jesus, the shepherd, sends the seventy to replicate his mission. As people become disciples in the Lukan narrative, God's mission becomes their mission. Perhaps this is why the motif of shepherd is so appropriate in the Miletus speech; Jesus has been presented as the faithful shepherd in the Gospel and so this is who the early church leaders become, faithful shepherds of God's flock. Mitchell's argument that Zacchaeus is justified by his good works is incorrect.[113] Further, Mitchell's use of Luke 3.8 to validate actions as the basis for repentance and salvation is therefore flawed. John the Baptist says to 'bear fruits worthy of repentance' (3.8) and goes on to list many examples. Luke uses καρπός in a physical and spiritual sense, but here Luke uses it to convey the idea that our actions are an appropriate and visible response by the people of God. Luke does not suggest they are the component on our part that brings us into salvation, but that they are the natural consequences of good fruit coming from a good tree (6.43-45).

Godet and Ravens' reading of σταθείς in v. 8 as standing firm in self-belief can equally be understood in its literal meaning, as in 18.11; Acts 2.14; 17.22; 27.21, or as prefacing a significant statement, as Marshall suggests.[114] It does not need to support a vindication reading.

The ethical response of Zacchaeus is generous and exceeds the requirements of the law. With respect to extortion, Leviticus 6.1-5 says you must return the principal amount plus one fifth of that sum, while 2 Kingdoms 12.6 and Exodus 22.1 require the amount plus a threefold penalty to be demanded of rustlers. In *Antiquities* Josephus writes similarly that the thief shall restore fourfold.[115] The Talmud required twenty per cent to be given to the poor rather than Zacchaeus' generous fifty per cent, and also twenty per cent for extortion rather than Zacchaeus' fourfold.[116]

The idea that these present tense verbs show Zacchaeus' customary behaviour runs contrary to the narrative which presents him as lost to the community and

---

113. Mitchell, 'Zacchaeus Revisited', pp. 169–72.
114. Marshall, *Gospel*, p. 697.
115. Josephus, *Ant.* 16.3.
116. Marshall, *Gospel*, p. 697; Bock, *Luke*, p. 1520.

therefore as excluded. If this extreme generosity was his norm, the crowd would not have called him a *sinner* and formed a physical barrier that he could not penetrate. Similarly, if this was his customary behaviour then Zacchaeus is more likely to have been called πτωχός and not πλούσιος. Money can only be given away this quickly a couple of times before you have little left.

There are two uses of κύριος in the verse: one by the author and one by Zacchaeus to Jesus. Zacchaeus' use of κύριος within the context of his statement of resolve most likely signals the reception of the 'Lord' of the house.[117] Rowe has convincingly argued that Luke shows Jesus to be ὁ κύριος from the womb,[118] and that 19.8 expresses Lukan Christology.[119] It is consistent with the narrative's thrust to interpret Zacchaeus' words here to indicate his prior reception of Jesus as κύριος.

Verses 9 and 10 give the pericope the final stamp as a salvation story. Jesus declares that today salvation has come to Zacchaeus' house, for the Son of Man came to seek out and to save that which is lost. Like the lost sheep in 15.3-7 Zacchaeus is now a person who is found, as is his house. As a Jew he is brought back into fellowship through Jesus' welcome of him, and as one cut off from his community he is now restored. The linguistic parallels of v. 5 and v. 9 make clear that it is in his house that salvation has occurred, and Jesus' statement simply echoes this reality. Just notes of vv. 9-10: 'Although "forgiveness" (ἄφεσις) is not pronounced in Luke 19:1-10, the declaration of salvation "today" implies the forgiveness of sins within the table fellowship of Jesus.'[120] O'Hanlon rightly suggests that the searching out of the lost along his journey to Jerusalem is the whole point of Jesus' journey.[121] To be lost, 19.10 clearly shows us, is to be in need of salvation.

As Mitchell has highlighted, Luke records Zacchaeus as υἱὸς Ἀβραάμ and through this reference the reader is encouraged to recall Abraham's story. Mitchell, however, makes a great deal out of Abraham's hospitality at the oaks of Mamre (Gen. 18.8), and that Josephus and Philo record the same encounter.[122] He argues Luke has built the Zacchaeus pericope using Genesis 18 as his source and provides parallels (see Table 3).

117. Matson, *Household,* p. 73; Moessner, *Lord of the Banquet,* p. 169.

118. Rowe, *Early Narrative Christology,* p. 27.

119. Ibid., p. 147.

120. Just, *Ongoing Feast,* p. 192.

121. O'Hanlon, 'Zacchaeus', p. 15.

122. Josephus, *Ant.* 1.196.

Table 3 A Linguistic Comparison Between Genesis 18 and Luke 19.[123]

Genesis 18	Luke 19
The Lord appears to Abraham at the oak of Mamre (Gen. 18.1)	Zacchaeus meets Jesus at the sycamore tree (19.5)
He entertains his guests under a tree (Gen. 18.8)	
Abraham looks up (ἀναβλέπω, εἶδον) and sees his visitors (Gen. 18.2)	Jesus looks up at Zacchaeus (ἀναβλέπω) (19.5)
	Zacchaeus seeks to see (εἶδον) who Jesus is (19.3)
When he saw them he ran (προστρέχω) to meet them (Gen. 18.2)	Zacchaeus runs to a tree (προτρέχω) (19.4)
He wishes they would not pass by him (Gen. 18.3)	(no parallel)
He runs to the herd (Gen. 18.7)	(no parallel)
Abraham addresses his visitor as κύριε (Gen. 18.3)	Zacchaeus addresses Jesus as κύριε (19.8)
Abraham hastens to the tent (Gen. 18.6)	Zacchaeus hurries down the tree (19.6)

There appears to be no doubt that there are linguistic parallels between the two stories, and that Abraham is an important figure for Luke (1.55, 73; 3.3, 34; 13.16, 28; 16.22-30; 19.9; 20.37). Mitchell therefore assumes that Abraham's act of hospitality is the point of the parallel, rather than the gracious action of God (Gen. 18.10). This overemphasis on Abraham's good works in providing hospitality means Mitchell fails to recognize the narrative thrust of the Abraham–Sarah story which was the fulfilment of the promise of Genesis 12.1-3, 15.1-6 that God would make them a great nation with many descendants, and not on Abraham's actions. The key barrier to the promise was of course Sarah's barrenness and Genesis 18 functions to show the progression of events whereby she falls pregnant with a son (Gen. 18.10). Mitchell is correct that the story of Abraham in Genesis 18 and the story of Zacchaeus have strong linguistic parallels, but to suggest these imply 'justification by works'[124] is to misread both stories.

The primary action in the story of Zacchaeus is Jesus who seeks out the man in the tree and invites himself to his home. It is Jesus' actions that are the reason Zacchaeus is transformed and is able to support the poor financially. Similarly, in Genesis 18 it is the Lord's actions in coming to Abraham through the three visitors that allow the promise to be fulfilled when Sarah falls pregnant with Isaac. While both Abraham and Zacchaeus offer hospitality, this is not the key event in either narrative, the key event is in the 'Lord' of each story coming to each and doing the impossible (Gen. 18.14; Lk. 18.27).[125] In Genesis it is providing a son to a couple who are old (Gen. 18.11), and in Luke it is in a Jewish toll collector who works for

123. Mitchell, 'Zacchaeus Revisited', p. 169.
124. Mitchell, 'Zacchaeus Revisited', p. 169.
125. Andrew E. Arterbury, 'Zacchaeus: "A Son of Abraham"?' in *Biblical Interpretation in Early Christian Gospels: Volume 3, The Gospel of Luke* (ed. Thomas R. Hatina; LNTS, 376; London: T&T Clark, 2010), p. 19.

the Romans, finding salvation. The parallel with the story of the rich man brings the idea that nothing is impossible for God, to the fore.

This study suggests that Luke's mention of Zacchaeus as a υἱὸς Ἀβραάμ works in three ways. First, it affirms that Zacchaeus is Jewish, as the reader has surmised from his name (19.2). We know this is significant to the story because it sets up the tension between his occupation as ἀρχιτελώνης and his fellow Jews.[126]

Secondly, it does help us recall the wider story of Abraham. As a son of Abraham we would expect Zacchaeus to be entitled to the blessings of Abraham, and yet the Lukan story has showed us this now comes through a response to Jesus rather than a right due to one's ethnicity.[127] Luke has already shown the reader that belonging to the Jewish race is not an automatic reason for blessing. John the Baptist says:

> Bear fruits worthy of repentance. Do not begin to say to yourself, 'We have Abraham as our ancestor'; for I tell you, God is able from these stones to raise up children to Abraham. Even now the axe is lying at the root of the trees; every tree therefore that does not bear good fruit is cut down and thrown into the fire. (3.8-9)

This is also reflected in Jewish tradition seen in *m.'Abot.* 5.19 which says:

> Anyone in whom are these three traits is one of the disciples of Abraham, our father;
> But [if he bears] three other traits, he is one of the disciples of Balaam, the wicked: (1) a generous spirit, (2) a modest mien, and (3) a humble soul – he is one of the disciples of Abraham, our father. (1) A grudging spirit, (2) an arrogant mien, and (3) a proud soul – he is one of the disciples of Balaam, the wicked.

Thirdly, it recalls the story of the crippled woman who is θυγατέρα Ἀβραάμ (13.16). Describing someone as a daughter or son of Abraham only occurs twice in the Gospel, giving these two stories a narrative link. Mitchell's argument that Luke is pre-eminently highlighting Zacchaeus' action of hospitality authenticating him as a child of Abraham, is further unseated here.[128] If his argument was true it should also be true for the crippled woman who is θυγατέρα Ἀβραάμ (13.16). Yet, the crippled woman pericope (13.11-17) does not justify her healing by any actions she performs on behalf of the poor. When Jesus approaches the crippled woman on the sabbath Jesus is the one who initiates the encounter, as with Zacchaeus. Jesus says to her: γύναι, ἀπολέλυσαι τῆς ἀσθενείας σου (13.12). She is set free by Jesus and not in any way through her own actions, as shown

---

126. Marshall, *Gospel*, p. 698; Fitzmyer, *Luke*, p. 1221. *Contra*, Arterbury, 'Zacchaeus: "A Son of Abraham"?' p. 18; Dahl, 'Abraham in Luke-Acts', pp. 139–58.

127. Fitzmyer, *Luke*, p. 1226.

128. Mitchell, 'Zacchaeus Revisited', p. 168.

by the passive form of ἀπολύω. The perfect tense further indicates the ongoing nature of this healing. Jesus' action is an act that releases her from the power of Satan (13.16), and so Jesus reasons it is very appropriate that she is set free on the sabbath day. However, nowhere is this status as θυγατέρα Ἀβραάμ justified by her ability to help the poor; quite the reverse, she is the poor person who is in need of help. Although Mitchell makes much of interpreting Zacchaeus' narrative in light of the reference to υἱὸς Ἀβραάμ, the same methodology does not hold for the parallel passage where the woman is θυγατέρα Ἀβραάμ.

The two stories noticeably show Luke's special interest in paired stories of women and men. I suggest that the use of the expression υἱὸς Ἀβραάμ, which inevitably recalls the θυγατέρα Ἀβραάμ, in this final pericope in the travel narrative shows another aspect of universal salvation; salvation for both genders. We have seen through a parallel with the rich ruler that salvation is available for both rich and poor and here we have salvation for both men and women. The Davidic shepherd king seeks out and saves the lost on every mountain (Ezek. 34.6) and he seeks for the lost sheep until he finds it (Lk. 15.4).

Further, in Luke's use of the expression that σήμερον σωτηρία τῷ οἴκῳ τούτῳ ἐγένετο, the reader sees that salvation is brought to the house rather than simply an individual. This is a fulfilment of the household mission (9.1-6; 10.1-12) but also a prefiguring of the Acts Gentile household conversion narratives. The house is the place where meals are shared and throughout the ministry of Jesus, a place where religious and social barriers are levelled.[129] When Jesus dines with Zacchaeus, the barrier of his uncleanness is broken, and the reader sees a further dimension to the radically inclusive Lukan salvation; salvation of both clean and unclean, and ultimately both Jew and Gentile. Matson goes so far as to suggest that 'Jesus converts a household by entering and staying in the house of a proto-Gentile'.[130] In many respects Zacchaeus is considered so unclean that he is like a 'proto-Gentile'. Jesus' encounter with Zacchaeus certainly gives a hint that mission is extended to both Jew and Gentile and that Lukan salvation is for all ethnicities. This resonates with the Davidic shepherd king, who did not leave any sheep on the hillside but sought out and found all the sheep (Ezek. 34.11-16), and the inclusive salvation of the Davidic shepherd king in Micah, Jeremiah, Zechariah and *PssSol* 17. It also coheres with Luke 15.1-7 and the lost parables in general, when Jesus criticizes the religious leaders who are not seeking the lost sheep. Faithful shepherds do not leave one sheep lost in the wilderness, but leave the ninety-nine and search until they find it.

It is true there is no crowd response in this salvation story, but coming at the end of the travel narrative, this pericope ends instead with a summary statement of Jesus' mission as the Davidic shepherd king. The shepherd's mission is complete

---

129. Matson, *Household*, p. 43. Sanders notes that 'it is among the outcasts, in the periphery, that Jesus finds appropriate response, and this periphery is to be the springboard to the Gentile mission'. Jack T. Sanders, *The Jews in Luke-Acts* (Philadelphia: Fortress Press, 1987), pp. 207–8.

130. Matson, *Household*, p. 75.

outside of Jerusalem, salvation is available to all socio-economic groups, both genders, and it points to all ethnicities. I therefore suggest that Luke does not end with a crowd response because he instead transitions the story line into the Jerusalem narrative, where Jesus will enter Jerusalem to battle Satan for the lost. Furthermore, not all salvation stories end with a crowd response. The healing of Simon's mother-in-law (4.38-39), the haemorrhaging woman (8.43-48) and the ten lepers (17.11-19) also do not finish with a crowd response and yet all are clearly salvific encounters.

Luke ends with a Son of Man saying (19.10) which is a well-accepted reference to Ezekiel 34.[131] The Lukan Jesus is the Davidic Shepherd who is the faithful shepherd; he looks for the lost (τὸ ἀπολωλός) until he finds it (Ezek. 34.4, 16; Lk. 15.4; 19.10), and he saves the sheep (Ezek. 34.22; Lk. 19.9-10). While the self-designation ὁ υἱὸς τοῦ ἀνθρώπου raises questions as to whether Jesus actually spoke these words,[132] in this pericope there is a clearly defined royal Davidic context where Jesus speaks with authority, and the historical question is outside the parameters of this study.

We have noted earlier that the Zacchaeus encounter is preceded by the blind man calling twice, Ἰησοῦ υἱὲ Δαυίδ (18.38, 39), a feature which marks an explicit return to the Davidic theme, and a royal thread in general.[133] Now in 19.11-27 we find a parable which is full of the language of royal power, followed by Jesus entering Jerusalem as ὁ βασιλεύς (19.38).[134] This shows a special interest of Luke. The Markan triumphal entry says, ὡσαννά· εὐλογημένος ὁ ἐρχόμενος ἐν ὀνόματι κυρίου (Mk 11.9) while Luke writes, εὐλογημένος ὁ ἐρχόμενος, ὁ βασιλεὺς ἐν ὀνόματι κυρίου. This redaction shows Luke deliberately positioning Jesus as king. It also suggests an echo of Zech. 9.9-10 is likely,[135] and that Jesus enters Jerusalem as a righteous and salvific king who brings peace.

Zechariah resonates with the Lukan Jesus on several levels: Jesus is δίκαιος (23.47; Acts 3.14; 7.52; 22.14), Saviour (1.69; 2.11; Acts 5.31; 13.23), and brings εἰρήνη (1.79; 2.14; 7.50; 8.48; 10.5; 24.36; Acts 10.36); features of Zechariah's king. Both figures ride on a πῶλος which has never been ridden (Zech. 9.9; Lk. 19.30), and bring salvation to all the earth (Zech. 9.10; Lk. 24.47; Acts 1.8). These linguistic parallels suggest Zechariah 9 is behind Luke's picture and that he is highlighting Jesus as the righteous and salvific king.[136] However, as Jesus is to enter Jerusalem to suffer and die (9.22; 18.31-33) this also coheres with Zechariah's picture of the *suffering shepherd*. The shepherd suffers for and with the people (Zech. 11.4-5) and his suffering leads to salvation for the house of David (Zech. 13.1).

---

131. Bock, *Luke*, p. 1523; Fitzmyer, *Luke*, p. 1226; Green, *Gospel*, p. 673; Marshall, *Gospel*, p. 698; Nolland, *Luke*, p. 906; O'Hanlon, 'Zacchaeus', p. 18; Lieu, *Gospel of Luke*, p. 148.

132. Nolland, *Luke*, pp. 254–5, 907.

133. Nolland, *Luke*, p. 898; Marshall, *Gospel*, p. 691; Green, *Gospel*, p. 663.

134. It recalls Psalms 117.26 where a pilgrim is welcomed into Jerusalem to worship at the temple. Bock, *Luke*, p. 1558; Nolland, *Gospel of Luke*, p. 926.

135. Bock, *Luke*, p. 1558; Green, *Gospel*, p. 686.

136. Bock, *Luke*, p. 1556; Green, *Gospel*, p. 687.

Furthermore, there is a narrative link back to the infancy narrative where the Davidic motif is explicit and where angels sing of God's salvific peace (2.14).[137] The two versicles (2.14; 19.38) can be considered as parallel through their similar hymn-like structure, the repeated use of δόξα, ὕψιστος and εἰρήνη in both hymns and the deliberately contrasted reference to γῆ in the birth narrative and οὐρανός in the triumphal entry. These linguistic and structural features suggest their messages are complementary.

The reader finds a deliberate return to the Davidic strand of the infancy narrative where Jesus has been indirectly introduced as the Davidic shepherd king. At the end of Jesus' ministry years and the beginning of the Jerusalem section, it is clear to the reader that Jesus enters Jerusalem as a particular type of king, a *Davidic shepherd king* who is still seeking the lost sheep on his journey.

5.4 Luke 19.10 and Luke 4.18-19

The logical step after recognizing the truth of Marshall and Miura's statements regarding Luke 19.10 and hearing the echoes of the Davidic shepherd king in the Gospel is to recognize its resonance with the programmatic saying of the Gospel (4.18-19) and then consider what this might mean for reading Luke.

We know Luke brings the Nazareth sermon forward in his Gospel and develops the content considerably from Mark; it holds a unique place in the Lukan narrative. We also know that the Lukan Jesus' care for the poor and marginalized is very prominent in the text. After the Isaianic quote in 4.18-19, which is at the beginning of the Galilaean ministry, we see Jesus demonstrating this mission in pericope after pericope in the narrative. Jesus is constantly stopping his journey for those in need, and this shows how he fulfils the programmatic saying.

As Jesus stops for each person however, we also hear the echo of the Davidic shepherd of Ezekiel 34 whose job is to reach to sheep who are lost on the hills and mountains, so that all are brought salvation. We further note that 19.10 ends Jesus' ministry years outside Jerusalem, and wonder about the placement of this saying at the *telos* of Jesus' journey, and the vision at 4.18-19 which begins his ministry. This leads me to propose that Luke has a second programmatic passage, and that 19.10 functions as a *programmatic inclusio* which echoes and defines the first saying. The Spirit of the Lord has anointed Jesus, Luke says in 4.18-19, so that he will bring good news to the poor, to proclaim release to the captives, recovery of sight to the blind, to let the oppressed go free, and to proclaim the year of the Lord's favour. We suggest that this ministry is carried out as a faithful shepherd. In many ways the two sayings make the same point, while the second defines how that ministry is carried out. It is carried out as God's faithful shepherd.

The impact of 19.10 as a *summative* statement of what has gone before ultimately paves the way for a recollection of 4.18-19, and allows us, perhaps even

137. Coleridge, *Birth*, pp. 143–5; Green, *Gospel*, p. 687; Nolland, *Luke*, p. 108; Marshall, *Gospel*, p. 715.

demands, that we hear as Miura heard, Luke summarize Jesus' earthly ministry as that of the *Davidic shepherd*. It is the blank in the narrative where the author 'does not set the whole picture before the reader',[138] but asks them to draw the inference for themselves. It is also an example of Buber's *estrangement* where two remote texts are related and the texts attract the reader to what is unique or exceptional. As he notes, this allows for significant meaning to emerge as the directing tool draws the reader to a conclusion.[139] Here, Jesus' ministry to the poor is enacted in his role as the Davidic shepherd king.

It is not just the placement of the two passages and that they echo each other thematically that lends support to this proposal; I think there are other signs that this may be a possible reading for Luke. First, we have already noted that the programmatic saying has a chiastic focus on the recovery of sight to the blind and that this idea of 'seeing' is used in a salvific sense for Luke. We have seen this confirmed in 7.21-22 and made visible when Jesus heals the blind man in 18.35-43. This is the pericope immediately prior to the Zacchaeus story when Jesus' ministry outside Jerusalem has its culmination or goal. While the healing of the blind man is a triple tradition passage, we have seen that Luke has inserted the Zacchaeus story immediately afterwards, suggesting that there is a cumulative sense of *telos*, whereby Luke has linked two passages together that bring a fulfilment to the programmatic saying. That is, we read Jesus fulfilling the heart of the Isaianic passage (Isa. 61.1-2) in the healing of the blind man, and then restating its message clothed in the language of Ezekiel's shepherd. This shows a significant narrative connection between the beginning and end of Jesus' ministry.

Secondly, the gospel for Luke is about the forgiveness of sins (5.17-26, 29-32; 7.36-50; 11.4; 15; 19.1-10; 23.39-43; 24.7, 47) and Luke has many pericopae revisioning the notion of ἁμαρτωλός, but it is as the Davidic shepherd that Jesus shows the way ahead. In particular, the Davidic shepherd gathers in the sheep and feeds them. While Jesus' ministry is characterized by moving from one meal to another, so too Ezekiel 34 has a key focus on the sheep being fed, so much so that we have seen the prophet use βόσκω eleven times in the one chapter. The prophet is convinced God is concerned that his people are fed. At the time of the Gospel's writing the religious elite had so many *halakhic* practices that they had become defined by their exclusion of people at meals. Jesus instead, went to the heart of the matter by dealing with sin and welcoming and eating with all who would dine with him. Further, he then sent the seventy as lambs in the household mission into Gentile territory, a prefigurement of the Acts household mission into Gentile territory. This Gentile mission is hinted at in the Nazareth sermon by the references to the widow of Zarephath and Naaman the Syrian (4.25-28), and is seen in the Zacchaeus pericope also with Zacchaeus' household mission as 'a proto-Gentile' mission. He is the final example in the ministry years where we see one who is materially rich to whom the good news of salvation is brought, and

138. Iser, *Implied Reader*, p. 282.
139. Buber, *Scripture*, pp. 114-28.

who finds forgiveness of sins (ἄφεσις; 4.18) and gives half of his possessions for the benefit of the poor.

These two sayings balance one another and both seek to describe Jesus' mission to the lost. Luke describes people as poor at the beginning of his ministry (4.18) and lost at the end of his ministry (19.10), and both summarize the vision of Jesus' earthly ministry. Their structural placement at either end of Jesus' ministry is an indicator of a theological feature for Luke. He has the Lukan Jesus going to the poor lost sheep, and with the care of a faithful shepherd, he gathers them in to the flock. As Luke understands salvation, not one is to be left out.

5.5 Summary

As we have examined Jesus' final encounter in the travel narrative, we have seen that the Zacchaeus story is a salvation story and not a vindication story. Although the present tense is used for the verbs δίδωμι and ἀποδίδωμι in 19.8, the thrust of the pericope is overwhelmingly that of a salvation story. Luke returns to language and themes of both the infancy narrative and the ministry years and ultimately shows that salvation is available for all people, clean and unclean, Jew and Gentile, rich and poor, men and women. The salvific act is centered in Zacchaeus' house, an example of household mission from the mission of the seventy and a prefigurement to the Gentile household mission of Acts. The ethical reform of the ἀρχιτελώνης is directly related to the salvific act of vv. 5–6 as salvation is multi-layered in Luke. Zacchaeus is saved to the community, from exclusion, and gains eternal life as he responds to Jesus with haste and with joy. At such a pivotal narrative juncture therefore, there is a completeness to Jesus' ministry outside Jerusalem. While the Gospel has laid particular emphasis on God's concern for the poor and his great demands on the rich, finally we see a rich person enter the kingdom. The crowd has recently called out, 'who then can be saved?' (18.26) after Jesus has asked the rich ruler to sell his possessions and give them to the poor, and in Zacchaeus an answer is finally given.

We then considered how 19.10 adds to our knowledge of the shepherd motif. We found the shepherd seeks out the lost sheep that they might be saved. He knows the sheep by name and is inclusive of ethnicity, status and gender. He is a shepherd who brings peace to the community and supports ethical action on behalf of the poor. The Davidic shepherd king desires a response of haste and joy when he calls to the one who is lost.

We finally made clear that Luke's narrative makes rhetorical use of the Davidic shepherd king motif by placing this saying, which echoes the programmatic saying of 4.18-19, as the final encounter of the ministry outside Jerusalem of the Lukan Jesus. The Zacchaeus pericope is an insertion into the Markan narrative and allows for the reader to see Jesus as he turns to his work in Jerusalem, with the clothes of a Davidic shepherd who cares for each individual sheep. Miura's statement that the Davidic shepherd sums up the earthly ministry of Jesus holds true.

We then suggested that the programmatic saying which comes at the beginning of the Galilaean ministry does not function alone, but is echoed by 19.10 and the two sayings work together to form a *programmatic inclusio*. The first saying describes the scope of Jesus' mission and the second saying describes how the mission is enacted. That is, Jesus' mission to the poor is as the faithful Davidic shepherd king, who is constantly seeking out and saving the lost.

6

THE DAVIDIC SHEPHERD KING IN THE LUKAN NARRATIVE

In this investigation, we have seen that Luke has crafted the narrative of Jesus so that the reader learns not only about his salvific mission to the poor and the lost, but also how he carries out his mission. That is, he does so as God's faithful shepherd constantly reaching to the margins of society for the lost sheep whom he saves and restores to the community. His ministry is characterized by dining and journeying with toll collectors and sinners from whom the Pharisees and scribes distanced themselves, and as he does so he enacts a radical inclusiveness, a gospel for all people.

As we noted in Chapter 1, Luke uses a variety of christological terms in his narrative[1] and the Davidic title stands alongside titles such as Lord, Messiah, and Saviour, which clearly take a central role.

The main result of this study is to give a more complete understanding of the character and task of Jesus as the Davidic Messiah in Luke-Acts who fulfils the role of faithful shepherd by his care of all people regardless of their ritual purity status or the cost of the task. He is the one in whom peace is brought to earth in the form of salvation and he is the one who exhibits the godly traits of a leader. The christological contribution this study offers is one of nuancing the already recognized Davidic Messiah in Luke, so that the shades of the shepherd who protects, feeds, guards, and cares for all God's flock, is recognized. It does not seek to overturn any other Christology, but shows that the role of Luke's Davidic Messiah reaches to the ends of the earth (24.47; Acts 1.8) because God's salvific peace is for all people and it is God's desire that not even one sheep should be lost. The theme of universal salvation which permeates Acts is thus the outworking of a Shepherd who saves both Jew and Gentile.

In Chapter 1 we established the rationale for a narrative methodology that draws on a solid exegetical base, noting that Luke has stated he is writing a διήγησις (1.1). We noted especially that narrative is cumulative and works toward its *telos*, and also how narrative is cohesive and the Lukan narrative is a whole which can interpret itself. We saw that the ordering of narrative is an important semantic tool, and especially that the beginnings of narratives are important as

---

1. Tuckett, 'Christology', p. 139.

they set the parameters for the ongoing story. Further, we considered how gaps and blanks in a narrative are deliberate and create opportunities for the reader to engage in the meanings of texts, and how repetition has a clear role in creating a *Leitwort* which reveals and clarifies an author's meaning. This repetition can involve an individual word or a semantic cluster of words and can happen with great effect over a distance in a text and also a motif's efficacy is strengthened when it occurs at strategic places in the narrative. In identifying gaps and blanks and *Leitwortstil*, the reader is logically restrained by the thrust of the text, and thus we considered criteria that strengthen the likelihood of a motif and its efficacy.

We noted the value of examining echoes in the Lukan narrative as Luke's writing style is more likely to allude to a passage rather than use a direct quote. We adopted Hays' seven tests for echoes and have used this tool repeatedly as we examined various passages.

In Chapter 2 we found that the motif of shepherd is used from the very earliest stages of the story of Israel conveying God's care and protection of his people, in the story of the exodus, and that David is seen as God's new shepherd for Israel. In the story of David the shepherd motif kept recurring during David's early years in Jesse's household to his anointing as the shepherd of Israel. It was in the background of the Davidic covenant, Nathan's parable, and the sin of the census which is at the coda of David's life. We found therefore, that when we talk of David and his kingship, his identity as a shepherd is an inseparable element.

With this in mind, in Chapter 3 we considered the Davidic theme at the beginning of the Gospel narrative (Luke 1–2). We examined each of the direct references to David, the related language of sonship, Bethlehem, shepherd, and echoes of David's story, arguing that these associated cluster of ideas formed a strong *Leitwort* which were deliberately chosen by the author to underpin the ongoing narrative. This led us to conclude that Luke 1–2 is crafted to highlight the Davidic story, but that this is coloured by the motif of the *shepherd king*. We found that the question of why the angels went to the shepherds in the birth narrative is best explained with reference to the messianic shepherd of Micah 5. Luke's reference to the πόλιν Δαυὶδ ἥτις καλεῖται Βηθλέεμ functions as a directing tool toward a new type of king and kingdom under the care of a Davidic shepherd. This is supported by Luke's genealogy which does not follow Matthew's line through Solomon, but instead, points to Jeremiah's prophecy (Jer. 22.28-30) where the kingly line would be superseded by the Davidic shepherd king from Jeremiah 23. This king's rule is characterized by justice, righteousness and salvation, which resonates with the Lukan Jesus.

Further, Luke points to Jesus' kingship as distinct from that of Augustus. Luke views the Davidic shepherd king as superior and vastly more powerful than the imperial world. He suggests that Jesus' kingship is characterized by righteousness and peace, features of Micah's messianic shepherd.

In Chapter 4 we considered the shepherd saying in 10.3 in the household mission mandate where Jesus sends the seventy out as a shepherd, and how in enacting his mission, the disciples act as faithful shepherds who eat with anyone and bring God's salvific peace. We noted the use of τὸ μικρὸν ποίμνιον in 12.32

in the context of Jesus' teaching on God's care and provision where we found an echo of Ezekiel 34 and how this placed Jesus in the role of Ezekiel's Davidic shepherd king. Further, in the parable of the faithful shepherd which conveys the heart of Luke's gospel, a faithful leader is like the shepherd who seeks out every lost sheep until it is found. While the parable is theocentric and speaks of what God does, Jesus is shown to be enacting the parable by hosting and welcoming the toll collectors and sinners, a burden of restoration he was willing to carry. This implicit polemic against the religious leaders of the day will have resonated in them, since they knew they were shepherds of God's flock and Jesus was implying they were in error. This pericope also echoed Ezekiel 34 with both its critique of the current leaders and its description of godly leadership.

We then turned to Paul's *Abschiedsrede* and noted that the motif recurred when he exhorted the Ephesian elders as he journeyed to Jerusalem. We observed how Paul and Jesus' lives are paralleled in the narrative, and in the same way Jesus strengthened the weak and cared for the flock in the Gospel in line with Ezekiel 34, so too did Paul in his ministry. We conceded that this motif was not prominent in Acts, yet it was found to be relevant and applicable for the early church in this, the only speech to Christians.

In Chapter 5 we found that the qualities of the Davidic shepherd king, particularly of Ezekiel 34, bore considerable resonance with the programmatic saying of Luke 4.18-19 and the Lukan Jesus' mission to the poor and marginalized. In using Hamm's analysis of the saying we found that the recovery of sight to the blind fell at the centre of the chiasm and yet Luke did not make this visible in the text until near the end of the travel narrative in the story of the blind man (18.35-43) which precedes the story of Zacchaeus. In the story of the blind man we noted that Luke made a clear return to the royal Davidic motif in the infancy narrative, and how 19.1-10 gave this a shepherd hue. Luke therefore describes Jesus' entry into Jerusalem as a *shepherd* king who had been constantly stopping on his journey for the lost sheep.

We especially considered the final encounter in the Lukan Jesus' journey to Jerusalem where Zacchaeus and his house are saved. Zacchaeus, a rich proto-Gentile, is saved in the encounter and demonstrates that for Luke, salvation is universal as now we have a rich person entering the kingdom. We also found that Zacchaeus a son of Abraham, is a narrative foil to the daughter of Abraham (13.10-17). This points to universal salvation in regard to gender. Luke's gospel really is good news for all people. This lent support to Marshall's comment that 19.10 sums up the message of the Gospel, and Miura's statement that Jesus' earthly ministry is characterized by his ministry as *Davidic shepherd*, for the Gospel shows the Lukan Jesus reaching constantly to the margins and saving the lost sheep.

Finally, this led to the conclusion that Luke has a *programmatic inclusio* where the mission statement at 4.18-19 is echoed in 19.10. They are similar sayings and are placed at either end of the ministry of the Lukan Jesus. The first saying explains Jesus' mission to the poor and the second comments on how this mission is fulfilled. For Luke, Jesus' mission to the poor is enacted as God's faithful Davidic shepherd king. Jesus seeks out the lost sheep, he heals the sick, and he binds up the broken hearted, and he saves each one. He searches for a lost sheep until he finds it; not one sheep is to be lost, for salvation is multi-layered and it is universally available for all people; in Acts we see this mission extended geographically.

Our study has shown that Ezekiel 34 is a scripture Luke drew on repeatedly, and it is a passage that is clearly significant for the Gospel. While the Davidic covenant and Micah's messianic shepherd are relevant for the narratives' beginning, Ezekiel 34 becomes a key text for Luke as he describe Jesus' ministry.

As I finish this study, the world and the church are struggling with leadership in this radically globalized and interconnected earth. From what I have seen in the Lukan narrative world, they struggled too. The Greco-Roman world was dominated by the imperial superpower, but Luke saw an inadequacy and impotence in their sphere of power. While Caesar issued a decree that all the world must be registered, Luke showed all that happened was Mary and Joseph arrived at the place God had already said, through the prophet Micah in the eighth century, that the messianic shepherd was to be born. Who really held real power here? For Luke it was God.

Similarly, the leadership shown by the religious leaders was negative for Luke. Their rules regarding ritual purity caused them to separate themselves from 'unclean' people around the meal table. As I have read Luke, I think Luke shows us another style of leadership, that of the Davidic shepherd king who feeds and even eats with the sheep, gathers them in, searches for one that is lost, and welcomes and saves the sheep. This radical inclusion is for all: women and men, Gentile and Jew, and for those at both ends of the social spectrum. It is this salvation which Jesus enacts and the disciples are called to follow, which Luke suggests can enable the gospel to go to the ends of the earth. Forgiveness of sins is paramount as social, ethical and gender barriers are broken down. This is good news for our current world, and the theological and practical implications of this work deserve some further study.

I have also suggested that Luke's household mission, where a new 'sacred space' is created, deserves further consideration. I have long considered that in Luke's writing there are the seeds of Jesus superseding the temple. I am aware that the temple is still very visible in Acts, but narratively it holds a unique place for Luke. In an apocalyptic Gospel passage, Jesus says, ἰδοὺ ἀφίεται ὑμῖν ὁ οἶκος ὑμῶν (Lk. 13.35) and Stephen states, οὐχ ὁ ὕψιστος ἐν χειροποιήτοις κατοικεῖ (Acts 7.48). In the mission mandate salvation is brought to households, but salvation for Luke is intrinsically tied to the forgiveness of sins (Lk. 1.77; 3.3; 4.18; 24.47; Acts 2.38; 5.31; 10.43; 13.31; 26.18). Luke seems to be suggesting a new locus for the forgiveness of sins which is tied to Jesus and his presence. I also note that Luke moves the story of the tearing of the temple curtain to before Jesus dies (23.45), which has not been satisfactorily explained. I wonder if Luke's passion takes the emphasis off the temple, for οὐχ ὁ ὕψιστος ἐν χειροποιήτοις κατοικεῖ. A fresh reading of the temple in the Lukan narrative would also be valuable.

Furthermore, as Jesus the shepherd comes into view in the narrative, it would be valuable to re-read Luke's use of Isaiah 53 with its sheep motif. Luke quotes Isaiah 53 twice in Luke-Acts (Lk. 22.37 – Isa. 53.12; Acts 8.32-33 – Isa. 53.7-8).

The most extensive quote is in Acts 8.32-33 where the images of a sheep and a lamb are used by Luke to explain the good news of Jesus. It is interesting that here we may have the functional opposite of the motif of shepherd, the motif of sheep for whom the shepherd cares.

It would be worth exploring whether there is a reversal of the motif of shepherd in Acts 8.32-33, and considering if within this, there may lie the embryonic seeds of an 'incarnational' understanding of Jesus. That is, is Luke presenting Jesus as becoming *one like us*, his flock, in his life and in his death? Scholars often comment that Luke's narrative lacks a strong work of the cross.[2] The Miletus speech is one of only two direct references to the vicarious work of the cross (Lk. 22.20; Acts 20.28). Yet, if Luke uses Isaiah 53 in the encounter of Philip with the Ethiopian Eunuch in such a way that Jesus is identified as the sheep led to slaughter, then we may have another way Luke is explaining the work of Jesus' death on the flock's behalf. The other quote in Luke 22.37 also contains some strong possibilities for a re-reading of the quote with a vicarious dimension. The essence of this idea comes from this study, but it was not within the scope of the study to explore.

Finally, it would be valuable to consider the relevance of this work to the study of the historical Jesus. The shepherd motif has already been recognized in the Gospels of Matthew, Mark and John, while our study has demonstrated this motif was also used by Luke. This raises the possibility that this was not simply a Lukan nuance, but one that has been influenced by the Jesus tradition or even Jesus himself. Our methodology has been primarily narrative, but now it would be valuable to move from the history within the narrative to a consideration of the picture of Jesus within his historical-cultural world. What was Jesus' self-understanding of his role and is there a historical basis for this motif?

2. Luke's theology of the cross is questioned for two reasons. First, if Luke 22.20 is authentic, then why is it entirely absent from the missionary sermons in Acts? Second, why does Luke omit the ransom saying in Mark 10.45? Green, *Gospel*, p. 764; I. Howard Marshall, *Last Supper and Lord's Supper* (Exeter: Paternoster, 1980), p. 101.

BIBLIOGRAPHY

Adams, D. H., *The Sinner in Luke* (Eugene: Pickwick, 2008).

Aland, B., K. Aland, M. Black, J. Karavidopoulos, C. Martini and B. Metzger, *The Greek New Testament* (Stuttgart: United Bible Societies, 4th ed., 1993).

Aland, K. (ed.), *Synopsis of the Four Gospels: Greek-English Edition of the Synopsis Quattuor Evangeliorum, On the Basis of the Greek Text of Nestle-Aland 27th Edition and Greek New Testament 4th Revised Edition. The English Text is the Second Edition of the Revised Standard Version* (Stuttgart: German Bible Society, 13th ed., 2007).

Alter, R., *The Art of Biblical Narrative* (London: George Allen and Unwin, 1981).

Alter, R., *The David Story: A Translation and Commentary of 1 and 2 Samuel* (New York: Norton, 1999).

Amit, Y., 'The Multi-Purpose "Leading Word" and the Problems of its Usage' *Prooftexts* 9 (1989): 99–114.

Anderson, A. A., *2 Samuel, Vol. 11* (Word Biblical Commentary; Dallas: Word, 1989).

Arterbury, A. E., 'Zacchaeus: "A Son of Abraham"?' in *Biblical Interpretation in Early Christian Gospels: Volume 3, The Gospel of Luke* (ed. T. R. Hatina; Library of New Testament Studies, 376; London: T&T Clark, 2010).

Bailey, K. E., *Finding the Lost: Cultural Keys to Luke 15* (St. Louis: Concordia, 1992).

Bailey, K. E., *Jacob and the Prodigal: How Jesus Retold Israel's Story* (Downers Grove: IVP Academic, 2003).

Bailey, K. E., *Poet and Peasant and Through Peasant Eyes: A Literary and Cultural Approach to the Parables of Jesus* (Grand Rapids: Eerdmans, 1983).

Bar-Efrat, S., 'First Samuel', in *The Jewish Study Bible* (eds A. Berlin and M. Zvi Brettler (Oxford: Oxford University Press, 2004).

Bar-Efrat, S., *Narrative Art in the Bible* (trans. D. Shefer-Vanson; Journal for the Study of the Old Testament Supplement Series; 70; Bible and Literature Series, 17; Sheffield: Almond Press, 1989).

Bar-Efrat, S., 'Some Observations on the Analysis of Structure in Biblical Literature', *Vetus Testamentum* 30 (1980): 154–73.

Bartholomew, C. G., J. B. Green and A. C. Thiselton (eds), *Reading Luke: Interpretation, Reflection, Formation* (Scripture and Hermeneutics Series 6. Grand Rapids: Zondervan, 2005).

Barton, S. C., 'Parables on God's Love and Forgiveness (Luke 15:1-32)', in *The Challenge of Jesus' Parables* (ed. R. N. Longenecker; Grand Rapids: Eerdmans, 2000).

Bauckham, R., *Jesus and the Eyewitnesses: The Gospels as Eyewitness Testimony* (Grand Rapids: Eerdmans, 2006).

Bauckham, R. (ed.) *The Gospel for All Christians: Rethinking the Gospel Audiences* (Grand Rapids: Eerdmans, 1998).

Bauer, W., W. Danker, W. F. Arndt and F. W. Gingrich, *A Greek-English Lexicon of the New Testament and other Early Christian Literature* (Chicago: University of Chicago Press, 3rd ed., 2000).

Benjamin, M. H., 'The Tacit Agenda of a Literary Approach to the Bible', *Prooftexts* 27 (2007): 254–74.

Bergen, R. D., *1, 2 Samuel* (The New American Commentary; Nashville: Broadman and Holman, 1996).

Biblia Hebraica Stuttgartensia: With Westminster Hebrew Morphology (Stuttgart; Glenside PA: German Bible Society; Westminster Seminary, electronic ed., 1996).

Black, D. A. and D. S. Dockery, *Interpreting the New Testament: Essays on Methodology and Issues* (Nashville: Broadman and Holman, 2001).

Blomberg, C. L., *Contagious Holiness: Jesus' Meals with Sinners* (New Studies in Biblical Theology, 19; Downers Grove, IVP/Leicester: Apollos, 2005).

Blomberg, C. L., *Interpreting the Parables* (Downers Grove: IVP, 1990).

Blomberg, C. L., 'Midrash, Chiasmus, and the Outline of Luke's Central Section', in *Gospel Perspectives III: Studies in Midrash and Historiography* (eds R. T. France and D. Wenham; Sheffield: JSOT Press, 1983).

Bock, D. L., *Acts* (Baker Exegetical Commentary on the New Testament; Grand Rapids: Baker Academic, 2007).

Bock, D. L., 'Echoes of Scripture in Luke-Acts: Telling the History of God's People Intertextually', *Catholic Biblical Quarterly* 68 (2006): 152–4.

Bock, D. L., *Luke 1:1-9:50* (Baker Exegetical Commentary on the New Testament; Grand Rapids: Baker Books, 1994).

Bock, D. L., *Luke 9:51-24:53* (Baker Exegetical Commentary on the New Testament; Grand Rapids: Baker Books, 1996).

Bock, D. L., *Proclamation From Prophecy and Pattern: Lukan Old Testament Christology* (Journal for the Study of the New Testament Supplement Series 12. Sheffield: Sheffield Academic, 1987).

Bock, D. L., 'Proclamation from Prophecy and Pattern: Luke's Use of the Old Testament for Christology and Mission', in *The Gospels and the Scriptures of Israel* (eds C. A. Evans and W. R. Stegner; Journal for the Study of the New Testament Supplement Series 104; Sheffield: Sheffield Academic, 1999).

Bodner, K., *1 Samuel: A Narrative Commentary* (Hebrew Bible Monographs, 19; Sheffield: Sheffield Phoenix Press, 2008).

Borg, M. J., *Conflict, Holiness and Politics in the Teachings of Jesus* (Studies in the Bible and Early Christianity, 5; Harrisburg: Trinity Press International, 1998).

Bovon, F., *Das Evangelium nach Lukas 1. Teilband Lk 1,1-9,50* (Evangelisch-Katholischer Kommentar zum Neuen Testament; Zürich: Benziger, 1989).

Bovon, F., *Das Evangelium nach Lukas 2. Teilband Lk 9,51-14,35* (Evangelisch-Katholischer Kommentar zum Neuen Testament. Zürich: Benziger, 1996).

Bovon, F., *Das Evangelium nach Lukas 3. Teilband Lk 15,1-19,27* (Evangelisch-Katholischer Kommentar zum Neuen Testament. Zürich: Benziger; Neukirchen-Vluyn: Neukirchener Verlag, 2001).

Bovon, F., *Luke the Theologian: Fifty-five Years of Research (1950–2005)* (Waco: Baylor, 2nd rev. ed., 2006).

Bowman, A. K., E. Champlin and A. Lintott (eds), *The Cambridge Ancient History: The Augustan Empire 43 B.C.–A.D. 69 Vol. 10* (Cambridge: Cambridge University Press, 2nd ed., 1996).

Brawley, R. L., *Text to Text Pours Forth Speech: Voices of Scripture in Luke-Acts* (Bloomington: Indiana University Press, 1995).

Brodie, T. L., 'Luke-Acts as an Imitation and Emulation of the Elijah-Elisha Narrative', in *New Views on Luke and Acts* (ed. E. Richard; Collegeville: Liturgical Press, 1990).

Brown, F., S. Driver and C. Briggs (eds), *A Hebrew and English Lexicon of the Old Testament.* (Oxford: Clarendon Press, 1906).

Brown, R. E., *The Birth of the Messiah: A Commentary on the Infancy Narratives in Matthew and Luke* (New York: Doubleday, 1977).

Brown, R. E., *The Death of the Messiah: From Gethsemane to the Grave, A Commentary on the Passion Narratives in the Four Gospels* (Anchor Bible Reference Library; 2 vols; New York: Doubleday, 1994).

Bruce, F. F., *The Book of Acts* (Grand Rapids: Eerdmans, rev. ed., 1988).

Brueggemann, W., *David's Truth: In Israel's Imagination and Memory* (Philadelphia: Fortress Press, 1988).

Brueggemann, W., *First and Second Samuel* (Interpretation; Louisville: John Knox Press, 1990).

Buber, M. and F. Rosenzweig, *Scripture and Translation* (trans. L. Rosenwald with E. Fox; Indiana Studies in Biblical Literature; Bloomington: Indiana University Press, 1994).

Bultmann, R. K., *The History of the Synoptic Tradition* (trans. J. Marsh; Oxford: Basil Blackwell, 1963).

Burger, C., *Jesus als Davidssohn: Eine traditionsgeschichtliche Untersuchung* (Göttingen: Vandenhoeck and Ruprecht, 1970).

Cadbury, H. J., 'The "We" and "I" Passages in Luke-Acts', *New Testament Studies* 3 (1957): 128–32.

Campbell, A. F., *1 Samuel. The Forms of Old Testament Literature, Vol. 7* (Grand Rapids: Eerdmans, 2003).

Cartledge, T. W., *1 & 2 Samuel* (Macon: Smyth and Helwys, 2001).

Ceresko, A. R., 'A Rhetorical Analysis of David's "Boast" (1 Samuel 17:34-37): Some Reflections on Method'. *Catholic Biblical Quarterly* 47 (1985): 59–74.

Chae, Y. S., *Jesus as the Eschatological Davidic Shepherd: Studies in the Old Testament, Second Temple Judaism, and in the Gospel of Matthew* (Wissenschaftliche Untersuchungen zum Neuen Testament, 2; Reihe 216; Tübingen: Mohr Siebeck, 2006).

Chatman, S., *Story and Discourse: Narrative Structure in Fiction and Film* (Ithaca: Cornell University Press, 1978).

Coleridge, M., *The Birth of the Lukan Narrative: Narrative as Christology in Luke 1–2* (Journal for the Study of the New Testament Supplement Series 88; Sheffield: JSOT, 1993).

Colson, F. H., G. H. Whitaker and R. Marcus (trans.) *Philo* (The Loeb Classical Library; 12 vols; Cambridge, MA: Harvard University Press, 1927–62).

Conzelmann, H., *Acts of the Apostles: a Commentary on the Acts of the Apostles* (Hermeneia; Philadelphia: Fortress Press, 1987).

Conzelmann, H., *Die Mitte der Zeit: Studien zur Theologie des Lukas* (Beiträge zur historischen Theologie; Tübingen: Mohr, 1954).

Conzelmann, H., *The Theology of St. Luke* (trans. Geoffrey Buswell; Philadelphia: Fortress Press, 1982).

Corley, J. (ed.), *New Perspectives on the Nativity* (London: T&T Clark, 2009).

Crook, J. A. 'Augustus: Power, Authority and Achievement', in *The Cambridge Ancient History: The Augustan Empire 43 B.C.–A.D. 69*, vol. 10, (eds A. K. Bowman, E. Champlin and A. Lintott; Cambridge: Cambridge University Press, 2nd ed., 1996).

Crossan, J. D., *The Historical Jesus: The Life of a Mediterranean Jewish Peasant* (Edinburgh: T&T Clark, 1991).

Culpepper, R. A., *Anatomy of the Fourth Gospel: A Study in Literary Design* (Philadelphia: Fortress Press, 1983).

Culpepper, R. A., 'The Gospel of Luke', in *The New Interpreter's Bible* (Nashville: Abingdon Press, 1995).

Curkpatrick, S., 'Parable Metonymy and Luke's Kerygmatic Framing', *Journal for the Study of the New Testament* 25 (2003): 289-307.

Dahl, N. A., 'The Story of Abraham in Luke-Acts', in *Studies in Luke-Acts* (eds L. E. Keck and J. L. Martyn; London: SPCK, 1968).

Danker, F. W., *Benefactor: Epigraphic Study of a Graeco-Roman and New Testament Semantic Field* (St Louis: Clayton Publishing House, 1982).

Danker, F. W., *Jesus and the New Age: A Commentary on St Luke's Gospel* (Philadelphia: Fortress Press, 1988).

Del Agua, A., 'The Lucan Narrative of the "Evangelisation of the Kingdom of God": A Contribution to the Unity of Acts', in *The Unity of Luke-Acts* (ed. J. Verheyden; Bibliotheca Ephemeridum Theologicarum Lovaniensium, 142; Leuven: Peeters, 1999).

Denova, R. I., *The Things Accomplished Among Us: Prophetic Tradition in the Structural Patterns of Luke-Acts* (Journal for the Study of the New Testament Supplement Series 141; Sheffield: Sheffield Academic, 1997).

Dewey, J., *Markan Public Debate: Literary Technique, Concentric Structure, and Theology in Mark 2:1-3:6* (Society of Biblical Literature Dissertation Series 48; Chico: Scholars Press, 1980).

Dibelius, M., *Studies in the Acts of the Apostles* (ed. H. Greeven; trans. M. Ling; Mifflintown, PA: Sigler Press, repr., 1999).

Dowling, E. V., *Taking Away the Pound: Women, Theology and the Parable of the Pounds in the Gospel of Luke* (Library of New Testament Studies, 324; London: T&T Clark, 2007).

Drury, J., 'Luke', in *The Literary Guide to the Bible* (ed. Robert Alter and Frank Kermode; London: Collins, 1987).

Dunn, J. D. G., *Jesus Remembered: Christianity in the Making* (Grand Rapids: Eerdmans, 2003).

Dunn, J. D. G., 'Pharisees, Sinners and Jesus', in *The Social World of Formative Christianity and Judaism: Essays in Tribute to Howard Clark Kee* (eds J. Neusner, P. Borgen, E. S. Frerichs and R. Horsley; Philadelphia: Fortress Press, 1988).

Dupont, J., *Études sur les Actes des Apôtres* (Lectio Divina, 45; Paris: Éditions du Cerf, 1967).

Dupont, J., *Sources of Acts: the Present Position* (trans. K. Pond; London: Darton, Longman and Todd, 1964).

Dupont, J., *The Salvation of the Gentiles: Studies in the Acts of the Apostles* (trans. J. Keating; New York: Paulist Press, 1979).

Eagleton, T., *Literary Theory: An Introduction* (Minneapolis: University of Minnesota Press, 2008).

Ehrman, B. D. (ed.) (trans.) *The Apostolic Fathers Vol. 1: 1 Clement, 2 Clement, Ignatius, Polycarp, Didache* (Loeb Classical Library; Cambridge, MA: Harvard University Press, 2003).

Ehrman, B. D. (ed.) (trans.) *The Apostolic Fathers Vol. 2: Epistle of Barnabas, Papias and Quadratus, Epistle to Diognetus, The Shepherd of Hermas* (Loeb Classical Library; Cambridge, MA: Harvard University Press, 2003).

Elliott, J. H., 'Purity' in *The Social World of the New Testament: Insights and Models* (eds J. H. Neyrey and E. C. Stewart; Peabody: Hendrickson, 2008).

Epstein, I. (ed.), *The Babylonian Talmud* (18 vols; London: Soncino, 1948–52).

Esler, P. F., *Community and Gospel in Luke-Acts: The Social and Political Motivations of Lucan Theology* (Society for the New Testament Studies Monograph Series 57; Cambridge: Cambridge University Press, 1987).

Eslinger, L., *House of God or House of David: The Rhetoric of 2 Samuel 7* (Journal for the Study of the Old Testament Supplement Series 164; Sheffield: Sheffield Academic, 1994).

Eslinger, L., *Kingship of God in Crisis: A Close Reading of 1 Samuel 1–12* (Sheffield: Almond Press, 1985).

Evans, C. F., *Saint Luke* (Trinity Press International New Testament Commentaries; London: SCM, 1990).

Evans, C. F., 'The Central Section of St. Luke's Gospel', in *Studies in the Gospels: Essays in Memory of R. H. Lightfoot* (ed. D. E. Nineham; Oxford: Basil Blackwell, 1955).

Evans, C. A., 'From Gospel to Gospel: The Function of Isaiah in the New Testament', in *Writing and Reading the Scroll of Isaiah: Studies of an Interpretive Tradition* (eds C. C. Broyles and C. A. Evans; Vetus Testamentum Supplement, 70.2. Leiden: Brill, 1997).

Evans, C. A., *Mark 8:27–16:20, Vol. 34B* (Word Biblical Commentary; Nashville: Thomas Nelson, 2002).

Evans, C. A. and S. E. Porter (eds), *Dictionary of New Testament Background* (Downers Grove: IVP, 2000).

Evans, C. A. and J. A. Sanders, *Luke and Scripture: The Function of Sacred Tradition in Luke-Acts* (Minneapolis: Fortress Press, 1993).

Farris, S., *The Hymns of Luke's Infancy Narratives: Their Origin, Meaning and Significance* (Journal for the Study of the New Testament Supplement Series 9; Sheffield: JSOT, 1985).

Fiedler, P., *Jesus und die Sunder* (Beitrage zur biblischen Exegese und Theologie, 3; Frankfurt: P. Lang, 1976).

Firth, D. G., *I and II Samuel, Vol. 8* (Apollos Old Testament Commentary; Nottingham: Apollos/Downers Grove: IVP, 2009).

Firth, D. G., 'Play It Again Sam: The Poetics of Narrative Repetition in 1 Samuel 1–7', *Tyndale Bulletin* 56 (2005): 1–17.

Firth, D. G., 'Speech Acts and Covenant in 2 Samuel 7:1–17', in *The God of Covenant: Biblical, Theological and Contemporary Perspectives* (eds Jamie A. Grant and Alistair I. Wilson; Leicester: Apollos, 2005).

Fitzmyer, J. A., *The Acts of the Apostles: A New Translation and Introduction and Commentary, Vol. 31* (The Anchor Bible; New York: Doubleday, 1998).

Fitzmyer, J. A., *The Gospel According to Luke I–IX: A New Translation with Introduction and Commentary, vol. 28* (The Anchor Yale Bible; Garden City: Doubleday, 1981).

Fitzmyer, J. A., *The Gospel According to Luke X–XXIV: A New Translation with Introduction and Commentary., vol. 28A* (The Anchor Bible; Garden City: Doubleday, 1985).

Fitzmyer, J. A., 'The Role of the Spirit in Luke-Acts', in *The Unity of Luke-Acts* (ed. J. Verheyden; Bibliotheca Ephemeridum Theologicarum Lovaniensium, 142; Leuven: Leuven University Press, 1999).

Fleddermann, H. T., 'The Doublets in Luke', *Ephemerides Theologicae Lovanienses* 84 (2008): 409–44.

Foerster, R. (ed.), *Scriptores Physiognomonici Graeci et Latini;* (2 vols; Leipzig: Teubner, 1983).

Fokkelman, J. P., 'Narrative Art and Poetry in the Books of Samuel', in *King David (II Sam. 9–20 & I Kings 1–2)* (Assen: Van Gorcum, 1981).

Fokkelman, J. P., *Reading Biblical Narrative: An Introductory Guide* (trans. Ineke Smit; Louisville: Westminster John Knox Press, 1999).

France, R. T., *The Gospel of Matthew* (New International Commentary on the New Testament; Grand Rapids: Eerdmans, 2007).

Freedman, N.. (ed.) *Anchor Bible Dictionary* (6 vols; New York: Doubleday, Logos Edition, 1992).

Freedman, W., 'The Literary Motif: A Definition and Evaluation', *Novel* 4 (1971): 123–31.

Friberg, B., Timothy Friberg, Kurt Aland and Institute for New Testament Textual Research (U.S.), *Vol. 1, Analytical Greek New Testament: Greek Text Analysis* (Baker's Greek New Testament Library; Cedar Hill: Silver Mountain Software, 2001).

Friesen, S. J, *Imperial Cults and the Apocalypse of John: Reading Revelation in the Ruins* (New York: Oxford University Press, 2001).

Fyfe, W. H. and W. R. Roberts (trans.) *Aristotle the Poetics, Longinus on the Sublime and Demetrius On Style* (Loeb Classical Library; Cambridge, MA: Harvard University Press, 2nd ed., 1991).

Gan, J., *The Metaphor of Shepherd in the Hebrew Bible: A Historical-Literary Reading.* (Lanham: University Press of America, 2007).

Garrett, S. R., *The Demise of the Devil: Magic and the Demonic in Luke's Writing.* (Minneapolis: Fortress, 1989).

Garsiel, M., *The First Book of Samuel: A Literary Study of Comparative Structures, Analogies and Parallels* (Jerusalem: Rubin Mass, 1990).

Gaventa, B. R., *The Acts of the Apostles* (Abingdon New Testament Commentaries; Nashville: Abingdon Press, 2003).

Gaventa, B. R., 'The Peril of Modernising Henry Joel Cadbury', in *Society of Biblical Literature Seminar Papers 87* (ed. K. H. Richards; Society of Biblical Literature Seminar Papers 87; Atlanta: Scholars Press, 1987).

Gaventa, B. R., 'Toward a Theology of Acts: Reading and Rereading', *Interpretation* 42 (1988): 146–57.

Guelich, R. A., *Mark 1–8:26, Vol. 34A* (Word Biblical Commentary; Dallas: Word, Incorporated, 1998).

Godet, F., *A Commentary on the Gospel of St. Luke* (trans. M. D. Cusin; 2 vols; Edinburgh: T&T Clark, n.d.).

González, J., *Luke* (Belief, A Theological Commentary on the Bible; Louisville: Westminster John Knox Press, 2010).

Gordon, R. P., *I & II Samuel* (Grand Rapids: Zondervan, 1986).

Goulder, M. D., *Luke – A New Paradigm* (Journal for the Study of the New Testament Supplement Series, 20; 2 vols; Sheffield: JSOT, 1989).

Gowler, D. B., *Host, Guest, Enemy and Friend: Portraits of Pharisees in Luke and Acts* (New York; Peter Lang, 1991).

Green, J. B., 'Internal Repetition in Luke-Acts: Contemporary Narratology and Lukan Historiography', in *History, Literature and Society in the Book of Acts* (ed. Ben Witherington III; Cambridge: Cambridge University Press, 1996).

Green, J. B., 'Learning Theological Interpretation from Luke', in *Reading Luke: Interpretation, Reflection, Formation* (eds Craig G. Bartholomew, Joel B. Green, and Anthony C. Thiselton; Scripture and Hermeneutics Series 6; Grand Rapids: Zondervan, 2005).

Green, J. B., *The Death of Jesus: Tradition and Interpretation in the Passion Narrative* (Wissenschaftliche Untersuchungen zum Neuen Testament, 2/33; Tübingen: Mohr (Siebeck), 1988).

Green, J. B., *The Gospel of Luke* (The New International Commentary on the New Testament; Grand Rapids: Eerdmans, 1997).

Green, J. B., 'The Problem of a Beginning: Israel's Scriptures in Luke 1–2', *Bulletin for Biblical Research* 4 (1994): 61–85.

Gros Louis, K. R. R., J. S. Ackermann and T. S. Warshaw (eds), *Literary Interpretations of Biblical Narrative* (2 vols; Nashville: Abingdon Press, 1974–82).

Grundmann, W., *Das Evangelium nach Lukas* (Berlin: Evangelische Verlagsanstalt, 1956).

Gunn, D. M., *The Story of King David: Genre and Interpretation* (Journal for the Study of the Old Testament Supplement Series 6; Sheffield: JSOT, 1978).

Haenchen, E., *The Acts of the Apostles: A Commentary* (trans. B. Noble, G. Shinn, H. Anderson and R. Wilson; Oxford: Basil Blackwell, 1971).

Hagner, D. A., *The Gospel of Matthew, Vol. 33B* (Word Biblical Commentary; Dallas: Word, 1995).

Hahn, S., 'Kingdom and Church in Luke-Acts', in *Reading Luke: Interpretation, Reflection, Formation* (eds C. G. Bartholomew, J. B. Green and A. C. Thiselton; Scripture and Hermeneutics Series, Vol. 6; Grand Rapids: Zondervan, 2005).

Hall, R. G., *Revealed Histories: Techniques for Ancient Jewish and Christian Historiography* (Journal for the Study of the Pseudepigrapha Supplement Series 6; Sheffield: JSOT, 1991).

Hamm, D., 'Luke 19:8 Once Again: Does Zacchaeus Defend or Resolve?' *Journal of Bibical Literature* 107 (1988): 431–7.

Hamm, D., 'Sight to the Blind: Vision as Metaphor in Luke', *Biblica* 76 (1986): 457–77.

Hamm, D., 'Zacchaeus Revisited Once More: A Story of Vindication or Conversion?' *Biblica* 72 (1991): 248–52.

Hatina, T. R. (ed.), *Biblical Interpretation in Early Christian Gospels: Volume 3, The Gospel of Luke* (Library of New Testament Studies, 376; London: T&T Clark, 2010).

Hays, R., *Echoes of Scripture in the Letters of Paul* (New Haven: Yale University Press, 1989).

Hemer, C. J., *The Book of Acts in the Setting of Hellenistic History* (ed. C. H. Gempf; Wissenschaftliche Untersuchungen zum Neuen Testament, 49; Tübingen: J. C. B. Mohr [Paul Siebeck], 1989).

Herrenbrück, F., *Jesus und die Zöllner: historische und neutestamentlich-exegetische Untersuchgen* (Wissenschaftliche Untersuchungen zum Neuen Testament, 2; Reihe 41; Tübingen: J. C. B. Mohr [Siebeck], 1990).

Hertzberg, H. W., *I & II Samuel: A Commentary* (trans. J. S. Bowden; Philadelphia: Westminster Press, 1964).

Hollander, J., *The Figure of Echo: A Mode of Allusion in Milton and After* (Berkeley: University of California Press, 1981).

Holmås, G. O., *Prayer and Vindication in Luke-Acts: The Theme of Prayer within the Context of the Legitimating and Edifying Objective in the Lukan Narrative* (Library of New Testament Studies, 433; London: T&T Clark, 2011).

Hood, J. B., 'Jesus as the Eschatological Davidic Shepherd: Studies in the Old Testament, Second Temple Judaism, and in the Gospel of Matthew', *European Journal of Theology* 17 (2008): 82–3.

Horsley, R. A., *The Liberation of Christmas: The Infancy Narratives in Social Context* (New York: Crossroad, 1989).

House, P. R. (ed.), *Beyond Form Criticism: Essays in Old Testament Literary Criticism* (Winona Lake: Eisenbrauns, 1992).

Howell, D. B., *Matthew's Inclusive Story: A Study in the Narrative Rhetoric of the First Gospel* (Journal for the Study of the New Testament Supplement Series 42; Sheffield: JSOT, 1990).

Irudhayasamy, R. J., *A Prophet in the Making: A Christological Study on Luke 4,16-30: In the Background of the Isaianic Mixed Citation and the Elijah-Elisha References* (Frankfurt: Peter Lang, 2002).

Iser, W., *How To Do Theory* (Oxford: Blackwell Publishing, 2006).

Iser, W., *The Act of Reading: A Theory of Aesthetic Response* (London: Routledge and Kegan Paul, 1978).

Iser, W., *The Implied Reader: Patterns of Communication in Prose from Bunyan to Beckett* (Baltimore: John Hopkins University Press, 1974).

Iser, W., 'The Reading Process: A Phenomenological Approach', in *Modern Critical Theory: A Reader* (ed. David Lodge; London: Longman, 1988).

James, M. R. (trans.), *The Biblical Antiquites of Philo* (London: SPCK, 1917).

Jeremias, J., *Jerusalem in the Time of Jesus: An Investigation into Economics and Social Conditions during the New Testament Period* (trans. F. H. and C. H. Cave; London: SCM, 1969).

Jeremias, J., *The Parables of Jesus* (trans. S. H. Hooke; London: SCM Press, 1963).

Jobes, K. H. and Moisés Silva, *Invitation to the Septuagint* (Grand Rapids: Baker Academic, 2000).

Johnson, L. T., *The Acts of the Apostles, Vol. 5* (Sacra Pagina; Collegeville: Liturgical Press, 1992).

Johnson, Luke Timothy, *The Gospel of Luke, Vol. 3* (Sacra Pagina; Collegeville: Liturgical Press, 1991).

Johnson, M. D., *The Purpose of the Genealogies: With Special Reference to the Setting of the Genealogies of Jesus* (Society for New Testament Studies Monograph Series 8; Cambridge: Cambridge University Press, 1st ed., 1969).

Johnson, M. D., *The Purpose of the Genealogies: With Special Reference to the Setting of the Genealogies of Jesus* (Society for New Testament Studies Monograph Series 8; Cambridge: Cambridge University Press, 2nd ed., 1988).

Jonge, H. J. de 'Sonship, Wisdom, Infancy: Luke 2:41-51a', *New Testament Studies* 24 (1978): 317-54.

Jung, C-W., *The Original Language of the Lukan Infancy Narrative* (London: T&T Clark International, 2004).

Kamesar, A., 'Biblical Interpretation in Philo', in *The Cambridge Companion to Philo* (ed. Adam Kamesar; Cambridge: Cambridge University Press, 2009).

Adam A. (ed.), *The Cambridge Companion to Philo* (Cambridge: Cambridge University Press, 2009).

Kariamadam, P., V. C., *The Zacchaeus Story Luke 19:1-10: A Redaction-Critical Investigation* (Kerala, India: Pontifical Institute of Theology and Philosophy, 1985).

Karris, R. J., 'Windows and Mirrors: Literary Criticism and Luke's Sitz im Leben', in *Society of Biblical Literature Seminar Papers* 16 (ed. P. J. Achtemeier; New York: Scholars Press for the Society of Biblical Literature, 1979).

Kimball, C. A., *Jesus' Exposition of the Old Testament in Luke's Gospel* (Journal for the Study of the New Testament Supplement Series 94; Sheffield: JSOT, 1994).

Kingsbury, J. D., *Matthew: Structure, Christology, Kingdom* (Philadelphia: Fortress, 1975).

Kingsbury, J. D., 'The Plot of Luke's Story of Jesus', *Interpretation* 48 (1994): 369-78.

Kistemaker, S. J., 'The Structure of Luke's Gospel', *Journal of the Evangelical Theological Society* 25 (March 1982): 33-9.

Kittel, G., G. W. Bromiley and G. Friedrich (eds) *Theological Dictionary of the New Testament* (10 vols; Grand Rapids: Eerdmans, electronic ed., 1964-76).

Klein, H., *Das Lukasevangelium* (Meyers Kritisch-exegetischer Kommentar über das Neue Testament 1; Bd., Teibd. 3; Göttingen: Vandenhoeck and Ruprecht, 2006).

Klein, R. W., *1 Samuel, Vol. 10* (Word Biblical Commentary; Waco: Word Books, 1983).

Koet, B. J., *Five Studies on Interpretation of Scriptures in Luke-Acts* (Leuven: Leuven University Press, 1989).

Koet, B. J., 'Isaiah in Luke-Acts', in *Isaiah in the New Testament* (eds Steve Moyise and Maarten J. J. Menken; London: T&T Clark, 2005).

Koole, J. L., *Isaiah III. Vol 1: Isaiah 40–48* (Historical Commentary on the Old Testament; Kampen: Kok Pharos, 1998).

Kugel, J. L., *Traditions of the Bible: A Guide to the Bible as it was at the Start of the Common Era* (Cambridge, MA: Harvard University Press, 1998).

Kuhn, K. A., 'The Point of Step-Parallelism in Luke 1–2', *New Testament Studies* 47 (2001): 38–49.

Kurz, W. S., *Reading Luke-Acts: Dynamic of Biblical Narrative* (Louisville: Westminster John Knox, 1993).

Lambrecht, J., 'Paul's Farewell-Address at Miletus (Acts 20:17-38)', in *Les actes des apôtres. Traditions, rédaction, théologie* (ed. J. Kremer; Gembloux: J. Duculot, 1979).

Laniak, T. S., *Shepherds After My Own Heart: Pastoral Traditions and Leadership in the Bible* (New Studies in Biblical Theology, 20; Nottingham: Apollos/Downers Grove: IVP, 2006).

Larkin, W. J., 'Luke's Use of the Old Testament as a Key to his Soteriology', *Journal of the Evangelical Theological Society* 20 (1977): 325–35.

Lieu, J., *The Gospel of Luke* (Epworth Commentaries; Peterborough: Epworth Press, 1997).

Litwak, K. D., 'A Coat of Many Colours: The Role of the Scriptures of Israel in Luke 1–2', in *Biblical Interpretation in Early Christian Gospels: Volume 3, The Gospel of Luke* (ed. T. R. Hatina; Library of New Testament Studies, 376; London: T&T Clark, 2010).

Litwak, K. D., *Echoes of Scripture in Luke-Acts: Telling the History of God's People Intertextually* (Journal for the Study of the New Testament Supplement Series 282; London: T&T Clark International, 2005).

Longenecker, R. N. (ed.), *The Challenge of Jesus' Parables* (Grand Rapids: Eerdmans, 2000).

Longman III, T., *Literary Approaches to Biblical Interpretation* (Grand Rapids: Academie Books, 1987).

Loewe, W. P., 'Toward an Interpretation of Lk 19:1-10', *Catholic Biblical Quarterly* 36 (1974): 326.

Louw, J. P. and E. A. Nida, *Greek-English Lexicon of the New Testament: Based on Semantic Domains* (New York: United Bible Societies, electronic ed. of the 2nd ed., 1996).

Lust, J., 'The Story of David and Goliath in Hebrew and Greek', *Ephemerides Theologicae Lovanienses* 59 (1983): 5–25.

Luz, U., *Studies in Matthew* (trans. Rosemary Selle; Grand Rapids: Eerdmans, 2005).

McCarter, P. K. Jr., *1 Samuel: A New Translation with Introduction, Notes and Commentary, Vol. 8* (The Anchor Bible; Garden City: Doubleday, 1980).

McCarter, P. K. Jr., *II Samuel: A New Translation with Introduction, Notes and Commentary, Vol. 9* (The Anchor Bible. Garden City: Doubleday, 1984).

'McCarter, P. K. Jr., The Apology of David', *Journal of Biblical Literature* 99 (1980): 489–504.

McComiskey, D. S., *Lukan Theology in the Light of the Gospel's Literary Structure* (Paternoster Biblical Monographs; Milton Keynes: Paternoster, 2004).

Mallen, P., *The Reading and Transformation of Isaiah in Luke-Acts* (Library of New Testament Studies, 367; London: T&T Clark, 2008).

Marguerat, D., *Les Actes Des Apôtres (1–12). Vol. Va.* (Commentaire du Nouveau Testament; Genève: Labor et Fides, 2007).

Marshall, I. H., *Acts: An Introduction and Commentary* (Tyndale New Testament Commentaries; Leicester: IVP, 1980).

Marshall, I. H., *Luke: Historian and Theologian* (Downers Grove: IVP, 1988).

Marshall, I. H., *The Gospel of Luke: A Commentary on the Greek Text* (The New International Greek New Testament Commentary; Exeter: Paternoster, 1978).

Matson, D. L., *Household Conversion Narratives in Acts: Pattern and Interpretation.* (Journal for the Study of the New Testament Supplement Series 123; Sheffield: Sheffield Academic, 1996).

Maxwell, K. Ri, *Hearing Between the Lines: The Audience as Fellow-Workers in Luke-Acts and its Literary Milieu* (Library of New Testament Studies, 425; London: T&T Clark, 2010).

Méndez-Moratalla, F., *The Paradigm of Conversion in Luke* (Journal for the Study of the New Testament Supplement Series, 252; London: T and T Clark International, 2004).

Metzger, B. M., *A Textual Commentary on the Greek New Testament* (New York: United Bible Societies, 2nd ed., 1971).

Metzger, J. A., *Consumption and Wealth in Luke's Travel Narrative* (Biblical Interpretation Supplement Series, 88; Leiden: Brill, 2007).

Meurer, H. J., 'Christliche Gotteserfahrung. Versuch einer Phänomenologie am Beispiel von Lk 19:1–10', *Trierer theologische Zeitschrift* 115 (2006): 181–99.

Minear, P. S., 'Luke's Use of the Birth Stories', in *Studies in Luke-Acts: Essays in Honour of Paul Schubert* (eds L. E. Keck and J. L. Martyn; London: SPCK, 1978).

Minear, P. S., *To Heal and To Reveal: The Prophetic Vocation According to Luke* (New York: Seabury, 1976).

Miscall, P. D., *1 Samuel: A Literary Reading* (Bloomington: Indiana University Press, 1986).

Mitchell, A. C., 'The Use of συκοφαντεῖν in Luke 19:8: Further Evidence for Zacchaeus's Defense', *Biblica* 72 (1991): 546–7.

Mitchell, A. C., 'Zacchaeus Revisited: Luke 19:8 as a Defense', *Biblica* 71 (1990): 153–76.

Miura, Y., *David in Luke-Acts: His Portrayal in Light of Early Judaism* (Wissenschaftliche Untersuchungen zum Neuen Testament, 2; Reihe 232; Tübingen: Mohr Siebeck, 2007).

Moessner, D. P. (ed.), *Jesus and the Heritage of Israel: Luke's Narrative Claim upon Israel's Legacy* (Harrisburg: Trinity Press International, 1999).

Moessner, D. P. (ed.), *Lord of the Banquet: The Literary and Theological Significance of the Lukan Travel Narrative* (Minneapolis: Fortress Press, 1989).

Moo, D., J., *The Old Testament in the Gospel Passion Narratives* (Sheffield: Almond Press, 1983).

Moore, S. D., *Literary Criticism and the Gospels: The Theoretical Challenge* (New Haven: Yale University Press, 1989).

Moyise, S., *Evoking Scripture: Seeing the Old Testament in the New* (London: T&T Clark, 2008).

Munck, J., *The Acts of the Apostles: Translation with an Introduction and Notes* (The Anchor Bible, Vol. 31; New York: Doubleday, 1967).

Muraoka, T., *A Greek-English Lexicon of the Septuagint* (Louvain: Peeters, 3rd ed. 2009).

Neale, D. A., *None But the Sinners: Religious Categories in the Gospel of Luke* (Journal for the Study of the New Testament Supplement Series, 58; Sheffield: Sheffield Academic, 1991).

Neusner, J., *From Politics to Piety: The Emergence of Pharisaic Judaism* (New York: Ktav Publishing House, 1979).

Neusner, J., *Introduction to Rabbinic Literature* (The Anchor Bible Reference Library; New York: Doubleday, 1994).

Neusner, J., *The Rabbinic Traditions about the Pharisees before 70* (3 vols; Leiden: Brill, 1971).

Neusner, J. (trans.), *The Mishnah: A New Translation* (New Haven: Yale University Press, 1988).

Neyrey, J. H., 'Ceremonies in Luke-Acts: The Case of Meals and Table Fellowship', in *The Social World of Luke-Acts: Models for Interpretation* (ed. J. H. Neyrey; Peabody: Hendrickson, 1991).

Neyrey, J. H. and E. C. Stewart, *The Social World of the New Testament: Insights and Models* (Peabody, MA: Hendrickson Publishers, 2008).

Nolland, J., *Luke 1-9:20*, Vol. 35A (Word Biblical Commentary; Dallas: Word, 1989).

Nolland, J., *Luke 9:21-18:34*, Vol. 35B (Word Biblical Commentary; Dallas: Word, 1993).

Nolland, J., *Luke 18:34-24:53*, Vol. 35C (Word Biblical Commentary; Dallas: Word, 1993).

Nolland, J., *The Gospel of Matthew* (The New International Greek Testamnt Commentary; Grand Rapids: Eerdmans/Bletchley: Paternoster, 2005).

O'Hanlon, J., 'The Story of Zacchaeus and the Lukan Ethic', *Journal for the Study of the New Testament* 12 (1981): 2–26.

Oliver, H. H., 'The Lucan Birth Stories and the Purpose of Acts', *New Testament Studies* 10 (1964): 202–26.

Osborne, G. R., 'Literary Theory and Biblical Interpretation', in *Words and The Word: Exploration in Biblical Interpretation and Literary Theory* (eds D. G. Firth and J. A. Grant; Nottingham: Apollos, 2008).

Osborne, G. R., 'Redaction Criticism', in *Interpreting the New Testament: Essays on Method and Issues* (eds D. A. Black and D. S. Dockery; Nashville: Broadman and Holman, 2001).

Osborne, G. R., *The Hermeneutical Spiral: A Comprehensive Introduction to Biblical Interpretation* (Downers Grove: IVP Academic, 2006).

O'Toole, R. F., 'The Literary Form of Luke 19:1-10', *Journal of Biblical Literature* 110 (1991): 107–16.

O'Toole, R. F., 'The Parallels Between Jesus and Moses', *Biblical Theology Bulletin* 20 (1990): 22–9.

O'Toole, R. F., *The Unity of Luke's Theology* (Wilmington: Glazier, 1984).

Pao, D. W., *Acts and the Isaianic New Exodus* (Wissenschaftliche Untersuchungen zum Neuen Testament, 2; Reihe 130; Grand Rapids: Baker Books, 2000).

Parsons, M. C., *Acts* (ΠΑΙΔΕΙΑ; Grand Rapids: Baker Academic, 2008).

Parsons, M. C., *Body and Character in Luke and Acts: the Subversion of Physiognomy in Early Christianity* (Grand Rapids: Baker Academic, 2006).

Parsons, M. C., '"Short in Stature": Luke's Physical Description of Zacchaeus', *New Testament Studies* 47 (2001): 50–7.

Parsons, M. C. and R. I. Pervo, *Rethinking the Unity of Luke and Acts* (Minneapolis: Fortress Press, 1993).

Perry, M., 'Literary Dynamics: How the Order of a Text Creates Its Meanings', *Poetics Today* 1 (1979): 35–64, 311–61.

Pervo, R. I., *Acts: A Commentary* (Hermeneia; Minneapolis: Fortress Press, 2009).

Petersen, N. R., *Literary Criticism for New Testament Critics* (Philadelphia: Fortress Press, 1978).

Phillips, T. E., 'Subtlety as a Literary Technique in Luke's Characterisation of Jews and Judaism', in *Literary Studies in Luke-Acts: Essays in Honour of Joseph B. Tyson* (eds R. P. Thompson and T. E. Phillips; Macon: Mercer University Press, 1998).

Pietersma, A. and B. G. Wright (eds), *A New English Translation of the Septuagint; And the Other Greek Translations Traditionally Included under that Title* (New York: Oxford University Press, 2007).

Plato, *The Republic* (trans. P. Shorey; The Loeb Classical Library; 2 vols; Cambridge, MA: Harvard University Press; London: Heinemann, 1982-7).

Polzin, R., *Samuel and the Deuteronomist: A Literary Study of the Deuteronomic History, Part Two: 1 Samuel* (Indiana Studies in Biblical Literature; Bloomington: Indiana University Press, 1989).

Powell, M. A., *What is Narrative Criticism?* (Minneapolis: Fortress Press, 1990).

Praeder, S. M., 'Jesus-Paul, Peter-Paul, and Jesus-Peter Parallelisms in Luke-Acts: A History of Reader Response', in *Society of Biblical Literature Seminar Papers 1984* (ed. K. H. Richards; Chico: SBL, 1984).

Price, S. R. F., *Rituals and Power: the Roman Imperial Cult in Asia Minor* (Cambridge: Cambridge University Press, 1998).

Pritchard, J. B. (ed.), *Ancient Near Eastern Texts Relating to the Old Testament* (Princeton: Princeton University Press, 3rd ed. with supplement, 1978).

Rahlfs, A., *Septuaginta: With Morphology* (Stuttgart: Deutsche Bibelgesellschaft, 1996).

Ramaroson, L., 'Le coeur du Troisième Évangile: Lc 15', *Biblica* 60 (1979): 338-60.

Ravens, D. A. S., 'Zacchaeus: The Final Part of the Triptych?' *Journal for the Study of the New Testament* 41 (1991): 19-32.

Rhoads, D., 'Narrative Criticism and the Gospel of Mark', *Journal of the American Academy of Religion* 50 (1982): 411-34.

Ringe, S. H., *Luke* (Westminster Bible Companion. Louisville: Westminster John Knox Press, 1995).

Robbins, V. K., 'By Land and Sea: The We Passages and Ancient Sea Voyages', in *Perspectives on Luke-Acts* (ed. C. H. Talbert; Danville: Association of Baptist Professors of Religion, 1978).

Robbins, V. K., 'The Social Location of the Implied Author of Luke and Acts', in *The Social World of Luke-Acts: Models for Interpretation* (ed. J. H. Neyrey; Peabody: Hendrickson, 1991).

Robbins, V. K., 'The We Passages in Acts and Ancient Sea Voyages', *Biblical Research* 20 (1975): 5-18.

Robinson, G., *Let Us Be Like the Nations: A Commentary on the Books of 1 and 2 Samuel* (International Theological Commentary; Grand Rapids: Eerdmans/Edinburgh: Handsel, 1993).

Rost, L., *Das kleine Credo und andere Studien zum Alten Testament* (Heildelberg: Quelle und Meyer, 1965).

Roth, W., 'You are the Man! Structural Interaction in 2 Samuel 10-12', *Semeia* 8 (1977): 1-13.

Rowe, C. K., *Early Narrative Christology: The Lord in the Gospel of Luke* (Grand Rapids: Baker Academic, 2009).

Rowe, C. K., 'Luke-Acts and the Imperial Cult: A Way Through the Conundrum?' *Journal for the Study of the New Testament* 27 (2005): 279-300.

Rowe, C. K., *World Upside Down: Reading Acts in the Graeco-Roman Age* (Oxford: Oxford University Press, 2009).

Safrai, S. and M. Stern in cooperation with D. Flusser and W.C. van Unnik. (eds), *The Jewish People in the First Century: Historical Geography, Political History, Social Cultural and Religious Life and Institutions* (Compendia Rerum Iudaicarum Ad Novum Testamentum; 2 vols; Assen: Van Gorcum, 1974–6).

Sanders, E. P., *Jesus and Judaism* (Philadelphia: Fortress, 1985).

Sanders, J. A., 'Isaiah in Luke', *Interpretation* 36 (1982): 144–55.

Sanders, J. A., 'Isaiah in Luke', in *Luke and Scripture: The Function of the Sacred Tradition in Luke-Acts* (eds C. A. Evans and J. A. Sanders; Minneapolis: Fortress Press, 1993).

Sanders, J. T., *The Jews in Luke-Acts* (Philadelphia: Fortress Press, 1987).

Schnackenburg, R., *The Gospel of Matthew* (trans. R. R. Barr; Grand Rapids: Eerdmans, 2002).

Schniedewind, W. M., *Society and the Promise to David: The Reception History of 2 Samuel 7:1-17* (New York: Oxford University Press, 1999).

Scott-Kilvert, I. (trans.) *Cassius Dio: The Roman History: The Reign of Augustus* (London: Penguin, 1987).

Scullard, H. H., *From the Gracchi to Nero: A History of Rome from 133BC to AD68* (London: Methuen, 1979).

Seccombe, D., 'Luke and Isaiah', *New Testament Studies* 27 (1981): 252–9.

Seccombe, D., *Possessions and the Poor in Luke-Acts* (Studien zum Neuen Testament und seiner Umwelt, 6; Linz: Fuchs, 1982).

Septuaginta: Vetus Testamentum Graecum (Göttingen: Vandenhoeck and Ruprecht, 1974–).

Siegert, F., 'Philo and the New Testament', in *The Cambridge Companion to Philo* (ed. Adam Kamesar; Cambridge: Cambridge University Press, 2009).

Smith, D. E., 'Table Fellowship as a Literary Motif in the Gospel of Luke', *Journal of Biblical Literature* 106 (1987): 613–38.

Snodgrass, K. R., 'From Allegorizing to Allegorizing: A History of the Interpretation of the Parables of Jesus', in *The Challenge of Jesus' Parables* (ed. R. N. Longenecker; Grand Rapids: Eerdmans, 2000).

Snodgrass, K. R., *Stories with Intent: A Comprehensive Guide to the Parables of Jesus* (Grand Rapids: Eerdmans, 2008).

Squires, J. T., *The Plan of God in Luke-Acts* (Society for New Testament Studies Monograph Series, 76; Cambridge: Cambridge University Press, 1993).

Stemberger, G., *Introduction to the Talmud and Midrash* (trans. Markus Bockmuehl; Edinburgh: T&T Clark, 2nd ed., 1996).

Sternberg, M., *Expositional Modes and Temporal Ordering in Fiction* (Baltimore: Johns Hopkins University Press, 1978).

Sternberg, M., *The Poetics of Biblical Narrative: Ideological Literature and the Drama of Reading* (Bloomington: Indiana University Press, 1985).

Strack, H. L. and P. Billerbeck, *Kommentar zum Neuen Testament aus Talmud und Midrasch* (München: Beck, 1922–61).

Strauss, Mark L., *The Davidic Messiah in Luke Acts: The Promise and Its Fulfilment in Lucan Christology* (Journal for the Study of the New Testament Supplement Series, 110; Sheffield: Sheffield Academic, 1995).

Strelan, R., *Luke the Priest: The Authority of the Author of the Third Gospel* (Aldershot: Ashgate, 2008–).

Talbert, C. H., *Literary Patterns, Theological Themes and the Genre of Luke-Acts* (Society of Biblical Literature Monograph Series, 20; Missoula: Scholars Press, 1974).

Talbert, C. H., 'Prophecy and Fulfillment in Lukan Theology', in *Luke-Acts: New Perspectives from the Society of Biblical Literature Seminar* (ed. C. H. Talbert; New York: Crossroad, 1984).

Talbert, C. H., *Reading Acts: A Literary and Theological Commentary on the Acts of the Apostles* (New York: Crossroad Publishing, 1997).

Talbert, C. H., *Reading Luke: A Literary and Theological Commentary of the Third Gospel* (Macon: Smyth and Helwys, 2002).

Talbert, C. H., *Reading Luke-Acts in its Mediterranean Milieu* (Leiden: Brill, 2003).

Tannehill, R. C., 'Freedom and Responsibility in Scripture Interpretation, with Application to Luke', in *Literary Studies in Luke-Acts: Essays in Honor of Joseph B. Tyson* (eds R. P. Thompson and T E. Phillips; Atlanta: Mercer University Press, 1998).

Tannehill, R. C., *Luke* (Abingdon New Testament Commentaries; Nashville: Abingdon, 1996).

Tannehill, R. C., *The Narrative Unity of Luke-Acts: A Literary Interpretation, Vol. 1* (Philadelphia: Fortress Press, 1986).

Tannehill, R. C., *The Narrative Unity of Luke-Acts: A Literary Interpretation, Vol. 2* (Philadelphia: Fortress Press, 1990).

Tannehill, R. C., *The Shape of Luke's Story: Essays on Luke-Acts* (Eugene: Cascade, 2005).

Tate, W. R., *Reading Mark From the Outside: Eco and Iser Leave their Marks* (San Francisco: International Scholars Publication, 1994).

Thackeray, H. St. J., R. Marcus, A. Wikgren and L. H. Feldman (trans.) *Josephus* (Loeb Classical Library; 9 vols; Cambridge: Harvard University Press, 1926–65).

Thiselton, A. C., *New Horizons in Hermeneutics: The Theory and Practice of Transforming Biblical Reading* (Grand Rapids: Zondervan, 1992).

Tooley, W., 'The Shepherd and Sheep Image in the Teachings of Jesus', *Novum Testamentum* 7 (1964): 15–25.

Tov, E., *The Greek and Hebrew Bible: Collected Essays on the Septuagint* (Leiden: Brill, 1999).

Tov, E., 'The Textual Affiliation of 4QSamᵃ', in *The Hebrew and Greek Texts of Samuel* (ed. E. Tov; Jerusalem: Academon, 1980).

Trebilco, P., *The Early Christians in Ephesus from Paul to Ignatius* (Wissenschaftliche Untersuchungen zum Neuen Testament, 166; Tübingen: Mohr Siebeck, 2004).

Tsumura, D. T., *The First Book of Samuel* (The New International Commentary on the Old Testament; Grand Rapids: Eerdmans, 2007).

Tuckett, C. M., 'The Christology of Luke-Acts', in *The Unity of Luke-Acts* (ed. J. Verheyden; Bibliotheca Ephemeridum Theologicarum Lovaniensium, 142; Leuven: Leuven University Press, 1999).

Turner, M., *Power from on High: The Spirit in Israel's Restoration and Witness in Luke-Acts* (Journal of Pentecostal Theology Supplement Series, 9; Sheffield: Sheffield Academic, 2000).

Tyson, J. B., *Death of Jesus in Luke-Acts* (Columbia: University of South Carolina, 1986).

Tyson, J. B., 'The Birth Narratives and the Beginning of Luke's Gospel', *Semeia* 52 (1990): 103–20.

Tyson, J. B. (ed.), *Luke-Acts and the Jewish People: Eight Critical Perspectives* (Minneapolis: Augsburg, 1988).

Uspensky, B., *A Poetics of Composition* (trans. by V. Zavarin and S. Wittig; Berkeley: University of California Press, 1973).

Vancil, J. W., 'The Symbolism of the Shepherd in Biblical, Intertestamental and New Testament Material' (Unpublished Ph.D. diss., Dropsie University, 1975).

Verheyden, J. (ed.), *The Unity of Luke-Acts* (Bibliotheca Ephemeridum Theologicarum Lovaniensium, 142; Leuven: Leuven University Press, 1999).

Verseput, D., *The Rejection of the Humble Messianic King: A Study of the Composition of Matthew 11–12* (Eurpoean University Studies; Frankfurt am Main: Peter Lang, 1986).

Vogt, J., 'Augustus and Tiberius', in *Jesus in His Time* (ed. H. J. Schultz; London: SPCK, 1971).

Walaskay, P. W., *Acts* (Westminster Bible Companion; Louisville: Westminster John Knox Press, 1998).

Walaskay, P. W., *And So We Came to Rome: The Political Perspective of St Luke* (Society for New Testament Studies Monograph Series, 49; Cambridge: Cambridge University Press, 1983).

Walker, P. W. L. (ed.) *Jerusalem: Past and Present in the Purposes of God* (Cambridge: Cambridge University Press, 1992).

Walker, P. W. L. (ed.) *Jesus and the Holy City: New Testament Perspectives on Jerusalem* (Grand Rapids: Eerdmans, 2006).

Wallace, D. B., *Greek Grammar Beyond the Basics: An Exegetical Syntax of the New Testament* (Grand Rapids: Zondervan, 1996).

Walton, S., *Leadership and Lifestyle: The Portrait of Paul in the Miletus Speech and 1 Thessalonians* (Society for New Testament Studies Monograph Series, 108; Cambridge: Cambridge University Press, 2000).

Watson, N. M., 'Was Zacchaeus Really Reforming?' *Expository Times* 77 (1965–6): 282.

Watts, R. E., *Isaiah's New Exodus in Mark* (Biblical Studies Library; Grand Rapids: Baker, 2000).

Weima, J. A. D., 'Literary Criticism', in *Interpreting the New Testament: Essays on Methods and Issues* (eds D. A. Black and D. S. Dockery; Nashville: Broadman and Holman, 2001).

Weiser, A., 'Die Legitimation des Königs David: zur Eigenart und Entstehung der sogen. Geschichte von Davids Aufstieg', *Vetus Testamentum* 16 (1966): 325–54.

Wengst, K., *Pax Romana and the Peace of Jesus Christ* (London: SCM, 1987).

White, R. C., 'Vindication for Zacchaeus?' *Expository Times* 91 (1979–80): 21.

Willitts, J., *Matthew's Messianic Shepherd-King: In Search of 'The Lost Sheep of the House of Israel'* (Beihefte zur Zeitschrift für die neutestamentliche Wissenschaft, 147; Berlin: Walter de Gruyter, 2007).

Winter, B. W. and A. D. Clarke (eds), *The Book of Acts in its Ancient Literary Setting* (Grand Rapids: Eerdmans, 1993).

Witherington III, B. (ed.), *History, Literature and Society in the Book of Acts* (Cambridge: Cambridge University Press, 1996).

Witherington III, B. (ed.), *The Acts of the Apostles: A Socio-Rhetorical Commentary* (Grand Rapids: Eerdmans, 1998).

Wolter, M., *Das Lukasevangelium* (Handbuch zum Neuen Testament, 5; Tübingen: Mohr Siebeck, 2008).

Wright, N. T., 'Jerusalem in the New Testament', in *Jerusalem Past and Present in the Purposes of God* (ed. P. W. L. Walker; Cambridge: Tyndale House, 1992).

Wright, N. T., *The New Testament and the People of God* (Christian Origins and the Question of God, Vol. 1; Minneapolis: Fortress Press, 1992).

Wright, Steven, 'Parables on Poverty and Riches (Luke 12:13-21; 16:1-13; 16:19-31)', in *The Challenge of Jesus' Parables* (ed. Richard N. Longenecker; Grand Rapids: Eerdmans, 2000).

Yamasaki, G., 'Point of View in a Gospel Story: What Difference Does It Make? Luke 19:1-10 as a Test Case', *Journal of Biblical Literature* 125 (2006): 89–105.

Yamasaki, G., *Watching Biblical Narrative: Point of View in Biblical Exegesis* (New York: T&T Clark, 2007).

Yamazaki-Ransom, K., *The Roman Empire in Luke's Narrative* (Library of New Testament Studies, 404; London: T&T Clark, 2010).

York, J. O., *The Last Shall Be First: The Rhetoric of Reversal in Luke* (Journal for the Study of the New Testament Supplement Series, 46; Sheffield: JSOT, 1991).

AUTHOR INDEX